Reading Roman Women

Reading Roman Women

Sources, *Genres* and Real Life

Suzanne Dixon

Duckworth

To my darling, Rob
viro perfectissimo

This impression 2003
First published in 2001 by
Gerald Duckworth & Co. Ltd.
90-93 Cowcross Street, London EC1M 6BF
Tel: 020 7490 7300
Fax: 020 7490 0080
inquiries@duckworth-publishers.co.uk
www.ducknet.co.uk

A catalogue record for this book is available
from the British Library

ISBN 0 7156 2981 6

Printed and bound in Great Britain by
CPI, Bath

Contents

List of plates and photo credits
(Plates between pp. 114 and 115)

1. Inscription on a memorial erected by Naevoleia Tyche, a freed slave, from the Street of Tombs, Pompeii, outside the Porta Ercolanea. Photograph from the German Archaeological Institute at Rome, neg. no. DAI 77.2085, by Rossa.

2. An inscription to a mother by a son from Rome. Courtesy Australian National University Classics Museum (inv. 71.03). Photograph by Professor Richard Green.

3. Tomb of the freed slave baker Publius Vergilius Eurysaces and his wife Antistia, outside the Porta Maggiore in Rome. Photograph by the author.

4. Statues of Antistia and Eurysaces, in which they are portrayed as a dignified married couple in traditional élite style. The current whereabouts of the statues is unknown. Photograph from the German Archaeological Institute at Rome, neg. no. DAI 32.1402, by Felbermeyer.

5. Copy of the statue erected by the fullers of Pompeii to their patron Eumachia. Photograph by the author.

6. Inscription over the entry to the building Eumachia donated to the fullers. Photograph by the author.

7. Ostian relief of the shoemaker Septimia Stratonice. Photograph neg. serie A n.1225, Ostia Mus. mag. inv. 1340. Photograph and reproduction permission courtesy Ostia Soprintendente Dott.sa Anna Gallina Zevi.

8. Funeral monument to a woman depicted with a woolbasket signifying her feminine virtue and industry, from Gallignano (Ancona). Photograph from the German Archaeological Institute at Rome, neg. no. DAI 81.2213, by Schwanke. Museo archeologico nazionale delle Marche, Ancona (8268).

9. Relief from Rome showing a butcher's shop. Photograph from the German Archaeological Institute at Rome, neg. no. DAI 62.1412, by Moscioni. Dresden Skulpturensammlung (ZV44).

10. The barmaid depicted here is part of an Ostian relief showing a harbour scene. Photograph from Fototeca Unione, American Academy in Rome, FU 5963. Museum, Ostia antica (inv. 1340).

11. A woman selling vegetables from a trestle table, Ostia. Photograph from Fototeca Unione, American Academy in Rome, FU 2383. Museum, Ostia antica (inv. 198, formerly 138a).

12. Remains of a shop at Ostia. These small shops, found in all towns of

Roman Italy, typically included an upper floor for the family and its dependants. Photograph by the author.

13. Shop-fronts opening onto a street in Ostia. My husband is standing at the separate entry-point to middle-grade apartments. Photograph by the author.

14. A Herculaneum street scene with a reconstructed balcony. Photograph by the author.

15. Mid-first-century CE stele of Menimani and Blussus, from Weisenau (Mainz). Photograph by Ursula Rudischer, Landesmuseum Mainz (inv. S146).

16. Third-century CE relief of a seated woman being attended by her maids, Neumagen-an-der-Mosel. Photograph from Fototeca Unione, American Academy in Rome, FU 11016. Rheinisches Landesmusum, Trier (inv. 184).

Acknowledgments

I have had the good fortune to gain help from different sources in the many years spent on this book, and wish to acknowledge the Australian Research Council for funding from a Small Grant 1993-1994 and the University of Queensland for an Enabling Grant in 1995. The month I spent at the Villa Serbelloni at Bellagio, courtesy of the Rockefeller Foundation, in 1994 was not only extremely valuable academically but indescribably pleasurable. I thank all the staff there, but particularly the Director, Pasquale Pesce, and the Deputy Director Gianna Celli.

I am grateful to Professor Susanna Morton Braund. Her encouragement at a crucial stage pushed me to finish the book and to offer it to Duckworth.

For photographs used in the book, I acknowledge the German Archaeological Institute at Rome for my Plates 1, 4, 8 and 9, Fototeca Unione, of the American Academy at Rome, for my Plates 10, 11 and 16, the Australian National University for permission to reproduce Plate 2; the Soprintendente of Ostia, Dott.ssa Anna Gallina Zevi, for permission to reproduce Plates 7, 10, 11, 12 and 13, Landesmuseum Mainz for permission to reproduce Plate 15, and the Rheinisches Landesmuseum, Trier for permission to reproduce Plate 16.

I was unable to include other photographs I wanted because, although personnel in those institutions were helpful in securing photographs, the prices required for reproduction rights by the Ashmolean and the Ny Carlsberg Glyptotek were beyond an academic budget and I could not risk the uncertainty of waiting for a price from the British Museum to be pronounced after publication. I therefore appreciated all the more the generosity of Dr Elizabeth Minchin of the Australian University and of Dr Marion Schroeder of the German Archaeological Institute at Rome.

Dr Devon Tully expertly drew the map (Appendix 1) and did the final conversion of the text files with efficiency, cheerfulness and aplomb.

Professor Marilyn Skinner and Ms Anna Taylor read Chapters 1 and 2 in earlier draft form. They were both patient with my relative theoretical innocence. The improvements owe a great deal to their tactful suggestions. The faults are mine.

My greatest thanks go, as always, to my husband Rob Wills, who has enthusiastically joined in my searches, listened patiently to my ideas, offered encouragement and suggestions, proofed the typescript and fed me wondrously.

Suzanne Dixon
The University of Queensland

Preface

This is a book about Roman women. Or is it? In spite of the proliferation since the 1970s of works on women in antiquity, I am now more sceptical than I was twenty years ago about the possibilities of extracting substantive information from the ancient sources, which exclude women altogether or fit them into a format which limits what they tell us. The cover of this book reverses the usual trend, for we have eliminated the husband of the woman who looks out at us over her writing tablets. We have a possible name (Terentius Neo) and occupation (butcher) for him, but we have to deduce from the picture that she is his wife and, though literate, uses her skill for the household accounts or some other ephemeral activity suited to the waxed wooden tablets she holds. Her excluded husband holds high a scroll which may proclaim his cultural aspirations or his status – for papyrus was used for permanent documents. Yet our knowledge of such commonplace visual signs is so slight that our conclusions are speculative.

It is not only the ancients who read women out of history or play down their roles. Outside the Herculaneum Gate of Pompeii stands a tomb erected by Naevoleia Tyche to herself, her husband and to their freed slaves, information she supplies in the inscription (Plate 1) below her portrait. The first line of the inscription has her name, the second (in smaller letters) that of her husband. Yet this very photograph has been captioned as 'relief from the funerary altar of C. Munatius Faustus, Pompeii' (Koortbojian 1996: 223).

I present in this book a series of self-contained essays which cross the traditional boundaries between literary and historical scholarship, to treat aspects of women's lives in Roman Italy c. 201 BCE – 180 CE: their sexuality, their morality, their legal and economic roles. The chapters serve as practical demonstrations of my key arguments: that *all* ancient texts – broadly defined – need to be read in new ways; that the *genre* of the text determines what it treats, how it treats it and what it leaves out; and that each text is designed to project ideology (e.g. of proper womanly behaviour) rather than circumstantial information about any given woman, even when it purports to record a specific, historicised woman.

My own wish to recover the history of women has survived the many developments I detail in the review of scholarship in my first chapter, but my initial confidence that the real Roman woman could be conjured up from a close reading of legal sources has dwindled. The quest has led me to consider wider questions about which texts might throw some light on the elusive women of classical antiquity and how to read them. It has led me to grapple with French feminist theories of discourse analysis, with film- and art-based theories of representation and with literary theories of reader-response in the hope of adapting some of their techniques to the basic material of Roman history.

That basic material also needs a new look. I have long since concluded that Roman satire, elegy and the novel are essential historical sources, although their use by historians clearly requires a lot of homework and serious thought about what we can expect from them. This conclusion strikes at the heart of our usual professional demarcation between literature and history and will arouse the suspicions of many of my fellow ancient historians with an aversion to theory.

My insistence that the *genre* shapes the information may seem at first glance a less confronting conclusion. It is fundamental to classical training to learn the conventions governing each literary *genre*. But the consequences are not always appreciated. David Konstan once remarked that historians of Greek and Roman marriage had a very different take on the subject from his own, which was grounded in imaginative literary *genres*. That observation, and discussions with John Sullivan and Amy Richlin about Roman misogyny, led me to elaborate on the idea. In fact, Roman marriage is a good illustration of Marshall McLuhan's dictum, that the Medium is the Message (or Massage). Marriage gets a good press in epitaphs but serves as a productive source of conflict in new comedy. It seldom appears in love elegy. Which brings me to the important question of exclusion. It is worth noting what is *not* in a particular *genre* and why, before drawing conclusions from its absence, e.g. inferring from the absence of references to women farmers that there were none. Exclusions might have more to do with the nature of the *genre* than with any direct reflection of practice, or 'reality'. Unhappy marriages, for example, have no place in epitaphs, happy marriages have none on the comic stage, and marriage does not fit into the formulaic narrative of illicit love promoted in elegy.

Exclusions and conventions can obscure the most basic information about women. Names are crucial to identity. We have already seen that we have no name for the woman on the cover. Many women are known to us only by such formulae as 'Wife of the consul Marcus Aemilius Lepidus' because literary and official sources focus on men's public activities. Naevoleia Tyche went to some trouble to ensure that we knew her name, paying a stonecutter to inscribe it in huge letters on a monument by the roadside. In many western societies, women change their surname on marriage to that of their husbands (which reduces them to 'wife-of-the-consul' status), a practice which makes it difficult for genealogists to trace a female line. In Roman inscriptions, the name is the key for the historian to status and relationship. A free Roman man had three parts to his name, but a woman's official name consisted only of the 'gentile' family name, such as Veturia. A slave-woman who had been Tyche became Naevoleia Tyche on being manumitted by a man (Naevoleius) or woman (Naevoleia). The first name of a free-born Roman's father is ofen included in that person's record. A freed slave would incorporate the name of his or her former owner (patron) with an abbreviation (M for Marcus, L for Lucius, for example) but the woman patron's name – whatever it was – was indicated only by a backwards C. It could be inferred from the former slave's name, which was based on the owner's, but it is suggestive that it was reduced to such a formula (Keegan 2000).

The format of this book is largely determined by the emphases of ancient *genre* categories, which inevitably raises the question of how these categories were defined. This issue is explored in Chapter 2, 'Reading the *genre*', but it should be stated from the outset that ancient authors sometimes perceived *genre* in more formal terms than moderns, always allowing for continuing debates about the boundaries (Braund, forthcoming). Even quite pedantic modern scholars refer, for example, to 'elegiac poets', those less pedantic to 'Latin love poetry', and they discuss Catullus under both headings, but ancient poetic categories were, strictly speaking, determined by the poets' metres. Catullus, who seems to us a trail-blazer in western love poetry, was more likely to be linked by the ancients with Horace. But there is nonetheless a connection in ancient terms between content and *genre*. It happens, for example, that references to the female body and female sexualities are concentrated in satire and elegy, so those *genres* are analysed in Part II for their very different perspectives on women and desire. Economic activity generally had no place in the more esteemed ancient literary *genres* but women's economic roles do figure in certain non-literary sources and in law-court speeches.

Throughout the book, my perspective is a modified version of an argument derived ultimately from the 'French feminists', that male-centred texts have employed constructions of Woman not as a reflection of known women or even of serious preconceptions about women in general, but as a category of discourse, *the other*, against which to define the insider qualities of the normative, hypothetical male (Irigaray 1995). Part I of the book, 'Readings', includes an elaboration of this argument as it applies to ancient texts (Chapter 2, 'Reading the *genre*'). This follows the review of scholarship on women in classical antiquity (Chapter 1, 'Re-readings'), which situates this work in historical context and notes that classical scholars are now more inclined to draw on wider theoretical perspectives, but to confine their attention more than ever to their particular speciality.

Part II, Reading the Female Body (Chapters 3-5) serves as an illustration of my interest in applying techniques of narrative analysis and feminist and post-modern approaches to constructions of sexualities and the body. In Chapter 3, 'Representations of female sexualities', I review the evidence of erotic poetry and satire for representations of female desire and of the female body as the object of desire. It emerges that when descriptions of sex or female bodies do occur in Latin literature, they tend to be either allusive (as in the atmospheric soft porn of Apuleius, *Metamorphoses* 2.17) or deliberately gross (e.g. Juv. 6.300-13). Female sexual initiative and desire are represented negatively, even grotesquely. Iconographic representations of sexual acts and the female body displayed in everyday contexts show quite different perspectives and suggest that any one 'take' on female sexuality is problematic.

In Chapter 4, 'Rape in Roman law and myth', I analyse the Lucretia and Verginia myths and the symbolic and political meanings of female 'purity'. The main ancient texts are Livy and legal sources. I also look at comparative material on the nexus of status, masculine honour and female chastity and aspects of the sexual-economic exchange implicit in ancient and modern legal systems. This chapter is a revised reprint of a 1982 article and has become a historical document in its own right because of its references to issues which have since been resolved or superseded.

Chapter 5, 'Woman as symbol of decadence', provides an excellent vehicle for testing the proposition that women in texts tend to be symbols rather than real people. I review the amazingly meagre 'evidence' from literature and the law for induced abortions in the Roman world. The literary references present a stock male fear-fantasy, the transgressive, adulterous woman flouting masculine control over her body. She frequently symbolises a general moral decline from a pure past and complements Chapter 4, where the virtuous women Lucretia and Verginia starred in exemplary death narratives from that mythic past.

Part III, Reading the Public Face: Legal and Economic Roles (Chapters 6-8), reviews varying source representations of the legal status and economic roles of Roman women in commerce, cloth-production and patronage, to assess how legal and conventional ideas of the feminine might have affected women's actual activities or representations of those activities. Chapter 6, 'Womanly weakness in Roman law', is a greatly edited version of an article published in 1984, on the gradual incorporation of a philosophic concept of female incapacity into the Roman legal system in spite of its inappropriateness. The concept took on a life of its own and re-surfaced in later European legal systems and from them to Roman-Dutch law in the old South Africa, an interesting example of the power of discourse to shape social institutions.

Natalie Kampen's 1981 study of Roman women and work first demonstrated the dramatic differences in representations of women's economic roles in various ancient media. I explore this theme in Chapters 7 and 8. In 'Profits and patronage' (Chapter 7), I examine the exclusions and biases of inscriptional tributes and statues as well as the letters, biographies and speeches recording women's roles in commercial and profit-oriented activities and the socially defined areas of patronage and loans. That chapter is therefore focused on élite and prosperous women, while Chapter 8, 'Women's work', looks at housewives and professional weavers and spinners, as represented in a range of sources. It becomes clear that concepts of women and work are mediated by literary and iconographic representations of the feminine and by epigraphic conventions generally favouring woman as wife and mother rather than as worker. Yet women's domestic role in cloth production was elevated culturally in Roman literature and epitaphs. In addition to addressing some of the apparent contradictions in these source representations, I critique modern scholarship on the subject, arguing that scholarly emphasis on ancient literary sources and economic categories derived from modern economies has vitiated the source-readings and therefore our understanding of ancient notions of work and of gender.

The concluding chapter, 'The allure of *la dolce vita* in ancient Rome', draws together many of the themes of the book. A critical look at some scholarly reconstructions of the Republican Clodia (Metelli) highlights the consequences of ignoring *genre* purpose. Roman women continue to be presented to new audiences as eternal fantasy-objects in what amounts to a wilful scholarly surrender to the lurid appeal of the deliberately shocking and extravagant imagery of Catullus, Cicero and Juvenal in invective mode, all drawing in appropriate contexts on one of the stock rhetorical themes of moral decline as symbolised by sexually transgressive women.

This book sets out ambitiously to read and combine *genres* in an attempt to gain maximum insight into chosen aspects of female experience and representation in the Roman world. It is an argument about method presented through examples. It is not a definitive or comprehensive view of Roman women. I necessarily make exclusions of my own. For one thing, I concentrate to a great extent on the women of Roman Italy. For another, I have made little use of the growing scholarship on medical authors in antiquity, which has contributed significantly to our understanding of ancient and modern constructions of the female body. I have scarcely touched on religion, which was surely an important aspect of women's lives, or on magic (a scholarly growth area). My use of visual sources has been affected by the limitations of my expertise. Although I include reprints of two earlier works, I have not re-visited important areas such as motherhood which I have treated extensively in the past. As it is, I had great difficulty in controlling the material of this study and the whole project has taken years longer than I intended.

But I hope I have suggested wider possibilities to other scholars and asked questions or raised issues which will encourage them to extend their particular skills across the sub-disciplinary borders. Since the excitement of the 1970s, we have become even more conscious of the problems of retrieving the women of the past but more skilled at teasing out dominant masculine ideas of the feminine which pervade our sources. I have tried to break down some of the remaining barriers to considering texts which people might be in the habit of overlooking as 'not their field' and to dispelling deep-seated notions about what kind of understanding we can derive from different texts, especially the idea that non-literary sources provide unproblematic historical data or that specific information about specific women can be accepted at face value. I argue that we should also be aware of the exclusions and biases which keep certain women or relationships out of some *genres* and heavily edit what aspects of their lives might be included or highlighted in others. Perhaps the most we can hope for from most sources, whatever they purport to record, is an idea of Roman social norms and ideals rather than actual behaviour and events.

Part I

Readings

1

Re-readings: a partial survey
of scholarship

Women in the title

It is more than twenty-five years – a generation – since the publication of
Sarah Pomeroy's book *Goddesses, Whores, Wives and Slaves: Women in
Classical Antiquity*, and there is no sign that interest in Greek and Roman
women (or Woman) is waning. The ancient sources we study are substantially the same ones available to earlier generations of scholars, but they
are now being mined for what they might reveal of women's *lives* and of
dominant masculine attitudes to women and gender relations in classical
antiquity. In the 1980s and 1990s, we have come to appreciate the difference.

The field, itself a sub-field, has since spawned many sub-sub-fields
(classical women poets; women in Roman Egyptian papyri; women in Attic
law court speeches; tragic heroines) and overlaps with many others (sexualities; history of the family; marginalities). The field is not exclusively
feminist, nor confined to academe. Some of the publications mentioned in
this chapter have appealed to more than one audience. Pomeroy's book, a
favoured choice for most undergraduate courses, is also read by the
general public.[1] Seltman's 1956 *Women in Antiquity* and Balsdon's 1962
Roman Women: Their History and Habits, both witty and readable, have
been unaccountably permitted to go out of print during the period of
greatest popular and academic interest, while Carcopino's appalling *Daily
Life in Ancient Rome* is unfortunately still available in book-shops and
libraries around the world and continues to influence popular ideas about
Roman women (Chapter 9).

Scholarship both reflects and forms contemporary ideas about women.
In this chapter, I review some of the approaches taken by scholars over the
last century or so to the history of women in classical antiquity and related
fields and, more briefly, look at the development of literary theory which
might be of use to historians in approaching ancient texts. This survey,
which puts my theoretical approach (Chapter 2) into historical perspective, is very much my own take on developments. It is neither exhaustive

nor detailed, so my omission of many important publications should not be taken as a reflection on the quality or importance of individual works. I refer in the text and in the endnotes to other surveys for readers to follow up, according to the level and type of their interest.[2] I concentrate on books because they are more accessible to the general reader, to students and to scholars from other fields who want to find out about trends in Roman history and Classics, but it is important to appreciate that articles in specialist journals were in the vanguard of scholarship throughout the 1970s and remained the prime medium of specialist exchange, particularly on Roman women, for a long time. It took a little while for individuals working in isolation around the world (many of them not professional academics at that stage) to get into print at all, then a few years more to consolidate their work into books and to persuade publishers there was a market for them.

Classical scholars wrote books and articles about women before the most recent wave of feminist publication. Leanna Goodwater's annotated bibliography (1975) indicates the kinds of writings available before the current crop, which can be dated from the 1973 'Women in Antiquity' special issue of *Arethusa* and Pomeroy (1975).[3] Pomeroy 1984b shows how interest had grown in the intervening period. Blok's 1987 historiographic essay reviews intellectual influences on the writing of history, particularly of Greek women, in the nineteenth and twentieth centuries, and establishes the precursors of the feminist writings of the 1970s and 1980s. My Roman-oriented survey is necessarily more specific and less detailed.

Many of the older studies are all but inaccessible, which is a pity, because some sound impressive.[4] Others now seem seriously misguided. The interest in women as a topic was sometimes driven by the nineteenth-century construction of the 'status of women', which was closely allied with colonialism and with a social evolutionary model of progress towards civilisation, as demonstrated by the way a society (i.e. its dominant men) treated 'their' women.[5] Studies of this type generally assumed that the 'status' of all women in the ancient world was low and oppressed, although Roman women were sometimes cited as being excessively free.[6] Authors of 'general' social and economic histories frequently omitted women without any apparent consciousness that they had done so.[7] Any references which did creep in were usually incidental to the main interests of the authors. The result was that, although many sound examples of classical scholarship on women, some from feminist perspectives, were published before the mid-1970s, each was produced in virtual isolation and therefore lacked developed theoretical perspectives and adequate points of comparison.[8] Some now seem simplistic in their literal readings of texts, their gender biases and their unawareness of what their sources left out.[9] There is no longer a theoretical vacuum and few have to start from scratch. Many anglophone ancient historians are empiricists. Denying any adherence to models and theories, they claim to follow, without preconceptions, where the evidence leads. But they, too, benefit now from the diversity of approaches and the atmosphere of scholarly exchange.[10]

The change was sudden and vigorous. Historians of ancient Greece and Rome joined the excited rush to compensatory history in the 1970s, many of us perhaps overly optimistic that ancient sources would, if examined carefully, yield an accurate picture of women's lives. In that sense we historians at least were all empiricists, believing in the existence of an historic reality which was waiting for us to approach 'it' in the right way. This might be termed the Sleeping Beauty view of history. The quest was inspired by the new stress on social history, especially 'history from below' and by the women's movement. The passionate determination to recover women's past, or 'herstory', was for many an expression of political commitment, even activism, and paralleled contemporary moves to retrieve Black and working-class history.

This radicalism was not initially evident in their methods or conclusions. Then, as now, most feminist historians were concentrated in the modern, post-industrial eras. While they were developing theories of patriarchy as a prime historical force, their classical equivalents, whether feminist or not, continued in essence to follow traditional empiricist techniques. They – we – focused on specific types of evidence (mostly inscriptions and historical literary texts) and produced intensive, small-scale studies – the kind Skinner has characterised (1987d: 2) as 'pointillist'. It was the subject rather than the method that was innovative.

The greatest activity, however, was – and continues to be – in the area of Greek literature and myth, and revealed a greater readiness to draw on psychoanalytic and non-classical literary theory. From the first, such publications differed from traditional or 'mainstream' literary studies in their readings of female characters. Classics as a profession tends to be conservative and these new approaches drew some strong reactions.[11] In the 1990s, Classics became more receptive to emblematic and complex readings of Greek and Latin literature, and feminist scholarship has been admitted to the fold. Even so, debates continue about the extent to which the gatekeeper periodicals should foster 'innovative' approaches – innovative in their application to the classical texts, that is, for such approaches are often established or even somewhat *passé* in cultural studies, Eng. lit. and modern language studies by the time they reach us.[12] The debates concern not only feminist readings but other kinds of modern theory, such as the application of reader-response and queer theory, post-modernist interpretations or the extraction of subversive readings from texts which appear to promote élite ideologies (dominant-subversive readings).

The eager reception in the 1970s of the '*Arethusa* Papers' and Pomeroy's book had demonstrated to publishers and academic policy-makers the appeal of Greek and Roman women to a huge potential audience of classical scholars, students and the wider public.[13] In 1975, Mary Lefkowitz and Maureen Fant produced a reader, *Women in Greece and Rome*, which made many of the relevant texts accessible to students with little or no Greek and Latin. Both Pomeroy's book and the Lefkowitz & Fant reader have been through many print runs since then and between them constitute a teaching staple.[14]

The *Arethusa* collections paved the way for many subsequent special issues of journals and edited collections in book form. This format has been central to the development of more specialist scholarship on women.[15] Some non-classical journals also produced special issues on classical topics.[16] As one would expect, individual articles and single-author books gradually expanded the body of knowledge and the issues for debate.[17] More remarkable is the fact that, as the once-new sub-disciplines have proliferated and diversified, the sense of community has persisted. Skinner (1987b: 70-1) credited the editors of the 'Arethusa Papers' with establishing the spirit of cheerful egalitarianism and non-competitive collaboration which has persisted in the field ever since.[18]

From the first, such enterprises, drawing together authors across a range of topics, showed another distinctive tendency: to review and sometimes to re-define or challenge the fledgling sub-discipline in its own terms. Introductory essays and keynote speakers or panel respondents at conferences have frequently performed this role, which is taken by the participants as a stimulant rather than a professional attack. Thus Phyllis Culham's reservations about the emphasis on literary representations of women in ancient male-authored (and male-centred) texts, expressed with vigour at a 1985 conference and incorporated in a 1987 paper, was integral to the debate continued in print in *Helios* (17) in 1990 and extending to contributions to the 1993 book, *Feminist Theory and the Classics*.[19]

Characteristically, that book also arose from a conference, and the 'Feminist Theory and the Classics' conference has since become a regular event. The 1993 book focused on current issues in feminism, confirming the North American role in setting the English-speaking agenda for classical scholars, although this dominance does not go unchallenged.[20] The presumption of a common aim and the tendency to review and re-define it provides a ready set of references to the changing *status quaestionis*, but it also highlights the complexities. Perceptive readers will by now have picked up on the fact that there is no longer a convenient expression for the field under discussion. Though still used by some, the once-standard 'Women in antiquity' has become problematic. Like 'Women's history', it conveys to many the assumption that our subject is a recoverable historical 'reality' (Rabinowitz 1993: 8). The 'image(s) and reality' juxtaposition which crept into historical writing in the 1980s seems presumptuous in a post-modern atmosphere which leads even the theory-shunners to acknowledge the multiplicity of 'realities' and the role of rhetorical constructions in ancient texts overwhelmingly written by, for and about men.[21] 'Women's studies' has fallen out of fashion and many consider that 'Gender studies' marginalises women. 'Feminist scholarship' is often, but not always appropriate, so that its use (or withholding it) almost becomes politically charged and has overtones of an *imprimatur*. My continual use of the term 'reading(s)' is a conscious attempt to avoid pre-empting conclusions about how retrievable the female experiences of the past might be and a reminder of the protean, elusive and subjective nature of the central activity employed by us all, whatever our specialities and whatever the nature of our preferred ancient materials.

However, the fact that many of us *are* avowed feminists with an interest in developing feminist perspectives has an impact on the issues and controversies which take centre stage.[22] Feminist classical scholars across the board show a recurrent concern with how best to recover 'our' history and how to find a female voice in the ancient texts. These issues arise in other disciplines but are particularly problematic for scholars of classical antiquity because of the male-centred and overwhelmingly élite character of the texts. The very term 'Classics' and its exclusive overtones, like the traditional emphasis on a restricted canon of literary texts worthy of study, has reinforced these élitist associations.[23] Committed feminist classical scholars sometimes feel as ambivalent and permanently displaced as feminists within the established monotheistic religions (Skinner 1986, 1987a). So apart from the difficulties of finding *references* to women, and the issue of whether we can actually ever know anything about women, serious questions are being raised about *which* women we should be studying – that is, how we can get to the women outside the ruling élite and beyond the narrowly defined 'classical' world of mainland Greece and Roman Italy. Given the nature of the evidence, such aims make the quest harder, but that is no reason to dismiss them. It has been suggested that even androcentric (male-oriented) texts are addressed in part to women and might provide some way of retrieving their voices. And Pomeroy has defended the study of Hellenistic queens on the grounds that royal models of womanhood might have had some impact on the mass of women.[24] In Part III of this book, I raise the issue of how far sources such as inscriptions, graffiti, legal documents and imperial rescripts might yield some female, lower-class voices. At this stage, these questions chiefly represent the liveliness of the sub-discipline(s) and its ability to generate new questions and possibilities.

Feminist scholars, like other radical theorists, are now more inclined to adopt a 'cultural studies' approach to literary texts in preference to the traditionally reverential attitude to the Great Books and the Great Fathers of Western Civilisation who produced them (Richlin 1992b: xi). Yet Classics has a way of taming and incorporating its rebels. In practice, feminist scholars continue to concentrate their efforts on the privileged

7

authors and, however radical their approaches, to demonstrate their expertise in close textual (even philological) analysis. Such caution, apparently designed to allay the fears (or forestall the criticisms) of traditionalists, must seem excessive to those unfamiliar with the tight culture of Classics and its entrenched suspicion of novelty or theory. Apprehension seems greatest in the USA.[25] Continental scholarship – especially French and Italian – continues to incorporate theory without any difficulty, while resistance in other anglophone classical circles is more torpid, but there is still a feeling in the USA that being innovative can affect a promising academic career.[26]

Oh, and ... Roman women

Romanists often feel like poor relations, on the periphery of the cheerful, co-operative, largely female, largely Greek realm of gynocentric classical studies.[27] When feminist historians say 'women's history', they mostly mean history since the Early Modern period. When feminist scholars theorise about classical literature, they mostly mean representations of women (or Woman) in a limited set of Greek literary works. A quick count of chapters in key publications will show that the exceptions occur in collections edited by Romanists.[28] Even Blok's 1987 historiographic essay, a *tour de force* which should be read by every serious student of Classics or 'Women's history', devotes barely three pages (one of them quotes) out of thirty-seven to trends in the study of Roman women from the nineteenth century to the 1980s. And that in spite of Blok's own acknowledgement that 'Roman history is populated with a rich assortment of noteworthy women, about whom we are more or less well informed'.[29]

There has always been a preponderance of scholarship on the Greek side, but the imbalance is not as extreme as such surveys suggest. Roman women – and Latin literature which claims women as its subject – have not been entirely neglected. If we look back over the differing approaches taken from the nineteenth century to the 1960s, we can discern a common interest in using Roman women to explore and explain the nature of women and the evolution of societies. Like its Greek equivalent, such scholarship isolated women as a category. It also sought explanations for the special character of Roman women. They were occasionally perceived as particularly oppressed by patriarchal institutions such as paternal power (*patria potestas*), the extreme powers held by a Roman citizen father over his children (for life) and in many cases over his wife (*manus mariti*, 'husband's hand': see Chapter 6 and Appendix 3). From the late nineteenth century until the 1940s, there was an interest in coding Roman marriage into an evolutionary and often racist view of human social development.[30]

More commonly, studies were driven by the perception, which existed also in the ancient world, that Roman women enjoyed greater freedom than their Greek equivalents, especially the women of classical Athens. In antiquity, Cornelius Nepos (Preface, *On Illustrious Lives (Vit. Ill.)*) noted the relative social freedom of respectable Roman women. Given the persistent interest shown in the alleged seclusion of Athenian women, it is curious that the freedom of respectable Roman women to go into public spaces and participate in mixed-sex parties has received so little attention post-1970s. Since the late twentieth century, the scholarly focus has been on the sexual, political and legal activities of Roman women and their family roles. Many of the studies from the nineteenth and early twentieth centuries sought to explain the position of Roman women and to develop from it a general argument about the nature of women and their impact on society.[31] All of these arguments were posited on the assumption that the Roman situation was an historical oddity and that the special position of the women was both an expression and a cause of Roman decline.[32]

Some authors frankly read 'Roman women', by which they meant married women of the upper classes in Rome in the imperial era, as moral signs (Chapters 5, 9). They ransacked literary sources with uncritical vigour and added a Gibbonesque, post-Christian prurience to the Roman satiric tendency to characterise élite women as sexually uncontrolled symbols of social decadence.[33] Quite sober scholars have felt obliged to address the well-known 'emancipation' (sometimes equated with an adultery habit) of Roman women and its putative link with general moral decay.[34] Roman sexualities have received great scholarly attention in recent years and the focus has shifted. Earlier, naive readings of satire as reportage and visual representations as 'realistic' have been superseded by sophisticated discussions of norms and representations (e.g. Chapter 3).[35] Roman sexual (and gastronomic) decadence remains a titillating rhetorical commonplace, or *topos*, of the popular media, and I shall suggest in the concluding chapter that its effects linger, but serious historical scholarship is now escaping from past fixations on uncontrolled female sexuality and associated ideas such as the decline of Roman marriage and the decay of the family in imperial times, concepts which were for some reason once taken as self-evident but have little academic currency nowadays, thanks to developments in Roman social history. Publications on the Roman family, marriage and childhood often deal with women and with gender relations, even if the words 'Roman women' are not in the title.[36] Treggiari's 1991 book on Roman marriage, for example, gives greater emphasis to male-female relationships and their cultural representations than its 1930 precursor by Corbett. The proliferation and greater sophistication of such studies since the 1970s has provided a core of material and useful models for relations between the sexes, the generations and the classes in the Roman world which has enriched approaches to Roman women.[37]

Even before recent developments in Roman social and legal history, there were scholars who were interested in aspects of Roman women other than their sexual and maternal shortcomings. Economic and legal aspects of female independence were explored from the nineteenth century onwards. On the face of it, that sounds more sober and positivist, but scholars used Roman law (usually sixth-century CE compilations) and comparative ethnographic material to legitimate evolutionary ideas about human social development. The legal status of Roman women was read as emerging from early Republican restriction to relative independence in the imperial period. The moral interpretation of the change varied: some saw it as a civilised progression, marked by the emergence of women from excessive male domination, while others saw it as a deplorable erosion of paternal rights.[38]

Modern treatments have also addressed this perceived improvement in women's legal standing, but with an underlying approval for the change based on feminist notions of equity – itself a covert moral narrative which we should make explicit. I have been guilty of reading the history of Roman women's legal capacities as a progressive narrative, but, like Gardner, I perceive it as a very uneven, *ad hoc* process. Change was achieved at times by manipulation (with masculine collusion) of legal structures which did not change substantially from the early Republic. The process makes it difficult to extrapolate any clear, constant ideology (Chapter 6).

Politics was once the core concern of Roman historians, and the political roles of Roman women have attracted the attention of scholars past and present. Women of the political élite who played an active role are either hidden in the spaces of our sources or loom out of them like monsters in a horror movie. Until quite recently, scholars tended to accept at face value claims by the historians and biographers of antiquity about women's 'interference' in the public, political spheres at Rome and generally to echo the moral disapproval of ancient authors, who introduced women into political narratives as symbols of disruption, like Nero's mother Agrippina, or as pitiable victims, like Verginia (Chapters 4, 9).[39] As historians of Roman politics became less inclined from the mid-twentieth century to explain events in terms of Republican chaos and imperial moral deterioration, women receded into the background, apart from occasional biographies of women of the imperial family. Roman political women re-appeared on the scene with the 1970s resurgence of interest in women's history, but have been divided up among scholars according to a public-private distinction ill-suited to Roman politics, which straddled the more public areas of senatorial debate and military commands and the private spheres of patronage, lobbying, kinship connections and political marriage. Ancient authors preserved the public-private distinction in literature and it lives on now, with many Roman historians who write about women specialising in the history of marriage and the family rather than politics. Those who treat political women vary in their use of sources and their theoretical perspectives, but are generally revisionist, concerned either to absolve specific women of the charge of unwomanly political ambition or to emphasise their political importance while stripping away its unfavourable and more sensational elements.[40] Few such studies make use of interdisciplinary models on gender and power/influence.[41]

1970s scholarship on Roman women specialised in the close-up. While feminist literary scholars were addressing representations of the feminine in Roman imaginative writing, historians were producing articles (seldom monograph books) on specific aspects of Roman women's history, often drawing on non-literary sources such as inscriptions.[42] The books began to appear in the 1980s, several of them claiming to fill in the gaps and correct the methodological shortcomings of earlier scholarship, which they reviewed.[43] Kampen, for example, pointed out (1981: 16-19) that earlier studies of Roman work, Roman women and Roman art, while valuable, tended not to combine those categories: 'To discuss the historiography of women's images is to consider gaps and absences.' Gardner noted the lack of a detailed study of Roman law relating to women and argued the need to place relevant legal developments in an historical framework, grounded in a range of historical sources.[44] The focus on method and on recovering the history of women's work, particularly from inscriptional and iconographic sources, continued into the 1990s, when words like 'gap' and 'silence' came to take on greater significance (Scheidel 1995 & 1996). Some historians began to express an interest in developing new approaches to reading such sources, not just to looking at more of them on the assumption that the truth would emerge of its own accord from collecting and cataloguing examples (Joshel 1992a: 3-24).

The 'status' and 'emancipation' of Roman women, which had dominated early scholarship, are markedly absent from these studies. For some time, there was a great gap between the sensational, highly sexualised images of Roman women in contemporary popular media such as the enormously successful television version of Robert Graves' *Claudius* novels, and these sober academic approaches. Perhaps there was a feeling that the new field had to look respectable if it was to be taken seriously. Although few followed Rawson's 1974 lead in explicitly challenging earlier portrayals of Roman concubinage and family life, historians' emphasis on the importance of élite women in the Roman family or the economic roles of lower-class women implicitly corrected earlier readings of 'the Roman woman' as luxurious and over-sexed or as wholly passive and subordinate to her father and husband. Such images, ancient and modern, are themselves now the subject of study: Coyne has examined the images of Livia in the *I, Claudius* television production and novels, Wyke (1997) has analysed images of the Roman world in film. Edwards (1993) has published on Roman political and literary images of 'immorality' and on women in disreputable professions, such as pantomime artistes (1997). Like

Joshel's work, these studies cross some of the traditional boundaries between history and literature. In the past, historians examined aspects of Augustus' moral programme and cautiously included the roles played in it by the poets Vergil and Horace, while literary specialists published on images of excess in satire.

The umbrella term 'ancient historians' used of classical scholars who specialise in ancient history conceals their traditional divisions not only by topic (e.g. Roman economy) but by source (e.g. as papyrologists or numismatists). Even combining different kinds of related written sources, such as lawcourt speeches and the law, is seen as adventurous and certainly requires varied expertise. Reluctance to expand their skill-base seriously limits the ability of historians to make considered judgements about sources outside their speciality and to combine the evidence of different sources (Chapter 9).[45] That is an obvious drawback in areas such as history of the family or women's history, which require such combinations, but it is also relevant to political history. Zanker's (1988) study of Augustan imagery and the greater interest in women of the imperial families who were publicised in coinage and statues have together influenced Roman political historians to give greater consideration to iconographic sources.[46] So far, in-depth analysis of such material is primarily carried out by art historians who vary in their approaches to its social and political meanings. Articles have, as always, preceded the books, which are now appearing in rapid succession and making this kind of material more accessible to text-based historians.[47] Such publications may undermine the professional boundaries of the past, which have divided text-historians even more firmly from art historians than from literary specialists or archaeologists. There are still few established scholars who combine the necessary skills and have the confidence to deal in print with both written and iconographic evidence. And to live with the consequences: fear of scathing territorial reviews is rational, not paranoid. The barriers have so far been bent more by joint publication in the edited collections of the 1990s on Roman sexuality (Chapter 3) and by the incorporation of visual evidence in the Fantham et al. 1994 textbook, which is more likely to encourage ancient history students to make greater use of iconographic evidence.

Theory continues to be a greater block to collaboration and boundary-crossing than doubts about acquiring new source-skills. Ancient historians, including those who specialise in women's history, are on the whole more likely to consider using social science statistical models and ethnographic findings than feminist historiography or the not-so-new historicism (Pomeroy 1991b). That has not changed radically since the 1970s. Individual historians develop various ways of dealing with the exclusions and generic emphases of specific texts relating to women, they provide careful documentation and their often novel findings, but they do not seem to regard the process as theorising or as contributing to a

12

developing methodological approach to the history of Roman women. Each punctiliously re-invents her wheel and modestly attaches it to a specific wagon going to a specific destination. Kampen, coming from an art history and marxist perspective, stood out in the early 1980s with her explicit discussion of theory. Others, such as Hobson (1984a and b), having developed highly interesting ways of reading particular texts, offered up their conclusions in classic empiricist fashion, as if they had no more general application. In practice, the growing corpus of work has had a visible impact across the board and even historians unaware of drawing on (let alone developing) new techniques have changed their methods and broadened their ideas of what texts they should be reading and what they should be looking for.

Theory has played a more overt role in literary studies by modern classical scholars, and traditional practices, such as the concentration on a single *genre* and respect for the divide between literature and history, have been undermined. Hallett's suggestion (1973) that Propertius' poetry, and the world he and his 'Cynthia' inhabited, posed conscious challenges to the Augustan moral rearmament programme was not only a precursor of the new feminist readings which continue to influence interpretations of Roman elegy, but showed a readiness by feminist literary scholars to take up historical issues. The converse is not true. Roman historians have been known to pale at the mere mention of literary theory and most approach poetry, if at all, with the conviction that it has nothing to do with history or 'real life'.

Unusually, Richlin (1983) identified a bank of Roman cultural stereotypes used in a range of invective *genres*, such as graffiti, satire and law-court speeches, for vilifying women, effeminate or sexually receptive males and others scorned by the voice and defined by the gaze of the dominant male narrator. Subsequent scholarship on masculinities and 'deviant' categories in literature, while not focused exclusively on women, continues to develop new and useful approaches to reading a number of literary and visual sources (e.g. Richlin 1992a, Clarke 1996, Walters 1997).

The problems of retrieving female voices and any trace of 'real' women from the self-obsessed writings of Roman poets preoccupied feminist literary specialists throughout the 1980s.[48] Different approaches have been taken, different conclusions drawn, but there is general agreement that the women who form the subject of Latin love poetry bear little relation to 'real' women.[49] Specific questions involving male representations of female bodies and female sexualities were raised again in Richlin 1992a with the help of models of the 'erotic' and 'pornographic' consciously imported from current debates outside Classics.[50]

The category of literary theory most familiar to Roman historians is historiography and ancient conventions governing biography (a distinct but often relevant *genre*). From the 1970s, studies of women in such

13

sources, varying greatly in quality and perspective, became more frequent and expanded the body of examples available to scholars. Even if the subjects of these studies have gradually been acknowledged to be not 'real women' but images (the 1970s word) or representations (the 1980s word) of women.[51] 'Constructions' came into their own in the 1990s, when studies began to emphasise the narrative purpose of authors such as Livy in introducing women into their histories (Joshel 1992b). Such developed feminist perspectives built on earlier critical studies of ready-made themes and characterisations in Roman historians (Woodman 1988). Like Richlin (1983), they stress the extensive and conscious use of what we would now call stereotypes in all kinds of Roman literary *genres*. Historical narrative, too, is viewed by some as a literary construction, its relation to 'fact' a complex and problematic business of disentangling ideologies and *topoi* (Joshel 1992b, 1997).[52]

Yet those who use Roman historians and biographers as historical sources have shown little interest in attempting this complex operation. On the whole, it tends to be the literary specialists who argue against the continued separation of history and literature – or, in feminist critical terms, of referential women and representational women (Rabinowitz 1993: 9-12). The familiar distinction between the empiricist, piecemeal approaches of ancient historians and the more analytic and self-conscious theorising of the literary specialists is as evident in this sub-field as in any other area of Classics.

What next?

In a survey of this kind, it is difficult to avoid a Whiggish tone, in which past efforts are viewed either as wrong-headed or as leading up to the current, 'right' approach. The racist, élitist and evolutionary perspectives of the past offend our sensibilities, but our own favoured approaches are often based on unacknowledged beliefs about women, humanity in general or history. Compensatory and political motives drive the wish to uncover women's voices and what we can of women's past experiences (including the experience of being excluded or constructed in certain ways by dominant masculine discourses). Rejection of the simpler and more popular motives – even if we once espoused them – leaves most of us in a twilight zone. Feminist scholars often display a sense of duty towards a wider public and a consciousness of conflict between inherited academic criteria and the hopes which other groups bring to the Classics of legitimating or rediscovering aspects of their own history.[53] We are not motivated solely by a disinterested search for knowledge – the guilty retreat from exclusively élite concerns suggests a more engaged approach, as does the fact that most who research women *are* women. Scholars continue to ask *themselves* about the problem of retrieving the voices or experiences of the mass of women.

Few of us would welcome suggestions that we are trying to establish the 'natural' state of affairs, or to recover our powerful past (the matriarchy) or to learn the secret of male domination. Yet all of those ideas are hovering in the background. If we doubt it, our students and public will remind us of it. I have stated elsewhere my belief that we should give up the idea of history as a narrative with a moral and a happy or unhappy ending. But we should face up to how hard we find it to refrain from 'status of women' judgements and arguments about overall improvement or decline under the empire or Christianity or whatever.

The starting-point for many who have laboured at the history and representation of Roman women was the discovery that their ready-made professional techniques were wanting. Their response was to develop new ways of looking at the evidence and, eventually, at what the evidence leaves out. Inspired adaptations of modern theories to classical sources have also been made by specialists who do not work specifically on 'women in antiquity' but on the Roman family, Juvenal or imperial propaganda. Studies explicitly addressing Roman women still lag behind their Greek equivalents – particularly on the literary and theory side – but they are in a healthy state and show no sign of falling off. The topic – whatever we call it – is now established.

We have certainly improved our understanding of representations of Roman women in ancient media, but part of that improvement has lain in our acknowledgement of the gaps and problems in reading. Behind our sober statements and academic language lurks the passionate wish to see through the veils of representations and read the women obscured by them, even if the one thing on which we all agree is that we cannot.

2

Reading the *genre*

Retrieving real women?

The study of women in ancient literature is the study of men's views of
women and cannot become anything else. (Culham 1987: 15)

The crucial question about women in the ancient world is whether – or how
far – we can actually reconstruct aspects of their lives. Or, in other words,
how *do* we 'read' the Roman women who appear as excellent mothers,
pious daughters and faithful freedwomen on tombstones, as wicked stepmothers in law and literature, as scheming trollops in history, biography
and law-court speeches, as desirable mistresses in elegiac poetry, as
witches in satire, as prostitutes in comedy and graffiti and as midwives in
tombstone reliefs, medical writings and epitaphs?

One way of answering could be that Roman women of the late Republic
and early Empire (*c.* 133 BCE – CE 211) obviously were mothers, step-moth-
ers, freed slaves, lovers, witches, prostitutes or midwives, that these
categories overlapped and that some women fulfilled the roles more satis-
factorily than others, according to ancient moral standards. It might also
seem self-evident that some literary works are more factually based than
others, that a generic witch in a satire or even a stereotypically demanding
mistress with a conventional name (Corinna, Cynthia, Lalage) is less
'historical' than the murderous Sassia of Cicero's speech *Pro Cluentio* or
the admirable Fannia whom Pliny the Younger knew personally and
described in his letters.

Let me counter these apparently commonsense responses with the
proposition that all such references amount to male-centred fantasies and
moral statements of what women should or should not be, whether they
are nominally attached to individuals, to fictitious characters or to groups
of women. What has been labelled women's history is largely history of
male-female relations or of men's musings about women, usually in terms
of women's sexual and reproductive roles and with more moralising than
observation.[1] This has led a number of classical scholars to take the French
feminist position that women appear in male-centred texts to define by
opposites the masculine ideal as the norm (Hallett 1989, Gold 1993). By
this reading, both men and women are constructions of discourse rather

16

than real, observed actors.[2] Henderson's argument (1989b: 94) that Roman
satire tells us nothing about Roman women but only about cultural
constructions of 'norms, ideals and fantasies' could be extended to other
kinds of imaginative literature and, indeed, to ancient texts generally,
including iconography.

The realisation came to me as I was working through a range of Roman
sources on mothers that what at first seemed a wealth of information
really consisted of variations on the theme of the cultural ideal of motherhood. Maternal breast-feeding, for example, was a recurrent topic. Male
moralists piously asserted its desirability and condemned contemporary
women for avoiding it. But references to the subject are of little use in
forming any idea of practice, even within a restricted group. For example,
when we read an inscription such as *CIL* 6.19128, in which an imperial
freed slave praised his dead wife:

> To Graxia Alexandria, an outstanding example of womanly virtue, who
> actually nurtured her children with her own breasts.

are we to understand it literally? Williams (1958), after all, dismisses
inscriptional praise of women's wool-working skills as emblematic, a way
of saying a woman was a good wife. If we accept that Graxia Alexandria
did indeed breast-feed her own children, are we to infer from her husband's
choice of words ('outstanding', 'actually') that it was unusual for such
women to do so? And even if we take that to be his meaning, should we
accept it as a true reflection of social custom, or should we read it as the
usual tendency to praise one woman by contrasting her with others, like
Juvenal's satiric contrast (6.592-3) between rich and poor women:

> And yet these [poor] women undergo the peril of childbirth and, pressed by
> hardship, endure all the aggravations of breastfeeding.

Such questions need to be asked of every source, although they can never
be answered definitively.

In quite a different medium, we find Aulus Gellius' rapturous praise
(*Noctes Atticae* 12.1) of a speech delivered by Favorinus on the benefits of
maternal breast-feeding. It is embedded in an account of a (purportedly
factual) visit by Aulus Gellius, Favorinus and others to a friend whose wife
had just given birth. The speech was delivered in response to the new
grandmother's stated intention of engaging a wet-nurse, to spare her
weakened daughter the additional strain of breast-feeding. Yet Aulus
Gellius' fascinating account does not tell us what happened after the
eloquent speech. We have no way of knowing its impact on the father
and grandmother of the new child. It takes a lot of intellectual detective
work to extract something about actual mothers from such anecdotes.
Maternal breast-feeding was essentially a moral commonplace, or

17

topos, in Latin literature and even inscriptions, of limited use in demographic reconstruction.[3]

Our response to the ancient material is also skewed by our own preconceptions about Roman women and women's roles in general. Underpinning this book is the contention that our readings of Roman women are themselves constructions – an amalgam of elements from ancient sources which we select on the basis of our professional specialities and to which we respond on the basis of our own prejudices and preferences. Acknowledging our own biases can be an important step. Even the commonplace modern preference for democracy and dislike of imperialism affect our moral responses to ancient characters and ideas. We should also be aware of the very different political and sexual presumptions of nineteenth- and twentieth-century scholars which have shaped inherited views about personalities from the Roman world such as Cicero and Messalina.

This brings me to how we 'read' individual Roman women. Most of us have favourites – whom we are loath to relinquish – in the gallery of named, historic Romans. The brief but vivid portrait of the reckless, cultured conspirator Sempronia in Sallust's account of the Catilinarian conspiracy of 63 BCE continues to make a strong impression on readers. Ideas have changed, so her boldness often appeals to young women. There was such a woman, but Sallust's 'Sempronia' is also a character in a literary-political narrative, presented to the reader as the female counterpart to the protagonist Catiline. Her social and sexual abandonment signals her revolutionary recklessness. Like Sallust's Catiline, she is a symbolic figure, her qualities all perversions of the virtues of her sex and class, indicative of the author's theme of the moral decay of the Roman élite. This literary description tells us no more about the historic Sempronia than the movie 'Cleopatra' does about Cleopatra Ptolemy VII or the first-century CE drama *Octavia* tells us about the 'real' Octavia and Poppaea, possibly known to the playwright. In each case the named woman is a moral and narrative device (Chapters 5 and 9). The epitaph of Graxia Alexandria, also a 'real woman', promotes the same ideals of womanhood implicit in Sallust's description of the wicked Sempronia, and the same implication that most of her contemporaries have failed to meet these ideals. She is explicitly upheld as an outstanding example (*insigne exemplum*) and, like the marble sarcophagus in which she was laid, proclaimed her husband's standing.

Genre

This book sets out to expand ideas of which texts ancient historians can use and how to read them. All social historians need to use a range of sources and my advocacy of including fiction and iconography in the repertoire clearly adds to the burden. To make things worse, whenever historians assess a reference to their chosen topic in a text, they need the skill to assess the impact of *genre* on its representation. Such skills are more commonly found in literary specialists who devote intense study to the conventions of the *genre* of their choice, such as lyric poetry. But the representation of a woman in any ancient source is strongly affected by its *genre*, which determines what is included, how it is treated and what is left out. All these things need to be taken into account in sifting evidence and combining versions from disparate *genres*.

Representations of women's work and leisure vary greatly by *genre*. In satire, female leisure symbolises decline from an earlier ideal of chastity and hard work (Juvenal 6.292-300), while the depiction of a dead wife's leisure on a tomb enhanced her husband's public image. But tombs themselves contain a mixture of *genres*. The visual depiction of a woman at her toilet with maids dancing attendance might be at odds with written praise on the same monument of her domestic industry, a popular theme in women's epitaphs. Men's jobs were rarely mentioned on funerary monuments, but women's occupations – sometimes noted in workplace memorials – were even less likely to be commemorated by their husbands or children. Even a woman with a clear job title might be represented by her 'private' virtues, which her family prized. Menimani's husband Blussus is shown with money on their family monument, while a wool-basket beside her portrait symbolises her domestic productivity and virtue (see Plate 15). A much narrower range of female jobs is depicted generally in iconography than in inscriptions and legal references (Kampen 1981: 117). Assessing the moral meanings of work and trying to reconstruct female participation in specialist jobs involves careful weighing up of these different impressions culled from diverse source-types, or *genres* (Chapter 8).

Because each part of this book explores specific aspects of female experience and representation, each chapter draws on the particular *genres* which highlight that aspect. Chapter 3, for example, reconstructs Roman ideas of female sexualities primarily from satirists and elegiac poets (with some input from invective and graffiti). Chapter 6 draws in turn on philosophical and literary stereotypes about women and compares them with legal constructions of female frailty (*infirmitas sexus*). In each case, 'reading' means bringing some understanding of the conventions and focus of each *genre* to bear, along with a method for sifting and combining differing generic constructions to throw light on the lives of 'real' Roman women and their relations with men or on the ways in which these differing cultural constructions might have interacted in the Roman consciousness.

References to women can serve more than one purpose in an ancient text. In different contexts, feminine ideals are paired with other Roman cultural values according to protocols which enabled a reference to women or a particular woman to express ideologies of kinship (Graxia Alexandria), work (Menimani) or social relations such as patronage. Again, the medium affects the message. There is a marked contrast between the favourable representations of female patronage in the many inscriptions and statue bases erected by beneficiaries (see Plate 5, with its dedication *CIL* 10.811 honouring Eumachia) and the sinister allusions by Roman historians to favours dispensed by governors' wives and the women of the imperial family. Recipients of benefactions were obliged by Greco-Roman protocols of reciprocity to acknowledge the favours publicly, by a personal visit or letter, by references in a speech in the forum, or by the erection of an inscription or even a statue of the benefactor, with a suitably inscribed base. The differing formats throw light on the interaction of class and gender. Inscriptional records (and statues) are more to be expected from beneficiaries of significantly lower social status than the benefactor. In the writings of Roman historians and biographers, the focus is on the men of the political élite. Although other sources suggest its importance to male political life (Dixon 1983), women's patronage is introduced into the literary accounts as a motif to demonstrate the corruption of a particular age and the inability of their menfolk to confine the women to their proper sphere. Women's private patronage is also more likely to be re-interpreted sexually by hostile observers (Chapter 7). Meanings of the female body and sexualities in Roman culture are explored in some detail in Part II, but the strong tendency of the male gaze to sexualise its female object means that sex frequently plays a role in other representations, including the vilification of political women (Chapter 9).

Exclusion and marginalisation

I have not been able to discover who Piso's mother-in-law was, since it appears the authors have not, in the case of the houses and families, passed on the names of the women as they have those of the men, except in the case of distinguished women. (Asconius, commentary on *In Pisonem* 10, tr. Clark)

Women are excluded altogether from some *genres*. They had no place in the consular lists (*fasti*) or the official senatorial records (*acta senatus*) which were important sources for the historians in Roman times. Those women who are mentioned by Appian, Livy or Tacitus typically perform very restricted roles, either demonstrating a general principle, or throwing light on the character of a leading male, rather than advancing the narrative in their own right.[4]

Traditionally, the argument from silence has been seen as a logical fallacy, but exclusions can be telling and the literary quest for the 'female voice' in male poetry or 'reading between the spaces' (Gold 1993) now has parallels in historians' attempts to develop methods of 'arguing from silence' (Joshel 1992a). Wives, babies, menstruation and older women figure scarcely at all in elegiac poetry and receive uneven coverage in medical writings and Pliny's *Natural History*. Collecting written and iconographic references to midwives yields precious little concrete information about such basic questions as who the midwives were, what they did or how they trained.[5] Arguing from silence – in this case, chiefly from the absence of references in standard medical texts to women's and children's everyday health – has led to the conclusion that these were the concern of ordinary women, who called in midwives for more demanding situations.[6]

One of the general problems of compensatory history is that the dominant groups who maintain the historical record are by definition likely to be poor observers of the outsiders. Jessica Mitford, reared in a country house in which the servants rose long before 'the family' they served, never quite caught on to what cooking and housework involved.[7] Even when surrounded by women, children and slaves, men of the élite might have been only partly aware of their actions unless those actions infringed on them.[8] The exclusions of our surviving sources owe something to this unconscious marginalisation of the subordinate groups. Sometimes Roman men were uninterested in or unaware of certain aspects of women's lives. They were vague in the extreme about relationships between mothers and daughters (Dixon 1988: 210-32). Adult men other than a small number of doctors were probably excluded altogether from childbirth.[9] A louder surviving female voice might have given wider coverage to some subjects. But it is not a simple question of male authorship. The dominant *voice* and *gaze* of ancient art and writings is male, élite, Italian, middle-aged and citizen Roman. Even authors who were themselves not Roman (Polybius) or not élite (Horace) wrote notionally for that tiny but powerful group based in the city of Rome.

Crossing the boundaries: professional transgressions

Ancient historians have always practised what was called 'thick description' by the new wave of Early Modern social historians of the 1960s and 1970s, influenced by the French *annalistes*. 'Thick description' involves filling out a bare-bones historical record such as census information with background material from contemporary sources, including literature and paintings.[10] Roman historians, with few documentary sources to draw on, had always used authors such as the biographers, historians and letter-writers of Roman times (who considered themselves to be writing literature), but they regarded other literary forms, such as poetry or the ancient novel, as outside their professional ambit. Justified criticism of historians who mined satire without an intelligent appreciation of its purpose and conventions (Braund 1989b, Henderson 1989a and b) confirmed the conservative belief that the traditional professional divisions should be maintained.

But the shift away from Roman political history has implications. In the last 50 years, the main topics of Roman historians have become slaves, the free lower classes, provincials, women, children and social institutions such as the family and patronage. Publication flourishes on Roman sexualities, the body, masculinity and health. The stress on social relations, attitudes and norms demands new approaches to historical material and wider reading. If we confine ourselves to a single *genre* or *genre*-type, we necessarily form a skewed picture of some relationships and activities. The fact that certain representations are found in particular *genres* does not mean that it is better to leave the more imaginative *genres* to the literary theorists to extrapolate ideologies ('Woman'), while the historians set to work on the more factual to retrieve the realities ('women'). Rather, there is an argument for applying some of the skills of intense literary analysis, on the cultural studies model, to non-literary sources, an exercise for which classically trained ancient historians are well equipped.[11] It is time to breach the conventional professional demarcation boundaries between historical sources and imaginative literature ('fiction').

The deep-seated, physical misogyny which Richlin and Sullivan have attributed to Roman men is arguably characteristic of satire and invective, but at odds with the very different picture of relations between the sexes to be found in Roman letters and epitaphs, for example.[12] The older woman figures, if at all, as an object of disgust in Roman satire and elegy, which treat women primarily as objects of desire, but is typically cited in respectful and affectionate ways in letters, epitaphs and law-court speeches. This does not mean that one *genre* necessarily yields a truer picture than another, but it should make us hesitant about drawing firm conclusions from a particular type of source (Chapter 3). The wealthy upper-class women who signify decadence in so many literary sources are the same ones honoured as individuals in contemporary statues for their gracious beneficence. Nobody could be harder on powerful older women than Martial, but his patron Marcella (a wealthy Spanish widow) is always invoked deferentially. It is a matter of horses for courses.

The role of the author is crucial to meaning. When a husband and daughter erect a tombstone to an old woman, they are – among other things – proclaiming their own *pietas* to the local community. Pliny gains *kudos* from his published praise of the venerable Fannia and demonstrates his regard for an older woman (who happens to be a stepmother, another vilified category). The interaction between ideologies, self-image, public image and lived experience is complex. Compare the different images of youth and individual young people in modern media and conversation. The 'youth' perceived as violent, lazy and disrespectful in one context becomes the hope of the nation in another. Neither construction has any visible effect on behaviour towards a cherished grandchild at the personal level.

2. Reading the genre

Finding the female?

The issue of the female voice and the female spectator/reader, prominent in feminist literary discussions, is particularly problematic for classical scholars. Although we know that Roman women wrote and published in many *genres*, few female authors are represented in surviving Latin literary texts.[13] That limitation alone should move us to look carefully at the *genres* which do, however imperfectly, transmit the voices of women of the Roman world: namely, the inscriptions (especially, but not only, epitaphs), imperial rescripts, and petitions and contracts on papyrus which purport to be authored by women, as well as funeral and occupational reliefs commissioned by them. Perhaps the techniques developed by scholars such as Rabinowitz or Gold to find some female voice in male literary texts (Euripides and Propertius) can be adapted to readings of the non-literary 'female' texts of these other *genres*.

Even an account by a woman of her own experience is filtered through the particular format of the *genre* she uses, whether it is love poetry by Sulpicia, an epitaph by Naevoleia Tyche to herself and her husband, a bequest from Iunia Libertas to her freed slaves and their descendants, a shop-sign commissioned by an Ostian vegetable vendor or a semi-draped statue of a matron showing her as Venus.[14] And indeed, who is to say whether women who commissioned tombstones simply chose stock epithets from the local stone-cutter's catalogue? In a wider sense, women who speak in a male forum are obliged to draw on the dominant cultural repertoire if they are to be heard at all.[15] Sometimes a papyrus from a woman was written physically by a man because she was illiterate, and in such a case we must consider whether the man actually shaped the form and content of the document. This applies in a different way to shop-front depictions commissioned from artisans. In each case, the woman concerned might have dictated her preferences authoritatively, as patron, or deferred to the expertise of the person carrying out the work. In each case, there is a strong conventional element, whatever the authorship and whatever the sex of the author. The voice may therefore be directed, distorted and even muted by these surely male-determined elements, but media of this type are among our more promising leads.[16]

Such sources broaden enormously the social base of our quest, for the women – and the men – who figure in them come from a much wider social spectrum than the authors of the dominant classical *genres*. The subjects of these texts are close to the daily lives of a great number of people – family relationships, death, inheritance, oppression by powerful neighbours, debts and loans, daily work, the benefits and burdens of patronage. They have the potential to give us some insight into relations between women of differing social standing – customer and saleswoman, owner and slave, patron and client. Each *genre* has its emphases and exclusions, just

23

as literary *genres* do, and any analysis must take them into account, but more productive readings might also employ ideological constructions – of public-private, for example – to interpret their yield. When a woman authorises her grandson in a papyrus to represent her in court because of the limitations of her age and sex, she may be employing a formula which actually has little to do with any relinquishment of effective control and much to do with appearances and proprieties (Chapters 6, 7).

Representation and reality?

The frequently encountered beliefs that historical texts as a genre are somehow more primal, or closer to reality, or safely composed of predigested historical data which require less manipulation before use, are simply naive. (Culham 1987: 15-16)

The information in documentary sources needs equally critical appraisal. Tax and census records are consciously falsified in all periods for obvious reasons, but we need also to consider the possibility that household registrations, wills and pre-mortem agreements detailing residence entitlements were also shaped and distorted by the desire of the author to appear properly dutiful or affectionate, even to make dispositions for which the resources were inadequate. A written guarantee of lifelong maintenance to a widow or parent recorded in such a document might have more in common with pious epitaphs than with reliable records. Montevecchi and Hobson have concluded that some loan and wet-nursing contracts actually represented fiduciary sales of children in times of economic hardship.

We all know that people do not always say what they mean. We are used to allowing for it in everyday contexts. In considering interpretations and omissions of the ancient material, we do well to remind ourselves of the difficulties encountered in data collection by modern researchers, who construct and administer questionnaires in the knowledge that anonymous responses are riddled with issues of self-presentation which confuse reportage with normative statements – 'I try to make the meals nutritious' (*translation:* not all the meals are governed by this admirable principle), 'I leave that sort of thing to the wife' (*translation:* I don't want even this telephone interviewer to know that I do unmanly jobs). Factual information has to be sifted out of prescriptive claims like these, which express ideals rather than practice.

Ideals and clichés can interact with practice in a complex way, which needs careful analysis. Many Romans were stepmothers or had stepmothers in a world of frequent remarriage and uncertain mortality. In Pliny's letters, such relationships among acquaintances are referred to casually, without any hint of the malign image of the murderous stepmother we know from so many surviving sources. But Seneca's reference to his

24

mother's stepmother, who brought her up lovingly and well, attests to the dominance of these folkloric stereotypes:

> You grew up under a stepmother whom you compelled by your total obedience and dutiful affection (equal to that which a daughter might display) to be a mother to you, but even a good stepmother is no small thing to endure. (Seneca *ad Helviam* 2.4)

Here Seneca has processed his own mother's apparently happy experience as a stepdaughter in terms of his common-sense 'knowledge' to fabricate a forced compliment which then becomes part of a work ostensibly directed to her but designed to publicise his own philosophical and literary merits.

This reminds us that certain stereotypes could travel between *genres* and contexts. The wicked stepmother belongs properly to satire and folklore, but can make a guest appearance elsewhere from time to time – in essays, history, biography and the forensic speech.[17] Pliny shamelessly exploited the stereotype of the wicked stepmother to further his client's cause in an important inheritance case (*Letters* 9.13.3).

The ancient texts have been there for our use and delectation for a long time. What changes is what we want from them and how we go about getting it. Given the complexities, is it expecting too much to try and extract 'real life', or real Roman women, from them? I think not. As long as we tread carefully. It is quite possible to be both bold and cautious. It is not a simple matter of setting real against fictitious women, factual accounts against literary creations, obvious generalities against what appear to be circumstantial and specific reports. If we do our homework about each type of source, we can afford to be brave and step outside 'our field'. After all, we have already revolutionised ideas of what history is all about and whose history is worth retrieving. And, like Socrates, we are prepared to admit how little we know. Confident equations of lawyers' rules or vase paintings with ancient practice are rarer nowadays. We should be very critical both of ancient testimony and of our own responses to it. There are no hard data, no easy routes to ancient lives. All sources have their uses, if only in revealing ancient prejudices, but we should be wary of accepting specific information about specific women at face value. Understanding *genre* means being alert to the gaps and biases which keep certain women out of some texts and to the rules determining which aspects of their lives will be highlighted in others. Above all, we should be suspicious of vivid portraits which appeal to our longing to get close to the personalities of antiquity. The best we can hope for are flickering glimpses of women's lives which (if we are honest with ourselves) leave us wondering if we really saw anything there at all.

Part II

Reading the Female Body

Introduction

It can seem to a modern student of Roman culture that pre-Christian Italy was remarkably uninhibited about the naked human body and sexual acts. Indeed, the freedom was too much for enthusiasts of the classical revival. The ubiquitous sculptures of phalli were knocked from Pompeian building exteriors for viewers who considered icons of painful death (crucifixes) more appropriate vehicles of blessing and regeneration than human sexual organs. Paintings and statuary deemed obscene were closed from the unfiltered public gaze (if still on site) or gathered in *gabinetti segreti* within museums or cherished private collections.[1] Much of Martial's poetry and certain passages in Juvenal's sixth satire or even Suetonius' *Lives* were either excised from Latin editions or not translated into an accessible modern language.[2]

It is now easier for the average person to gain access to the texts and the Pompeian penis is at last emerging from the closet, but the works of Martial, Catullus and Juvenal retain the power to shock modern audiences.[3] Students gasp delightedly on hearing examples of Cicero's pointed repartee, including outrageous sexual accusations made in the senate.[4] At Caesar's triumph – a time of ritual licence for such ribaldry – his soldiers cheerfully celebrated in song his status as serial adulterer and erstwhile bum-boy of the Bithynian king.[5] The much-vaunted modern sexual liberation has not extended to so many public areas.

This apparent freedom proves on closer examination to have a number of gaps and skewings. While visual depictions of the naked human body, of reproductive parts and of sexual acts were certainly far more commonplace in the Roman world than in the modern west, sex and the body were confined to a narrow range of literary sources. When the male gaze is fixed on women, it is likely to type them by their sexual and reproductive characteristics. That should mean that we learn a lot about the female body and female desire. But it doesn't usually work that way. As always, *genre* dictates treatment: the female body repels the gaze of the satirist and arouses the desire of the elegiac narrator. But Latin love poets were actually fairly reticent about the body of the beloved and elaborated the poet-narrator's desire, not hers. In Latin literature generally, female desire is played down, ridiculed or associated with transgression. Women's bodies – like men's – are described more graphically and cruelly in satire and epigrams, the proper site for the grotesque (Braund & Gold 1998), but in idealising, impressionistic terms in elegy (Chapter 3). The 'sexuality' of the beloved in Latin love elegy is largely a matter of projection, telling us more of the poet's desire than hers.[6] In more elevated *genres*, women's desire plays a cautionary role: the licentious (and idle, luxurious and grasping) women of the author's own era are contrasted with the chaste and industrious matrons of an earlier age (Chapter 5). Sex and women's bodies take on noble political meanings: in Livy's narrative of Rome's history from its founding, the display of Virginia's sexually intact corpse parallels the heroic suicide of the raped Lucretia as a founding myth of the Roman state and a perennial example of proper sex roles: chastity for women and its protection or vengeance by their men (Chapter 4).

Sexualities are a growth area in classical publications. They followed the usual pattern of focusing first on Greek sexualities, or collapsing Greek and Roman into a general 'ancient world' category. Hallett and Skinner felt the need in 1997 to preface their *Roman Sexualities* collection with a justification for separating out the Roman element from a general Mediterranean coverage of the subject. 'Greek love' took on particular meanings in the nineteenth century, and the history of what is still called 'homosexuality' by the populace at large has driven many scholars to retrieve aspects of same-sex love from Roman writings, partly to define the differences from Greek attitudes. The reader interested in the ensuing debates, in the latest re-vamping or denunciation of Foucault or in search of an overview of related publications needs to look elsewhere.[7] My concern is with how particular *genres* shape the representations of women which we have to use to reconstruct 'Roman attitudes' to women and aspects of Roman women's lived experience. Like others, I treat the female body as a cultural construct and Roman sexualities as types of discourse. Like others, I reject the cosy assumption that the Romans were just like us, but it is important to know that they were not always telling us directly and literally just what they were.[8]

Roman men saw women's (and men's) naked and semi-draped bodies on statues, coins, wall-paintings, on dinnerware, on the stage and in the arena, perhaps also in the baths and certainly in brothels and in their own homes.[9] They also saw in sculpture the heavily draped figures of respectable matrons in the so-called 'Modesty' (*Pudicitia*) posture.[10] Impeded by our own heritage, we find it difficult to know how these bodies might have been read.

In discussing sex, rape and the body, I have, like others, played the academic game of pulling examples of a particular kind out of certain *genres*, thereby perhaps putting them in a special category which may distort the meanings they held for ancient authors and audiences. The consistency of satiric and epigrammatic castigation of female desire and female homoeroticism have led commentators to conclude that they reflect strong cultural norms. But do publicly espoused rules and jokes, even if consistent, express the anxieties of a specific group – in this case, the dominant elite citizen male? It is a complex question, one that has direct implications in the modern world, where there are debates about the impact of jokes that target particular out-groups. It is hardly to be doubted that such attitudes reinforce stereotypes and are painful to their objects, that they express differing power relations. But do they tell us the 'real' attitude to a particular social category? Is it the truth and nothing but the truth about dominant attitudes? Why should recurrent jokes at the expense of the ugly old lustful woman or the effete pathic male be more informative than funeral *laudationes*? The same individuals can be represented in both *genres*. Calpurnius Piso, painted by Cicero as a hedonistic Epicurean swine, and Augustus, stigmatised by Mark Antony as a boy-prostitute, are elsewhere treated with respect. The stereotypic widowed mother of biography balances the sex-hungry old bat of satire. Both the generic and individual portrayals are flexible.

We might agree that public morality, humour and sex are all expressions of power relations, but it is hard to know where to go from there, particularly in the area of representations. Male literary neglect of female desire might be just a self-centred oversight, like the neglect of mother-daughter relations – it need not be based on a *fear* of female sexuality. The virtual exclusion of masturbation from ancient and modern *genres* might simply reflect the poor narrative possibilities of a solitary activity rather than deep cultural abhorrence.[11] Am I joking, you ask, or do I mean it? That's the kernel of the problem. A hint: I do think it is important to review our own perspectives and to remind ourselves not only of what is and is not in the ancient text before us but what we are, for one reason or another, leaving out of our own studies and analyses.

31

3

Representations of female
sexualities

Once [Yogi Berra, US baseball player] declined an invitation from teammates to go with them to a porn movie. They persisted. He still refused. They
persisted some more. Berra hesitated. 'Who's in it?' he asked. Dumbfounded,
his teammates retreated. How do you explain to somebody who really wants
to know that there is *nobody* in a porn movie, only moving parts? (Frank
Devine, 'That's Language' feature, *The Australian Magazine* 27-8 May 1995)

Genre and desire

In an evocative first-person account of an afternoon rendezvous with
Corinna, the poet Ovid describes her beauty:

There was no flaw anywhere in her whole body: what shoulders, what arms
I gazed at and caressed! The beauty of her nipples – perfect for squeezing!
How flat the belly beneath the slender breast! What a long and lovely flank!
What a lusty thigh! But why should I single out her features? Not a one did
I see unworthy of praise. (Ovid *Amores* 1.5.18-23)

The role of women in the male-authored and male-centred Latin writings
is prescribed (and therefore limited) by *genre*. In the passage above, Ovid
conforms to the conventions of Latin love poetry, or elegy, which celebrates
illicit love but glosses over the physical aspects of the beloved. The persona
of the poet-narrator is constructed as unconventional and passionate,
glorying in transgressive aspects of his love, but he is still a gentleman
and *never* mentions the buttocks or genitals of his love-object (Richlin
1983: 47).[1]

Castigated by the rhetorician Quintilian (*Institutio Oratoria* 10.193) as
'more lascivious' than his literary predecessors, Ovid has provided us with
one of the most explicit descriptions in so-called erotic poetry of a sexual
encounter and of a woman's body, but it is highly impressionistic. Not so
much a matter of moving parts as of discreetly disembodied bits – choice
cuts. He leaves it to the individual fantasy of the reader to flesh out the
details of 'Corinna's' beauty. Her body and self are merely hinted at.
Although given a name, the woman has no personality. Her sexuality? To

be inferred from her attendance at the tryst and the ritual modesty with which she resists the removal of her clothing (13-16).

The elusive object of the elegiac poet's passion is always charming, beautiful, wilful, often faithless (to the author's persona), venal and probably young. These elements were all inherited from Greek lyric poetry on erotic themes to or about male and female objects of the poet's desire. The Roman contribution to the Greek tradition was the idealisation of a more longstanding illicit passion between the author's persona and a named mistress: Catullus' Lesbia, Propertius' Cynthia, Ovid's Corinna, Tibullus' Delia. The focus of such poetry is on the feelings of the author (mostly male), writing in the first person. Extrapolating any female identity – let alone, female sexuality – from them is a challenge (Gold 1993, Wyke 1987a&b). Sexuality is itself a problematic concept in a post-Foucauldian world, but, given the tendency of the male gaze to sexualise its female object, it seems important to include in our readings some attempt at reconstructing Roman (male) attitudes to female desire and sexual behaviour.[2]

The womanly ideal of Roman culture was reflected in many media. As mothers, women were expected to be firm moral guides; as wives, to be chaste, domestically industrious and eager to please their husbands. Some epitaphs note a wife's lack of interest in social life outside the house as an advantage.[3] These wifely virtues are reflected in sexual praise and invective. Prose *genres* such as history and biography consciously presented models of good and bad behaviour in both men and women. It is notable that women who appear in the historical narratives as transgressing in one way, for example by intruding in the masculine political sphere, are usually credited with sexual transgressions as well.[4] Most women who appear in oratory and satire do so as objects of invective. Those are the literary *genres* which provide the greatest space to female sexuality and bodies. In letters, where women are more likely to figure as people with more credible, individual characteristics, their sexual activity is discussed only in the context of malicious gossip, with an emphasis on adultery.[5] Similar typings are apparent in non-literary written sources: the women of inscriptions are overwhelmingly praised as benefactors and patrons or as much lamented wives, mothers and daughters, but women who figure in graffiti by name or by occupation (especially *caupona*, landlady of a pub) are more likely to be sexualised and stigmatised.[6]

It will be evident that although the proper roles of the Roman woman as a good wife and mother entailed sex, this was not a type of sex likely to feature in most surviving writings.[7] The fact that female sexuality and the female body receive greatest attention in invective and satire has led scholars to concentrate on such representations when considering the subject. Popular works on Roman life – notoriously, Carcopino's *Daily Life in Ancient Rome*, which is still being reprinted – took Juvenal's sixth satire as reportage. Sophisticated modern scholarship has read invective and satiric treatments as evidence for strong Roman misogyny and distaste for the female body.[8]

Before drawing general conclusions about either behaviour or attitudes, we need to remind ourselves of the aims of ancient authors and the limitations (including ones of metre and prosody) imposed on them by form and tradition (Williams 1968). Take Cicero, for example. Many of his forensic speeches were as much part of political exchange as his senatorial repartee – it is not surprising that Clodia, elder sister of his arch political enemy Publius Clodius Pulcher, was the object of his biting wit in both venues.[9] The law-court was a theatre in which the public and the huge juries expected entertainment from the famous speakers of the day.[10] All Cicero's law-court speeches – designed for an adversarial performance in which evidence might take second place to innuendo – draw on a pool of comic and scurrilous tropes and stereotypes (the murderous stepmother, the tight-fisted old father, the untrustworthy whore) familiar from a range of media, including new comedy, folklore and political graffiti.[11]

As for satire, the political and sexual lampoons of Catullus' or Martial's 'sexual' epigrams – they thrive (like gossip and popular jokes) on shock and malice. In extracting the material and dissecting each theme in sober academic terms, in isolation from its literary context, we run the risk of forgetting that the author's main aim was to impress, to entertain, to raise a (shocked) laugh. The lack of comic potential in virtuous wives and loving husbands is amply attested by the succession of dreary US sitcoms to which the world has been subjected since the proliferation of television.[12] Wives who get drunk at religious festivals and mount donkeys or each other and who pee on imposing statues so that the unwitting husband wades later through the evidence of his wife's incontinence capture the attention more effectively.[13] The stunning punchlines of Catullus' and Martial's pithy epigrams become limp and loathsome (to ape their own imagery) outside their natural habitat.

This is not to say that we cannot analyse humour. It necessarily encodes cultural values and reflects important presumptions about norms. Our appreciation of Roman sexual attitudes has been enormously advanced by scholars who have rightly pointed, among other things, to the specific biases of the narrative stance – male, citizen-Roman, dominant-conservative – and the direction of the reader's gaze.[14] But when we attempt to reconstruct women's sexuality from such materials, we must allow for the likelihood that the grotesque, the transgressive, the aborted experience will dominate humour and invective, just as the pain of unrequited or betrayed love dominates erotic poetry.

All the same, it is notable how little we do hear of female desire in Latin literature. Greek myth, drama, philosophy and even law-court speeches reveal a strong male vision of the terrifying female principle, directly related to uncontrolled female sexuality and probably to a deep-seated fear of the female reproductive organs – consider the figures of the Gorgon and Medusa, to take two obvious examples.[15] The masculine apprehension of female sexuality (a feature of many early Christian writings) is literally proverbial in many contemporary Mediterranean cultures:

> Viewed from this perspective, women are perceived as powerful and danger-ous. Indeed, many Mediterranean societies conceptualise them as the sexual embodiment of the demonic. (Cohen 1991: 140-1)

This elemental construction of the female and her overwhelming sexuality is not prominent in Latin texts. Any study of Roman sources inevitably invites comparison with their Greek forerunners. Not only were Roman literary forms consciously derived from Greek originals, but Greek philo-sophic and medical thinking dominated Roman approaches to a number of spheres, including legal reasoning. It is all the more striking, therefore, that Roman sexual codes are equivocal. Sexual ideals and norms are fairly straightforward: women should be chaste and men should be discreet and self-controlled. Neither should engage in adulterous affairs or in oral or homoerotic sexual acts. And so on. Some illicit sexual activities were even subject to legal penalties.[16] But in practice the social and legal conse-quences of discovery were not usually as grim as their Greek equivalents. Even the most savage Roman husbands seem to have been more inclined to exact painful and humiliating revenge on the lovers and slaves of their wives than on the adulterous women themselves.[17]

Roman authors credit 'bad' women with sexual offences, but we seek in vain substantial evidence of a deep-seated, consistent masculine fear of female sexuality to correspond with that striking feature of Greek litera-ture. The result is that the sexuality of Roman women – even as a construction of male fantasy – is somewhat elusive and incoherent. Women's sexual behaviour is primarily glimpsed as a spur and a response to the desire of the male narrator rather than as an independent entity. Where we do encounter an elaborated construction of female sexuality it is that of gross and inappropriate sexual appetite – Lesbia combing the back alleys to 'peel' men; women copulating with other women; the woman of lineage eloping with a gladiator; the ugly old woman importuning a young lover – in the context of invective or caricature.[18] *Protervae* (forward) women these, who make sexual advances, rather than responding to male overtures.

To put it rather simplistically, the Greek model was posited on strict and interdependent notions of female chastity, male honour and obsession with (legitimate) biological paternity, while the Roman norms and practices were more flexible. The difference is encapsulated in two *causes célèbres*, the prosecution of Neaira by Apollodorus in Athens in the 340s BCE and Cicero's defence of Caelius Rufus in 56 BCE. In each case, a woman's sexual reputation was savagely and very publicly demolished in order to discredit men associated with her. Neaira and her descendants stood to lose their civic status. The jokes about Clodia's sex life gave the audience a good giggle and probably helped to acquit Caelius.[19]

There *was* a sexual double standard at Rome, which Cicero invokes in the *pro Caelio* to excuse Caelius' involvement with Clodia and to undermine her testimony. But it had none of the life-and-death force of the rigid code of honour and shame, tied to female chastity, which operated in classical Athens. Cicero was politically indiscreet to joke to Metellus Celer's and young Crassus' face about the virtue of their mothers, but they did not feel obliged to prosecute him or to kill him on the spot for his comments, as their Renaissance descendants might have done.[20]

The proper role for the free-born élite male author and his persona was that of penetrator – of women and of slave-boys – by whatever orifice he pleased. This was another double standard, between penetrator and penetrated, but distinguished Roman men (Caesar and Augustus among them) readily survived strong public accusations that they had been buggered. The ultimate double standard was the double standard of status, which denied any human rights, including sexual choice, to slaves. There were doubtless many technically free poor then, as now, whose circumstances put them in much the same category. But marriage could change that. It was not uncommon for a slave-woman to be freed for the purpose of marrying her owner.[21]

The consequence is that we must confront a number of ambiguities and silences in the Roman material, and attempt a nuanced reading of what is and is not there. Certainly women as a group were not accorded the relative sexual freedom of their male equivalents, but the control mechanisms were weak in the late Republic and early Empire and seem to have been regarded as options rather than moral imperatives. Female chastity was praised and illicit female sexual activity deplored and gossiped about, but the stronger sanctions like divorce and prosecution for adultery seem to have been employed intermittently and half-heartedly. As in the modern west, there was a double sexual standard but it was not absolute. Compliance with male desire was valued over any troubling assertion of sexual initiative by a woman, but female pleasure in sex was also acknowledged and even advocated. If we explore these complexities and assess the literary skewing towards repression or hostile representation of female desire we find the subject is not cut and dried.

Wicked women

Contemporary western constructions of women as less sexual than men are historical oddities. Until the eighteenth century, men of those same cultures (not only Fathers of the Christian church) considered women's sexual appetites and capacity for pleasure to be frightening and dangerous. In his anti-marriage sixth satire, Juvenal pillories Roman wives and claims that *libido* drives women of all social groups.[22] He vilifies a female gladiator for encroaching on a male activity, and harumphs that she would not be willing to forego the feminine prerogative of greater sexual pleasure.[23] He was invoking a commonplace: Roman authors adopted and re-worked the Greek myth of the prophet Teiresias, who had experienced life as a woman and reported that women enjoyed nine times the degree of sexual pleasure men derived from copulation.[24] Underlying the inherited models was the Greek belief that women were in general more animal than men and, being less capable of self-control, required external (i.e. masculine) monitoring to enforce their purity which, as we shall see in the following chapter, is frequently perceived as a necessary condition of the integrity of a group (the family, the *polis*, the tribe).[25]

Roman attitudes are more difficult to pin down. Female desire is problematic. Acknowledged and encouraged in some contexts, it is most likely to be associated in literature with the transgressive woman. There were two schools of thought on the female orgasm, some Roman medical authors favouring the view that it was essential for conception.[26] In book 3 of *The Art of Love*, a supplementary volume addressed (allegedly in response to demand) to women, Ovid acknowledges the female orgasm (802-4) and insists that the man and woman should both enjoy the sexual act to the full:

> The woman should feel the pleasurable melting in her innermost fibre, and that act ought to delight them both equally. (3.793-4)

but this assertion is undercut by the following passage, a much longer set of instructions (3.797-803) on how to fake it if you are so unfortunate as not to have that capacity!

Female sexual initiative is associated with wickedness. In his famous description of the Catilinarian conspirator Sempronia, Sallust mentions as one of her vices that 'her sex-drive was so inflamed that she made overtures to men more often than they did to her'.[27] Invective is therefore the natural repository for woman as desiring subject. Consider Catullus' vicious portrait of Lesbia prowling the back alleys for sex (Catullus 58.4-5), or his 'girl' being given a farewell message (Catullus 11.17-20) to go on breaking the pelvises of numberless lovers. Or Juvenal's description of the disgraced empress Messalina sneaking out of the imperial palace to a brothel to compete with a prostitute (Juvenal 6.115-32). The three authors show a similar disapproval of female lechery and immodesty and associate them with other vices (treason, indebtedness, cruelty, insincerity) but vary by *genre* in the degree of physical and sexual detail they provide.

Any discussion of Roman sexual attitudes and literary descriptions necessarily draws heavily on Martial, whose epigrams exploited the licence of the *genre* to dwell on the grotesque and deliberately gross physical detail. Desiring women are often the object of his ridicule, even when they suit the poet-narrator's purpose. 9.67 is a first-person boast about a lascivious girl (*lasciva puella*) who cheerfully acceded throughout the night to the poet's most embarrassing sexual wishes. The punch-line is a gloat, that the poet avoided granting her special wish (*cunnilingus*, perhaps?). In a society which revered faithfulness to the contract, it was apparently a good joke, to thwart female urges after gratifying one's own.[28]

Such poems seem to confirm the view that Roman men in general and Martial in particular were misogynist and fearful of female desire, but Martial's perspective varies.[29] Many of his epigrams are not about sex or the body, many are not attacks. The epigrams, viewed as a body of work, do not provide a consistent view of Roman society or Martial's own life – for example, we cannot tell whether he was married, although many poems are notionally addressed to a wife. There is truth in Richlin's observation that the élite male gaze of the satirist virtually defines the sexuality of the 'inferior' party – the (often lower-caste) boy or woman penetrated by the poetic *persona* – as irrelevant or aberrant, but this may be a feature of the context rather than an absolute credo of the individual author or of Roman men in general.[30]

Role reversal was a popular device of Roman love poetry: the woman became mistress (*domina*), the man her slave. Although female and notionally of a lower status than the poet-ego, the poet's mistress was able to exert her power over him. But other sources express masculine anxiety about any such reversal. The young empress Messalina is represented as forcing herself on men, the older woman who attempts to satisfy her desires is a particular object of ridicule.[31] Her body is described in detail never accorded the love-object of elegy. Apart from graffiti, the main references in Latin to female genitalia seem to be in this highly aggressive genre, full of death imagery and other deliberately disgusting bodily descriptions and associations.[32]

One of the repellent aspects of the older woman which features in such *genres* is her attempt to impose her sexual will. Typically, she tries to win over her lover with gifts or, as in Petronius *Satyricon* 134-8, attempts rape – activities which are not stigmatised if performed by the male author or a hero (such as a god).[33] Other manifestations of active female desire are also represented as physically grotesque and as transgressing proper social bounds, as in Juvenal 6.63-5 where one woman wets herself and another gasps as if having an orgasm over the performance of a popular artiste at the pantomime. A frightening voracity is sometimes a feature of such descriptions, and reflects a well-known male *angst* about the greater female sexual capacity. In the brothel, Messalina exhausts her many customers but not her own lusts:

still burning with the urgency of her stiff vulva, she withdrew, having exhausted the men but not yet satisfied. (Juvenal 6.129-30)

In his message to his girlfriend, Catullus urges:

Let her live and prosper with her lovers, embracing and grasping three hundred at once, loving none of them truly, but simultaneously cracking all their pelvises. (Catullus 11.17-20)

Sullivan (1991: 198-200) saw in such references a deep-seated masculine resentment of women asserting their sexual desires and interpreted it as unease with the growth of female wealth and social power in the early Empire.[34] This seems to me to give undue weight to one motif in one *genre*. Juvenal's sixth satire, riddled with uppity women who display unseemly desires, falls into the longstanding Greco-Roman tradition of attacks on marriage and particularly on the power a wealthy wife could exert over a husband. Such diatribes appear in comic *genres* throughout Roman history:

I can't stomach those women of great family, with their attitudes, their great dowries, their shouting, their bossy ways, their prestige carriages, their cloaks, their dyed cloth. They reduce their husbands to slavery with their extravagance. (Plautus *Aulularia* 168-9[35])

Anti-marriage (=anti-women) anecdotes and aphorisms were also kept alive in 'serious' prose *genres* in connection with the issue of whether the philosopher should marry. Such chestnuts had no more serious relation to life-choices than their modern equivalents. Augustus, happily married to Livia, allegedly began a hectoring address to recalcitrant élite bachelors in 9 CE with the words of a second-century BCE censor who was himself a husband and father:

Since nature has decreed that we cannot live at all comfortably with our wives, or live at all without them, we should consider the long-term benefit rather than immediate happiness.[36]

A selective emphasis on such jokes and traditional sayings gives a false impression of cultural consistency. They coexisted with institutionalised praise of erotic love (elegy) and marriage (epithalamia, letters, epitaphs). Older women were vilified as inappropriate sex-objects and even more inappropriate sexual subjects in invective *genres*, but are typically revered in serious prose *genres*, moral essays and epitaphs. There is no overwhelming reason to read one view as the 'true' one.

The rich literary sources of the late Republic and early Empire make it clear that, by and large, discreetly conducted adulterous affairs were tolerated. Illicit sex was celebrated in Latin love poetry, as was the charm and allure of women who practised it. Serial marriage was the norm. Female desire was acknowledged in principle and the extent and impor- tance of female sexual pleasure was enshrined in tradition and science. But epitaphs, literature and sculpture preserve the cultural stereotype of the virtuous woman as effectively asexual, devoted for life to one husband, self-effacing and deferential. The desiring woman is invoked as a trans- gressive category. Her sexual preferences, particularly if she takes the sexual initiative, arouse venom and ridicule in Roman authors, who group them with other aberrant or distasteful characteristics: smell, ugliness, homoeroticism, cruelty, oral sex, bossiness or an unseemly interest in masculine preserves.

Dream lovers

The ideal Roman woman was above all compliant. This sexual attribute was an extension of the virtue enshrined in tributes to the perfect wife, who was *morigera* and *obsequens*: 'agreeable' in every sense.[37] We have seen that references in Roman literature to the independent expression of sexual interest by a woman are met at best with male ambivalence, frequently with panic and loathing. Ovid's advice to women to display themselves in the most attractive way during the sexual act and to fake orgasm if necessary has no equivalent in his advice to men.[38] More aggressively, Martial takes the part of a husband ordering a classically modest wife to accede to his every sexual wish:

> Wife, adjust to my fancies or get out of the house! ... You don't see any need to wriggle or cry out or use your fingers – as if you're performing a solemn rite of sacrifice. The Trojan slaves used to masturbate outside the bedroom door whenever Andromache straddled Hector like a horse ... You don't let me bugger you, but Cornelia used to offer her arsehole to Gracchus, Julia to Pompey and Porcia to you, high-minded Brutus; ... If you like to be staid and proper, you're welcome to be virtuous Lucretia all day, but I want lascivious Lais at night. (Martial *Epigrams* 11.104)

In the novel *Metamorphoses*, the first-person narrator Lucius describes his sexual encounter with the maid Photis:

> While she spoke, she climbed on to the couch. Straddling me, she would lean back sensually and jig up and down repeatedly and, shaking my limber prick with her provocative movements, she satisfied me with the pleasure of a hovering Venus right up to the moment we both crashed simultaneously into a mutual embrace, panting out our last breath, our stamina exhausted and our limbs worn out. We passed the whole night wakefully with these grap- plings and others like them, until dawn's first light. (*Metamorphoses* 2.17)

Three different approaches in three different *genres*, but in each case female compliance with male preferences is expected in wives and mistresses alike.[39] It is not that women's sexual pleasure is denied or criticised as such but it is eclipsed in Latin literature by the masculine prerogative, which preoccupies each author. Representations of sexualised women follow the usual pattern of polar opposites: women who assert their own sexual wishes are bad or undesirable, the butt of male jokes; 'good' women inspire male desire and minister to it.

In this context, good women include the mistresses of elegy who hold the first-person poet in sexual bondage which purportedly flouts Roman conventions of class and marital propriety.[40] I subscribe to the now-dominant feminist view that the mistress of Latin love elegy is a construction of discourse, a poetic device rather than a 'real-life' beloved (Wyke 1987b; Gold 1993). Though tempestuous and lacking many of the virtues of the respectable Roman matron commemorated in epitaphs, the mistress also serves as a show-case of alternative desirable traits: she is beautiful, charming and fascinating. Latin love poetry is by definition illicit and sexual and the conflict-narrative is driven by sexual jealousy. But there is very little explicit sex in the *genre*. As we have seen, even the description of the beloved is restrained. Witty Ovid played dangerously with this *genre*, which had been established for two poetic generations.[41] His relatively detailed account of a pleasant afternoon with Corinna (whose status is uncertain) actually gives very little away.[42]

Ovid's poem has much in common with Apuleius' prose description of the narrator's encounter with the slave-girl Photis (Apuleius *Metamorphoses* 2.17), although Apuleius includes explicit detail about the sexual act. Both take some care in setting the scene and in both cases the woman shows a modesty or resistance which is discounted by the narrator.[43] Photis gets a richer characterisation, with dialogue to illustrate her wit and sauciness (*Metamorphoses* 2.9-10), and greater description of her energetic sexual enterprise (2.16-17). But just as Ovid glosses over the sexual act itself ('Who does not know the rest?' l. 25) so – having omitted the area between her belly and thighs – he cuts short the description of Corinna – 'Why should I list all her features?' (l. 23).[44]

Sex, like beauty, is implicit in certain *genres* and requires no elaboration. All the fantasy women of Latin love elegy have huge, expressive eyes and gleaming hair, but their beauty is otherwise left to the reader's imagination.[45] Compare the proverbially beautiful but modest Roman bride enticed from her home in Catullus' wedding hymn by the assurance that the groom is ready to foreswear adultery and to seek out the sexual delights of his new wife. We hear occasionally of the breast or shoulders of bride or mistress, but neither elegy nor *epithalamia* (wedding songs) are appropriate media for great bodily detail.[46] The reader must take the beauty and the consummation of sexual passion on trust.[47]

In spite of modern scholarly views to the contrary, there are indications that sexual passion was expected between married couples.[48] Catullus refers to the groom as burning with a deep flame of desire as great as the bride's (ll. 165-72) and the Stoic Seneca (himself renowned for his passion for his much younger wife) cautioned husbands against excessive sexual infatuation with their wives.[49] Pliny the Younger adopted motifs from Latin love elegy to describe his longing for *his* young wife Calpurnia during her absence:

> I am seized by unbelievable longing for you. The reason is above all my love, but secondarily the fact that we are not used to being apart. That is why I spend the greater part of the night haunted by your image; that is why from time to time my feet lead me (the right expression!) of their own accord to your room at the times I was accustomed to come and see you; that is why, in short, I retreat, morbid and disconsolate, like an excluded lover from an unwelcoming doorway. (Pliny *Letters* 7.5)

The expression is artificial (as is that of love poetry), but the existence of such a convention and the readiness of Roman husbands to publish such sentiments contradicts any blanket presumption that Roman men were expected to confine their romantic and sexual leanings to adulterous and déclassé liaisons.[50] Of course, this letter tells us as little as elegy about the sexuality of the woman addressed, in this case Pliny's wife, who definitely existed. We do, however, have some poetry by a woman, Sulpicia, apparently addressed to her fiancé or husband:

> I burn more than the other girls. The fact that I burn, Cerinthus, is no trial, if the same flame burns in your breast for me. (3.11 [4.5], 5-6 (in the Tibullan *corpus*))

> At last love has come – such love as it would be more of an offence to my modesty to conceal than to expose to anyone.
>   Won over by my prayers, Venus has brought him here and delivered him to my embrace. (3.13 [4.7], 1-4)[51]

Passion and its consequences were not necessarily equal. There were greater expectations of sexual fidelity on women than men, and women were adjured (like their modern equivalents) to work on their sexual allure to secure their husbands' interest. Consider the advice from the choir to the bride in Catullus' hymn:

> Bride, you, too, make sure you do not deny
> what your husband asks,
> lest he go elsewhere to look for it. (61.144-6)

This wording is echoed in the more outrageous advice to a wife in Martial

12.96.7-8: that her husband will have recourse to boys if she denies him her anus.

In the *Fasti*, a poetic version of the Roman religious calendar, Ovid gives a rather confused account of April rituals performed by married women in honour of 'Virile Fortune' and of Venus. He explains that married women drank special potions of poppy, milk and honey and bathed in warm water wearing only a myrtle garland in the course of annual rites designed to make them sexually attractive to their husbands.[52] This suggests an institutionalised acknowledgement of women's responsibility for the sexual success of their marriage, in line with women's more general appeals to Juno 'Husband-Pleaser' (*Viriplaca*), to ensure marital happiness.[53]

Women's sexuality (like most female characteristics) was of marginal interest to Roman authors. Women's sexual behaviour was introduced into appropriate *genres* to serve specific purposes of humour, social satire, moral *exempla*, gossip, promotion of a plot or exploration of an elegiac theme. With the exception of medical discourse, wedding hymns, some religious rituals and their political/narrative potential as victims, good women are not usually discussed in sexual terms. Bad women are almost always sexualised. The scholar looking for written references to female sexuality – and, indeed, to sex and the body in general – therefore concentrates on legal rulings on adultery or on satire and invective *genres* such as epigram, lawcourt speeches, graffiti and political lampoons. These not surprisingly adopt a negative, outrageous and often grotesque view of the female body and female sexuality. Rather than reading satiric derision of the female body as an expression of deep-seated hatred, we might see it as one of many indicators that bodily detail belongs primarily in such *genres*. The men pilloried by Martial, Juvenal and Catullus have bad breath, clean their teeth with their own urine, are physically gross and gluttonous or effete.[54] Sex is simply one aspect of such treatments. Juvenal's sixth satire and Martial's *Epigrams* provide the nastiest and most detailed literary attacks on women's sexualities and bodies, but they are not differentiated from equally savage denunciations of boring or ill-mannered women. It is our culture which places special emphasis on the sexual. The woman who repeatedly drinks and vomits in front of her pained husband, or corrects his grammar in public, is as odious to the satirist as the one who pees on the shrine of Chastity, then drunkenly copulates in the street with her girlfriend.[55]

Such figures exploit the comic and repulsive possibilities of the physical (Braund & Gold 1998) without the all-encompassing revulsion characteristic of later Christian references to the body. Unlike us, these Roman authors regularly saw a range of real (naked) bodies and displayed their own on appropriate occasions, such as attendance at the baths. In public and private settings, they were surrounded by idealised and naturalistic representations of the human form, draped and undraped. Male human genitals appeared on housefronts and corners and some female ones were in evidence. Graphic depictions of copulation decorated dinner services, elegant mirror-backs and wall-paintings in the public and semi-public areas of Roman houses (Johns 1982, Clarke 1998). This is the context in which we must assess the neglect and the specific treatments of female sexuality and bodies in various *genres*.

What can legitimately be said of Roman literature is that it privileges a dominant perspective which is primarily male, élite, citizen, Rome-centred and middle-aged.[56] This perspective marginalises other groups: children, slaves, women, foreigners, the free urban poor, peasants. Such groups are typically excluded from particular *genres* altogether or idealised or demonised as 'other.' In comic, satiric and invective forms, their foibles are exploited in stock ways. In *genres* which feature sex and the body – whether by implication, as in love elegy, or directly, as in satire – the sexual gaze is that of the penetrating, élite citizen male. This desiring gaze is fixed on the boy-slave or girl-mistress (in elegy) who can legitimately be penetrated.[57] Their sexuality is essentially irrelevant.[58] It is their desirability to the author which is of interest. Their role is to be pursued and penetrated. Elegy highlights the pursuit and the poet's feelings, while the coarser invective *genres* highlight the penetration. The selective authorial tunnel-vision may reflect literary convention as much as a pervasive cultural norm.

4

Rape in Roman law and myth

The following text is a revised reprint of an article originally published in 1982 as 'Women and Rape in Roman Law' in *Arbejdsnotat* 3/82, by the Women's Research Centre in Social Science, Copenhagen. Rape had become part of the political agenda around the world but was slow in reaching academe. Radical feminists saw rape and attitudes connected with it as crucial to women's oppression (Brownmiller 1976). This article is an early fusion of my political and academic concerns and draws on my experience of agitating for rape law reform in Australia and co-founding a Rape Crisis Centre in Canberra. Many of the circumstances I wrote about have (happily) changed.

Since then, rape has been incorporated in historical studies and the focus has shifted. Judith Evans Grubbs' classic (1989) analysis of abduction marriage was also written from a predominantly legal and anthropological perspective. More recent authors such as Sandy Joshel, Mary Beard and Carol Dougherty no longer need to justify writing about rape, using myth or being 'theoretical'.[1]

Readers unfamiliar with Roman law terms might like to consult Appendix 3.

*

In this survey of Roman laws on rape and related offences, designed to tease out underlying cultural assumptions about female 'purity' and its control, I necessarily simplify developments which spanned many centuries and fall back on theory because the legal sources by their nature provide few concrete examples of rape. My focus is on the legal assessment of the rapist's act and the consequences for the female victim. The study concentrates on the period *c.* 80 BCE to 530 CE, but begins with two stories which precede this period and have no legal force – which are, indeed, of dubious authenticity. Their importance lies in the place they occupied in the Roman national myth.

The first story is set notionally in the late sixth century BCE, when Rome was still a monarchy, and it concerns the noble matron Lucretia. During a military campaign, her husband and other nobles – including the royal

45

prince, Tarquin – fell to discussing their wives. It was evening, they were drinking, and they became vociferous on the relative merits of the women they had left at home while they made war. The camp was apparently not far from their estates, so one of the quarrelling men suggested that they ride immediately around their homes to surprise the women and settle the question of how well each wife conducted herself in her husband's absence. Accordingly, they mounted their horses and set off (Livy 1.57-9).

Lucretia easily won the title of most virtuous wife: all the other women were found lolling about, drinking wine and enjoying themselves (as their husbands had been doing), but Lucretia sat spinning with her slaves in spite of the lateness of the hour. All the men admired her and envied her husband. It is difficult to know how many of these elements were retained from earlier versions of the story. Tradition held that women had been forbidden wine in early Rome (certainly not the case in Livy's day), so the presence of alcohol at the all-female parties may once have added shock value to the tale (Pomeroy 1975: 154). Romans of the Republic also characterised Etruscan women as lax, so Livy's readers might have seen their behaviour as reinforcing a familiar stereotype (since Lucretia was retrospectively naturalised as quintessentially 'Roman'). In any case, Prince Tarquin's response to Lucretia's signal virtue was the usual one of the wicked tyrant of fable: her virtue inspired his lust. He returned to her home a few days later and, brandishing his sword, tried to force himself upon her. Undeterred by the prospect of death, Lucretia resisted. But when he threatened to kill a male slave and place his body in the same bed with hers, she submitted. As a relative – a connection not usually stressed in Roman nationalist tradition – Tarquin could claim to have killed noblewoman and slave in righteous outrage.[2] Having established Lucretia's courage and the fact that her good name was more important to her than her life (or the technical preservation of her virtue, for that matter), Livy moves the narrative through its established sequence, with an elaboration typical of the Roman declamatory tradition whereby schoolboys recreated great moments of history with set speeches by the participants.

Once Tarquin left, the ravished Lucretia summoned her husband and father, instructing each to bring a reliable friend to hear grave news. After telling her story to this family court, she took out a dagger and, in spite of their remonstrances, stabbed herself before their eyes. The men then stirred up a revolt against the monarchy. Her violation was held up as a symbol of royal abuse, a pretext for driving out the king and establishing a republic. Henceforth, Lucretia was the embodiment of the prime virtues of the Roman matron: industry and chastity.

The second story bears many similarities to this one. It is traditionally placed in the mid-fifth century BCE when the patrician and plebeian orders were engaged in savage class warfare in which the patrician Appius Claudius plays the part of the villain (Livy 3.44-8). His refusal to lay down

46

his extraordinary office as a member of a ten-strong committee (decemvirate) charged with publishing the law threatened the newly won representation of the *plebs* in the political hierarchy. He exploited his position to gain sexual access to a plebeian girl, Verginia (a word suggestively reminiscent of the Latin *virgo*), whose fiancé Icilius and father Verginius were prominent in the opposition to the patricians.[3]

Appius had one of his own social dependants (a *cliens*) declare that Verginia was not really Verginius' daughter but the child of a slave. The case, a blatant set-up, was tried before Appius himself in the market-place, where he ruled that Verginia was a slave and should be handed over instantly to the claimant. When her father and some bystanders tried to resist, Appius ordered armed men to seize the girl. In the certainty that the corrupt judgement was designed solely to put Verginia in Appius' power and that her seizure was tantamount to her sexual violation, her father Verginius took up a knife from a nearby butcher's stall and stabbed his daughter to death. Once more, a dead woman became a political symbol. Verginia's corpse was displayed by mourning women as testimony to patrician oppression (Mustakallio 1999). The plebeian response forced Appius and the other corrupt patricians out of their decemviral offices and constitutional rule was restored.

These stories, learned by all Roman children as an inspiring part of their early history, fall into an established tradition in ancient discourse of 'wicked tyrant' excesses. To the modern reader, they suggest other historical parallels, such as the story of the Sicilian Vespers, which presume that a woman's chastity is not merely an individual concern, or even solely a matter of family honour, but could implicate the wider community of her class, status group or nation.[4] The purity of a woman's body could thus be a sign for the purity, safety or political autonomy of the group.[5]

To the Livian Lucretia, neither death nor rape was quite as terrible as the shameful prospect of her body found in apparent adultery with a slave. Once violated, she took care to make the facts clear to her husband and her male relations before ending her life. Verginia's honour was, if anything, even more closely bound to that of men. As an unmarried girl, she plays a passive role in her own tragedy, defended by her fiancé and then killed – for her own protection – by her father. Where Lucretia's virtue is underscored by her physical courage and determination, Verginia's purity is a contingent quality, like her beauty. In each case, the woman's chastity is a family attribute, a cause which the men of her birth family *and* her husband/fiancé are prepared to defend as their own.

Should we take these stories to mean that chastity was defined 'objectively' in early Roman society? Did it make no difference to family honour whether a woman willingly lost her virtue or was taken by force? This notion is implicit in the Verginia story: when the court case was first scheduled for the following day, to enable her father to travel from his

47

military camp, her fiancé Icilius insisted that the girl must not pass the intervening night in the custody of the man who claimed her as a slave:

> I wish to wed a maiden Verginia and to have a chaste Verginia as my wife. The fiancée of Icilius shall not spend the night away from her father's home. (Livy 3.45.6)

Addressing his fellow plebeians after the incident, Verginius said that it had pained him to kill his daughter who was dearer to him than life, but that compassion had compelled him to commit this act of apparent cruelty to prevent her rape as a slave without rights (Livy 3.50.6).

In Valerius Maximus' version of the story, designed for rhetorical use, Verginius is praised because he 'preferred to be the killer of a chaste girl than the father of a despoiled one' (Valerius Maximus 6.1.2). This strongly suggests the view, evident in so many cultures throughout history, that a woman's worth was largely defined in terms of her chastity – that is, the guarantee of exclusive sexual (and reproductive) rights to her body. If this sexual access was abrogated by an unauthorised male, whether with the woman's complicity or against her will, she lost her value as an object of exchange between families and could redeem herself only by death. Solon's early sixth-century BCE reforms purportedly made it illegal to sell any Athenian citizen into slavery, the only exception being an unmarried girl who had been seduced or raped.[6] A deflowered Verginia, returned to her family by Appius Claudius, would not have been accepted by the father to whom she was dearer than life, and her fiancé Icilius, prepared to fight for her, would not have wanted to marry her unless her dowry came with her virginity.

Livy's account of Lucretia's story is a little more complex. The men to whom she told her version pronounced her innocent. It was Lucretia who insisted that she should die. Both she and the men had made the point that it was her body, not her spirit which had committed the offence.[7] The Livian Lucretia insists on her own death as a necessary *external* proof of her innocence. She demands of the men that they swear to avenge her by punishing her violator, she demands of herself that she commit suicide:

> You will see to it that he gets his deserts. As for me, I absolve myself of wrongdoing, but not of its punishment. Nor will any unchaste woman justify her continued existence by invoking the example of Lucretia. (Livy 1.58.7)

The corollary being that a dead Lucretia will be a very suitable testimony – or monument – to chastity, which is what she did become (cf. d'Ambra 1993: 85-6). Perhaps this is a recognition by Livy of the value and varied potential of stories – only too appropriate in an age of important myth-making by himself, Vergil and Augustus about the origins of the Roman state.

4. Rape in Roman law and myth

The concept of guilt (*culpa*) as defined by intention rather than action seems rather sophisticated for the sixth-century BCE setting of the story. Perhaps Lucretia's argument represents Livy's attempt to explain to his contemporaries an element in the traditional account which they might find puzzling. While Romans of his day (probably 59 BCE – CE 17) could accept the notion that a man might 'save' his virgin daughter from enslavement and rape by killing her *before* these could take place, they might have had more difficulty in seeing why a married woman who had satisfied her menfolk of her innocence after the event should nonetheless take her own life. Perhaps there had been a shift in the intervening years, whereby the woman's *intention* was taken into consideration. This would emanate from the socially current notion of what constituted chastity (and its opposite), and would have an effect on its legal expression.[8]

Until the marriage laws of 18 BCE, adultery was generally judged within a family council similar to that described in Lucretia's case. Augustus' legislation translated adultery into a criminal charge which could be brought before the courts by any public-spirited citizen.[9] It was specifically and repeatedly stated in subsequent judgements that a married woman who had been raped could not be charged with adultery.[10]

So the reasoning attributed by Livy to Lucretia's kinsmen, that no blame attached to the woman who had been an unwilling partner, seems to reflect the thinking of his own era. The men of archaic Rome probably took the same line apparent in so many cultures, past and present – that the act itself sullied the woman inescapably. The interesting thing about the Roman equivalent is that it should have developed into a more sophisticated notion, recognising an individual concept of guilt by intention rather than passive complicity. The transition was not necessarily neat and wholesale. In a speech delivered in the very late Republican era, Cicero spoke as if some raped women of his own day committed suicide, and the highly artificial speeches of the rhetorical schools of the early empire refer to hypothetical cases of young boys and girls who take their own lives from shame after such an attack – so such instances, even if fantastic, were not unimaginable (Cicero *Pro Scauro* 2.6). But, as far as the law was concerned, blame attached only to the rapist, and in general by the late Republic the victim was seen as someone who had suffered an outrage.

The legal definition of rape was closely tied to a woman's status and circumstances. As in most states, a husband could force himself on his wife without breaking any law. Lord Hale pronounced in the eighteenth century that 'by their mutual matrimonial consent and contract the wife hath given up herself in this kind unto her husband, which she cannot retract'.[11] Despite recent moves for reform, it is still virtually impossible for a woman in any modern state to have her husband charged with rape unless she has at least begun proceedings for a formal separation – the archaic wording of Hale's judgement expresses a view which still holds at law.[12] The modern woman and the woman of ancient Rome differed from women of early modern England in their access to divorce. A Roman citizen woman of the late Republic or early Empire (*c.* 200 BCE – 330 CE) who considered herself ill-used could speedily leave her marriage – but we have no way of knowing whether, like so many women throughout history, she accepted a certain amount of sexual abuse and physical assault from her husband as part of the natural order.

A female (or male) slave in Roman society had no recognised right to sexual choice or even the right of refusal – she was a piece of property. Verginia's father and fiancé regarded her enslavement as tantamount to sexual violation. This concept had undergone no alteration between early and imperial times. Thus we should be aware that great numbers of women – whether actually in brothels, serving primarily as agricultural workers or urban domestic slaves – were by virtue of their servile status condemned to endure any sexual inroads dictated by their owners, who could not only exercise such rights themselves but instruct the women to submit to the demands of others. Cato the Censor wrote in the second century BCE that it was economical for a master to charge his male slaves a fee each time they had sex with the female slaves.[13]

At law, rape was classified as a form of violence, and covered by the *lex Iulia de vi publica*, the 'Julian law on public violence', which was probably established *c.* 45 BCE. The law, and subsequent judgements, are recorded in later compilations, which give as the definition of rape forcible sexual intercourse with a boy or a woman 'or anyone', though the terms sometimes specify – or imply – that the offence is wholly criminal only if the victim is *free-born*.[14] The characterisation of rape as criminal violence suggests that it was seen as an offence against public order, to be punished by society rather than the individual victim. As a 'capital' offence, it could be punished by banishment and diminution of civil status or by death. The status of the criminal probably determined the punishment (Garnsey 1970).

Civil proceedings arising under the law *de iniuriis* covered a greater range of sexual nuisance. This very broad heading encompassed a variety of insults, physical or verbal, of which sexual approaches formed only a small part. A charge *de iniuria* could be brought by the victim or by someone who could reasonably represent the victim at court – thus a man could bring a charge on behalf of his son or daughter and at the same time on his own behalf, since any insult to them affected him also. I should point out that a Roman citizen did not normally become independent (*sui iuris*) at law until his or her father died. In this respect, women were on the same footing as men, though convention discouraged even independent women from appearing in court on their own behalf, and the law from the early empire forbade them to appear on behalf of another, as men did.[15] It is expressly stated that a husband may appear for an insulted wife but not vice versa (Justinian *Institutes* 4.4.2). The reason for bringing such a suit was to gain monetary compensation for damage suffered: the seriousness of the damage was assessed not only in terms of the actual injury, but the circumstances in which it occurred and the social standing (*dignitas*) of the victim.[16]

The rulings *de iniuriis* bear a certain resemblance to modern notions of 'sexual harassment' which some feminist reformers are currently trying to introduce into penal codes.[17] Such actions are carefully defined in the Roman law: for example, *adsectatio*, the offence of following about a free-born girl or boy or a matron, and making lewd suggestions. A man brought to court on such a charge could argue in his defence that the woman was dressed like a prostitute or slave, not as a respectable married woman (*materfamilias*).[18] In modern cases of rape a victim deemed to be dressed immodestly might also find herself penalised for not dressing like a respectable matron, but the standard is based more on undefined notions of propriety (although class bias is by no means unknown) and the cultural presumption that men cannot be held entirely responsible for their own sexual responses (our version of *infirmitas sexus*). As in most legal systems, the rapist and harasser (but not the abductor) was constructed as a stranger, attacking the stronghold of the family/household from outside. Roman law displays the familiar refusal to acknowledge the greater likelihood of his being an intimate.

A significant development in Roman law on sexual violence was the emergence of the crime *raptus*, defined in 320 CE under Constantine, the first Christian emperor, as the abduction of a girl without the agreement of her parents. The punishment was death. If the man accused of *raptus* tried to plead in his defence that the girl had gone willingly with him, this would not prevent his execution but would have the result that the girl would also be put to death. The crime is therefore defined as a theft from the parents rather than as physical violence or an infringement of the girl's personal rights. The wording of this ruling was very severe – servants who carried messages from a seducer were to have boiling lead poured down their throats, and a girl who failed to cry out loudly for help on being violently attacked by someone who broke into her home lost the right of succession to her parents' property.[19]

Another development was the insistence that parents were not permitted to conceal the crime afterwards by quickly marrying the girl off to her ravisher. Anyone who discovered such a marriage was encouraged to report it – a slave who did so, for example, would be granted freedom – and the guilty parents would be exiled. If the concealment went undiscovered for five years, the parties were safe thereafter from prosecution and any children of the union were legitimate (*Codex Theodosianus* 9.24.3). There are procedural similarities to the Augustan laws on adultery, which punished any husband who had retained a wife he knew to have been guilty of adultery. In that case, too, outsiders were encouraged by the law to bring charges and immunity was gained by husband and wife alike after five years without a prosecution.[20]

The scope of the law *de raptu* was gradually extended to include both maidens and widows consecrated to God, i.e. nuns. A man even attempting to persuade a nun to marry him could be deprived of citizenship under this law. Again, informers were encouraged to report instances of the crime (*Codex Theodosianus* 9.25.1-3). In the sixth century CE the definition of *raptus* seems to have covered all single women: honourable or free-born virgins, whether betrothed or not, widows and even freed slaves and slave women (if they belonged to someone other than the ravisher). Married women were cursorily included, as an afterthought. The crime, stated the emperor Justinian, should rightly be punished by death since it is as bad as homicide – it is, he pronounces, particularly bad if committed against virgins or widows dedicated to God because it is an offence not only against humanity but against the Almighty himself – especially since 'virginity or chastity, once corrupted, cannot be restored'.[21] It would seem that the wheel had come full circle, back to the archaic notion.

It is interesting that this separate legal category, *raptus*, should have arisen in the first place. Forcible rape of any woman was already covered by the Julian law on violence (*lex Iulia de vi publica*), lesser sexual offences could be prosecuted privately, under the law 'on insult' (*de iniuriis*), and consensual but unlawful sexual intercourse with a married woman or young girl was punishable as criminal adultery or fornication (*stuprum*) under Augustus' moral legislation.[22]

The law on *raptus* therefore added little, but underlined the importance of parental consent. Like the Augustan law(s) of some three and a half centuries earlier, it added the voice of imperial authority to the cause of private morality, which was thus translated into the realm of public concern. Adultery and elopement, like rape, were species of theft from husband and father but *also* offences against morality which husband and father had no business to ignore, whatever their personal inclinations.

And what of Justinian's official statement in 533 CE that a woman's virtue, once lost, was irredeemable? Ancient morality had decreed that it was so, with the consequence that the woman in question became unmarriageable and therefore worthless in social terms.[23] This had apparently ceased to be the necessary result of a 'loss of virtue' in the last century of the Roman Republic, when adultery in the upper classes was not viewed as strictly and women could initiate divorce fairly easily or re-marry even after having been themselves divorced for adultery. The tone of the fourth-century laws suggests that at least some parents preferred to sanction the hasty marriage of a daughter who had been raped by – or willingly eloped with – a man of whom they disapproved. They clearly thought the situation could be retrieved (as it could in Sicily under the prevailing *onore* system) by subsequent marriage. So some, at least, felt that lost chastity *was* recoverable as long as the neighbours did not find out.[24]

Not only does the imperial code on *raptus* dismiss as irrelevant the question of a young girl's consent, but Constantine makes the (inaccurate) point that women had traditionally been excluded from judicial processes because of their imperfect powers of judgement.[25] This bears some similarity to the reasoning behind the modern notion of a 'minimum age of consent', whereby girls below a certain age are deemed incapable of deciding for themselves whether to have sexual relations. It has been argued by some modern jurisprudents that such laws, which claim to protect the young from sexual exploitation, rest in effect on the assumption that a young girl is incapable of appreciating the 'market value' of her sexual favours:

> A popular conception of a girl's sexual indulgence or virginity as a single 'thing' of social, economic and personal value explains in part, the law's concern with her desire to 'understand'. An 'unwise' disposition of a girl's sexual 'treasure', it is thought, harms both her and the social structure which anticipates certain patterned uses. Hence, the laws of statutory rape intervene to prevent what is predicted will be an unwise disposition.[26]

Such an analysis would have made immediate sense to any Roman parent. In a culture in which marriages were regularly arranged by the older generation, and in which girls were married very young, it was taken for granted that a girl could not be trusted to make important decisions such as whom she married or whom she had sex with.[27] Rape could not therefore be seen as an invasion of her right to choose her own sexual partner so much as the destruction of her chief commodity in the exchange which accompanied marriage, and which she was not equipped to negotiate.

The elaborated rules of 533 CE (*Codex Iustinianus* 9.13) throw some light on the connection between virginity and the matrimonial trade-off. The *raptor* must suffer death, but the fate of his property depends on the status of the woman concerned. If she is a slave or former slave, she receives nothing. If she is free-born she receives the estate of the *raptor* and of anybody who helped him in the abduction. If unmarried, she may take this property as her dowry – that is, she is not entirely unmarriageable, though she may, if she wishes, refuse to marry at all (a possibility unlikely to occur to a pre-Christian legislator). This notion of compensation seems to assume forcible abduction rather than elopement as the usual case, just as it assumes that the 'typical' victim is a young virgin (a common modern assumption in culturally elaborated rape discourse).

These laws could be read as a decline (in very general terms) in women's standing from the last century of the Republic (*c.* 133-27 BCE) to the era of the Christian emperors from Constantine to Justinian.[28] The primitive, unyielding notion of chastity preserved in the traditional tales of Lucretia and Verginia reappears under Christian regimes with a more sophisticated rationale based on a categorical notion of sin and a strong sense of the general importance to the community of chastity – as opposed to a family-based notion of honour. The Julian law on public violence relegated rape to the class of violent assault from which any citizen could expect the protection of the state. *Raptus*, as dealt with by the Christian emperor Constantine, was defined in terms of parental rights and public morality and allowed for the legal penalisation even of the victim of sudden violence. The rights of the father, the purported basis for the rulings on *raptus*, were in fact abrogated, for parents were not permitted to yield to a social sense of shame but had to put public morality above all other considerations. Sexual purity as such was now officially a community concern. Consider the fifth-century ruling that someone who brought an accusation against a family for conniving at a 'rape/abduction' (which could include elopement) by agreeing subsequently to marriage was himself immune to charges of being an informer, 'for a person must not be considered an informer if his humanity invited him to this course for the sake of the purity of religion'.[29]

The Christians are not entirely responsible for this development. The ground was laid by the Augustan relegation of adultery to the sphere of criminal activity which could be denounced by a member of the public as well as the 'injured' father or husband. But the elaboration of an 'absolute-purity' principle seems to have been reinforced by Christian ideology. Throughout Roman history, chastity was an important attribute of a (free) woman, and enhanced her value in the marriage stakes. Significantly, it was by marriage that major property redistributions were carried out, by means of the dowry which the bride took with her, and, from about the third century CE, the substantial gift the groom customarily gave her on or before marriage (bridewealth).[30] Inheritance, the other chief mode of re-distribution, was eventually determined by marriage links. Hence the connection noted above between the purity of the wife/mother and the reproductive rights, which would ensure the legitimate issue of their right to inherit.[31]

The importance of female chastity was therefore implicit in the Roman economic scheme, but there was a period between rustic simplicity and Christian severity when the notion would appear to have been a little more flexible. This may have been the background to classifying rape as one of many unacceptable forms of violence. The later, increasing emphasis on the 'theft' aspect of rape/abduction, the stress on the absolute duty to put public morality before private shame, the inclusion in the definition of criminal *raptus* of persuading a young girl to elope, or a nun to marry – all these seem to mark a hardening of official attitudes.

All this is necessarily speculative. I offer this study of rape in Roman law as a tentative contribution to those researchers of women in history, of rape in modern society or of the relationship between women's overall status and economic exchanges, in the hope that it might stimulate their own quests. It seems to me, for example, highly suggestive that the periods of 'absolute chastity' in Roman history coincide with those times when divorce was least acceptable in general and when its initiation by the wife was well-nigh impossible. It would be interesting to see if this association between divorce and ideals of feminine purity had parallels. Modern western shifts away from the traditional stress on female chastity are often linked with developments in contraception, but I suggest that they could be influenced as well by the decline in importance of inheritance and immovable property in predominantly urban economies. Comparisons from feminist historians of post-industrial cultures might be productive.

I have not dealt here with the vital issue of male motivation, which is not discussed in Roman law. This should not be taken to mean that I discount its importance, particularly in dealing with the radical feminist argument that rape is universally used by men as a means of intimidating women as a group. In limiting this chapter to two early myths and the later law, I have necessarily placed all my emphasis on the consequences of the act for the woman. I also view rape as a crime of violence, an expression not so much of male sexuality as of male aggression towards women by means of sex. Historically, it has been associated with the woman's devaluation in the overall social pattern of exchange, and I see this as the basis of the view, common to so many diverse cultures, that the crime shames the victim more than the criminal. The laws which define the crime in any society reflect some dominant attitudes to women and can determine the fate of the victim herself after the event. There are women in Pakistani prisons now because, having been raped, they are technically guilty of the crime of adultery.

Law, however, is only part of the picture. A spokesman for Kosovar refugees in Australia stated (March 2000) that women who had been raped in the war were viewed as 'damaged' by many in their own honour-based culture. We all take on the heritage of a past age in every society. We may reject the heritage and eradicate it from our legal system, but its vestiges can still affect us all. Popular responses to rape may echo other times and other views. If we are to combat them, as we combat the anachronistic laws, we can benefit from a deeper understanding of the traditional basis of these views, which have outlived the conditions that gave rise to them.[32]

5

Woman as symbol of decadence

Once upon a time, want used to keep Latin women chaste. Their hovels were protected from vice by their hard work, their lack of sleep, their rough hands, coarsened from teasing out Tuscan wool; by the prospect of Hannibal descending on Rome and their husbands doing guard duty at the Colline Gate watch-tower.

Nowadays we suffer the drawbacks of long-established peace. Decadence (*luxuria*) – more savage than enemy arms – has invaded us and takes its revenge for our conquest of the world. (Juvenal *Satires* 6.287-93)[1]

The good old days

It was a truism of antiquity that the current age had degenerated from lofty ancestral standards. Roman historians and epic poets were particularly prone to shape works around this view, but it pervaded a range of literary sources. The decline revealed itself in various ways, but some themes – such as the corrupting power of luxury and foreigners – were dominant and the symptoms were particularly evident in the aristocracy of the capital, especially its young men and married women (a trend possibly related to the fact that literary works were notionally aimed at older men of this group). Indeed, when authors of any period wrote generically of the women of their day, it was usually to contrast their luxurious, promiscuous or frivolous behaviour with that of their venerable ancestresses. Juvenal's sixth satire is simply the most famous and memorable example.

The great mothers of Roman history were upheld as guardians of traditional culture and values, but rejection of maternity by contemporary women formed a part of ancient (as of modern) popular moral discourse.[2] This reflects a common tendency to type women by their sexual and reproductive characteristics. Tut-tutting about upper-class resistance to parenthood became the literary fashion from the beginning of the Principate and women were often blamed for deliberate childlessness although it was men, not women, who actively resisted Augustus' attempts to promote marriage and parenthood by legislation in 18 BCE and 9 CE.[3]

Claims by Roman authors that women aborted children, treated by some scholars as reportage, are better viewed as part of a moral discourse

56

in which women, particularly élite women, serve a symbolic purpose. Such literary references to abortion appear to be based on gossip or moralising fantasy rather than circumstantial knowledge of an established practice. The historical value of such claims is moot. The presumed association of abortion with adultery – and with lesser offences, such as vanity – made it a fit subject for misogynist denunciations and speculative gossip but not for personal confidences by offending women to male authors. Juvenal's rhetorical statement:

> Rarely does a wife give birth on a gold-plated bed. So great is the power of the magical arts, the potions of the woman who makes them sterile and murders the humans in their bellies for a fee. (Juvenal *Satires* 6.594-7)

might attest the cultural reality of a specific masculine anxiety (like his references to women poisoners in the same satire) but tells us nothing of behaviour in any social sphere. The lines following the quote make the suggestion – scarcely a serious one – that a well-born husband might as well give his wife the appropriate drug to guard against the shame of a child which proves his wife's doubly transgressive adultery with an African slave (598-601). Lower-class women, whom he grudgingly praises in the following lines for at least having to endure childbirth, were also criticised in the preceding passage (588-91). Juvenal knew little and cared less about the Roman lower classes – like women, they were a device to be used to make a satiric point.[4]

Moralists bewailing the degeneracy of women might praise individuals who served, like Juvenal's lower-class women, to highlight the vices of the targeted group. Seneca, honouring his own mother, contrasted her with her contemporaries who, he claimed, avoided pregnancy for fear of spoiling their figures (*Ad Helviam* 16.3). This is the classic mark of a stereotype: counter-examples are treated as exceptions, while transgressive women are cited with some relish as confirmation.[5] The secrecy of abortion, its disreputability and its strong association with adultery make it highly improbable that any of Seneca's women friends actually told him (or anyone else) that she had had an abortion to preserve her looks.

The great mass of women presumed to be morally inferior to their forebears was also differentiated by a hierarchy of virtue according to class and region. The towns of the provinces and Italian municipalities were held to preserve an ancestral standard of probity unknown in the corrupt capital of the author's day; the country was agreed to be morally superior to towns, lower-class women to be more virtuous than their élite counterparts.[6] It will be apparent that the worst examples were, all things being equal, to be found among upper-class women at Rome (other than mothers, friends and patrons of the author).

In the modern world, social darwinism and adherence to the intrinsic benefits of continued technological progress dominate public discourse, but they somehow co-exist with the idea that the present age is less good and happy than the past. This proposition surfaces, for example, in protests against the displacement of regional culture, especially cuisine, by global (i.e. US) culture and the alleged decline of nebulously defined 'traditional family values'. Food, television, teenage pregnancy and divorce are problematised and can all be invoked as symbols of moral degeneration, to be juxtaposed with images of past practice which are assumed rather than defined and described.

Ancient authors, too, could represent the decline in various ways. The simplicity and virtue of the past were typically contrasted with the extravagance, effeteness and selfishness of the current age. Young Roman men, like (married) women, often signified these vices. The Greek historian Polybius (c. 200-118 BCE) contrasted the virtue of his friend and patron Scipio Aemilianus with the decadence of his contemporaries:

> Some of the youth were preoccupied with courting boys, others given to frequenting female prostitutes. Many had a craze for musical performances and drinking-parties and the associated expenditure. In the course of the war with Perseus, they had soon succumbed to the easygoing Greek attitude to this kind of thing. The extravagance entailed in this kind of lifestyle was so out of control that many would pay a talent for a pretty boy and three hundred drachs for a pot of salt fish from the Black Sea. This was why Cato said before the popular assembly that it was a sign of a state's degeneracy that cute boys commanded a better price than paddocks and pots of imported fish fetched more than farm labourers. (Polybius 31.25.4-6)

Clearly Polybius agreed with Juvenal that the defeat of Hannibal had been a mixed blessing for the Roman state. Livy (c. 59 BCE – 17 CE)[7] and Pliny the Elder (23-79 CE) also dated Roman extravagance and the public display of wealth from this period of imperialist expansion beyond the Italian peninsula.[8] But Valerius Maximus (fl. 27-37 CE) and Plutarch (c. 49-120 CE) preserved proverbial examples of archaic simplicity from the second century BCE itself.[9] Sallust (probably 86-35 BCE) wrote in the late Republic of the moral decline of the Roman senatorial order of the late second century BCE, showing its members as venal and incompetent in contrast to the municipal purity of the lower-born general Marius.[10] The philosopher Posidonius (c. 135-51 BCE) blamed Lucullus' eastern campaign (73-67 BCE) for the corruption of Roman austerity. Tacitus (c. 56-118 CE) later used the autocratic principate and the fawning acquiescence of the senatorial order to it as his major theme.[11]

Thus bribery, epicurean or greedy eating habits, extravagance and political cowardice could be invoked to illustrate the presumed decline, although its date and specific cause were variously assigned.[12] But some symbols were particularly popular – food and women among them.[13] In

5. Woman as symbol of decadence

Latin literature, women – particularly those of the upper classes at Rome itself – were invoked both as a group and through named examples as signs of the historic deterioration which everyone knew as a given. Condemnation of their Roman counterparts is implicit in Tacitus' praise of the German women:

> And so they preserve an unassailable virtue. They are not corrupted by the licentious atmosphere of public festivals or the excitements of dinner parties. Men and women alike are innocently unaware of clandestine notes. (Tacitus *Germania* 19.1)[14]

Abortion: sources and scuttlebut

Oddly enough, *genres* which celebrate romantic/sexual love routinely exclude its consequence. References to pregnancy and childbirth are as rare in Latin love poetry as in modern music videos.[15] Ovid breaks the silence in two poems on the subject of 'Corinna's' abortion, *Amores* 2.13 and 14 (or 14 and 15, by an alternate system). The first poem, of 28 lines, consists primarily of a prayer to Isis (7-18) and to Eileithyia, who presides over women in labour (19-28). The prayers are preceded by four lines of scene-setting: Corinna is at death's door after secretly procuring an abortion. Her pregnancy was caused by the poet – at least, he *thinks* it was his doing (5) since he had often performed the act likely to cause this result (6). She therefore deserves his anger, but it is eclipsed by his fears for her safety (4).

Amores 2.14 (15), clearly intended to be read with 2.13 (14), approaches the same subject from a different angle, denouncing abortion at greater length, but also concluding with a prayer (41-4): that the monstrous act go unpunished this once. The customary contrast between the morals of ancient and modern Woman (9-18) leads to specific reference to the relationship of the poet and his mistress. The poem veers throughout between the general and the personal. Each figure is rounded off by a reproach addressed to the mistress (7-8; 23-4; 33-4). What is the good, asks the poet, of achieving respite from war if girls wound themselves and wrench fragile fetuses from their wombs (1-4)? The bald statement that the first woman who committed this act deserved to die from her own warfare (5-6) leads into a rhetorical question:

> Do you have to choose the sorry arena for your battleground, just to avoid the charge of a wrinkled belly? (7-8)

The poet goes on (9-18) to contrast such behaviour with that of the distant past in an increasingly preposterous series of 'What-ifs': if the nymph Thetis or the goddess Venus had behaved in this way Rome would never have been founded.[16] You yourself (presumably Corinna) and I would have perished if our mothers had done this (19-22). Why do you cruelly spoil the burgeoning fruit (23-4)? Why not let the embryo develop naturally? Why dig out your internal parts with weapons and inflict poisons on the unborn? And so on (23-8).

The women of mythology who killed their children had – unlike the addressee – suffered cruelties from their fathers (29-32). Not even the brute beasts kill their young (35-6). And, indeed, girls suffer themselves from this act. Often, the girl who kills her own progeny *in utero*, dies herself and those who hear about it say 'Serve her right!' (37-40). The tone changes once more in the final lines, 41-4: may these words not prove a potent omen, but dissipate; and may the gods allow a safe outcome to the wrong done this time. Punishment can follow a repetition.

Ultimately too clever for his own good, Ovid was not always to be taken at face value, at least by his favoured audience – witness his closing prayer that his words evanesce, which is undercut by his publication of those words. Juxtaposition of arms and poetry was a commonplace of love poetry which perhaps took on new meanings in the charged atmosphere of Augustus' total propaganda programme.[17] Ovid's apparently respectful reference at the outset of the poem to the benefits of the much-vaunted Augustan peace is countered by the incongruous association of combat with abortion. Mockery of the state's moral rearmament programme is likely in the parade (lines 9-18) of mythic/historic characters who figure in the imperial promotion of Rome's founding myths – notably, Vergil's *Aeneid* – linking its origins with those of the ruling Julian family.[18]

Ironic overtones apart, Ovid's surface meaning reflects (and cheekily exceeds) conventional sentiments. To these, he adds detail quite inappropriate to the *genre*: namely his reference to implements and to abortifacient pessaries, lines 27-8 (although *dira venena* might refer to drugs taken orally). Many twentieth-century novels, especially those written by women, have covered emotional and physical aspects of abortion, but ancient authors referred to the practice briefly, in more general terms, to make a moral point – usually to confirm the flightiness or sexual immorality of the modern woman. We have seen the uniform sentiment expressed in the diverse *genres* of satire (Juvenal), philosophical essays (Seneca) and elegiac poetry (Ovid), all stressing the furtiveness of the process and the triviality of the motive – vanity, rather than social shame, health fears or economic desperation.

Vanity is presumed also in *Nux*, an odd poem included in the Ovidian corpus:

Nowadays, a woman who wants to look beautiful defiles her womb (*uterum vitiat*); anyone *wanting* to be a mother is a rarity in this day and age.[19]

and in Aulus Gellius' Latin version of the eloquent sentiments of a Greek philosopher, Favorinus, in support of maternal breast-feeding. Favorinus (85-155 CE) employed a number of analogies to highlight the disadvantages of putting an infant out to nurse, abortion among them:

> In so doing, [mothers] display the same folly (*vecordia*) as women who strive by certain secret devices (*commenticiis fraudibus*) to abort the fetus of the very creature conceived in their own body, for fear that the smooth surface of their belly might be spoilt with stretch-marks and droop from the weight of the burden and the labour of birth. (*Noctes Atticae* 12.1.8)

This frivolous motive is belied by the authors' own stress on secrecy and deceit (e.g. *clam*, *Amores* 2.13.3; *fraudas*, *Amores* 2.14.23; *fraudibus*, *Noctes Atticae* 12.1.8), which implies fear of disgrace following the exposure of an illicit union rather than a concern about 'wrinkles' (stretch-marks) which would normally be concealed from view (even during love-making, if one followed Ovid's own advice: *Ars amatoria* 3.785-6). And in the *Heroides*, Ovid uses the example of an unmarried girl desperate to destroy the result of incest.[20] Tacitus claims that the emperor Nero accused his young wife (and stepsister) Octavia of procuring an abortion to cover up her adultery. Tacitus treats the suggestion as the depraved act of a cruel tyrant, a clear pretext for judicial murder. Elsewhere, however, imperial biographers lend credence to such imputations when it suits their narrative purpose.[21] In each case, abortion is associated with adultery and sometimes incest, sources of great shame.[22] Juvenal's sarcastic assurance (6.598-601) that abortion will cover up scandalous misalliances is posited on the same adultery-abortion nexus.

These literary references, though taken for centuries as evidence of the moral decline of Roman society, are useless as historical information. Rather, they express masculine fears about secret female practices, on a par with fears of poisoning (of husbands or stepchildren) or the introduction by women of 'suppositious' children into the family.[23] Such fears have many parallels and almost infinite variations in many cultures.[24]

Their divorce from reality is shown not only by the stereotypic representation of motive but even by accounts like Ovid's or Suetonius' which make a moral cause-and-effect argument from the dangers of abortion to the mother, passing over the fact, which they knew perfectly well, that childbirth was also dangerous.[25] Moreover, the masculine distaste for abortion stemmed from the idea that women might thereby control their own fertility, not from any disinterested horror of child-murder. These men lived, after all, in a world in which fathers had (and exercised) an absolute right to determine whether a new-born baby was to be reared or put out with the rubbish, to die of exposure or be attacked by feral animals.[26]

The extreme power of the Roman father – *patria potestas* – was never challenged as such in Roman literary, moral or legal writings. The equivalent to the rather casual denunciations of abortion and women's morals lies in literary head-shaking about the avoidance of parenthood *these days* by the wealthy. From the time of Augustus this becomes a literary commonplace, articulated at different times over more than a century by the childless Horace, Seneca and Pliny.[27] Just as women were assumed to have abortions for trivial reasons, so upper-class couples or men were assumed to avoid procreation for selfish, materialistic reasons. Again, such guesswork is not very useful to historians wanting to reconstruct family limitation practices and the means employed. While the upper classes of the late Republic and early Empire appear to have restricted the size of their families, there is little to support the proposition that the wealthy opted for childlessness.[28] Pliny's own letters support the conclusion that he tried and failed to have children.[29] Abortion could easily have been prohibited by Augustan legislation, as adultery was, if it had genuinely been perceived as a social problem. But there is no attested Roman statute on the subject, just a tradition that in archaic Rome child exposure (except in cases of proven disability) was outlawed and women could be divorced for 'poisoning children'.[30]

In a complicated and sensational law-suit in 66 BCE, Cicero claimed that the stepfather of his client had murdered his own sister-in-law to prevent her child taking its proper inheritance. He likened the deed to a case he had heard of years before of a widow in the Greek island of Melos, bribed by potential heirs to abort a rival heir, who had been condemned to death as a result. Cicero endorsed her punishment on the ground that such an act deprived the husband's family and even the state of its rightful expectation.[31] This anecdotal tale was later embedded in Roman legal writings in connection with an imperial ruling that a married woman who procured an abortion should be exiled for a fixed term for having defrauded her husband of children. The case of the Melian woman and Cicero's reasoning was cited.[32] Although the later crime was classed as '*vis*' (violence, or murder), it was not punished as such and the rationale made it clear that it was perceived as a theft from the husband.[33] The implication is that it would have been acceptable if the husband had instructed his wife to have the abortion. It was not until Christian times that the Roman state legislated against abortion as such.[34] On balance, I think it improbable that procured abortion was a regular, approved method of birth control in Roman Italy, but I readily concede that our knowledge of the subject is too meagre for any definite conclusions. We simply do not know how upper-class Romans restricted family size.[35]

The limitations of ancient works – even those on medicine and natural history – as sources of information on this subject are apparent from any attempt to recover some notion of how abortions were performed in antiquity. Terms like *medicamina* (corresponding to Greek *pharmaka*), drugs, do not always distinguish between pessaries and oral abortifacients.[36] A declamatory reference to a woman drinking a *sterilitatis medicamentum* makes the method of administration clear, but suffers from that other common ancient blurring of abortion and contraception.[37] Even Pliny the Elder, who draws both on literary sources and on traditional Italian folklore, shares this vagueness.[38]

The lack of hard information in 'masculine' medical and scientific works may be because female practitioners – also demonised by Juvenal and Pliny the Elder – were more likely to attend women and children and perhaps the training of these midwives and wise-women took the form of practical apprenticeship rather than the book-learning of the (mostly male) doctors.[39]

Even Ovid's deliberately harsh reference to digging out the innards with weapons (*telis*, *Amores* 2.14.27) is uninformative. Like twentieth-century allusions to crochet hooks, it invokes an obvious method without revealing any definite knowledge. The violence and unpleasantness drive the description. The frantic Cana's account (*Heroides* 11.39-42) of her unsuccessful attempts:

> What herbs, what drugs did the nurse not bring and place inside me with an intrusive hand, to excise the burden growing deep within my parts!

sounds more like a pessary in a medicinal mixture, rather than sharp metal designed to pierce the amniotic sac.

But none of these references was intended to inform. Abortion, like adultery, threatened legitimate masculine control over women and progeny. Its condemnation elides with denunciations of women's sexual misbehaviour as a sign of contemporary decadence. The good woman is a chaste wife and good mother, the bad woman an adulteress who aborts her offspring to conceal her affairs or for more frivolous reasons – because she values her beauty over her fertility. The husband is thus cheated of his rightful enjoyment of exclusive sexual access to her body and his right to determine its consequence.

Men's ideas on how abortions might have been induced were vague, but their views on women's motives for procuring them were definite. That alone should give us pause about treating the literary commonplaces as evidence. Since spontaneous and induced abortion are not readily distinguishable to any but the most involved participants, the basis of popular knowledge is unlikely to have been sound.

Seneca's contribution neatly illustrates the literary function of abortion. In condoling with his mother in her bereavement and, in the usual style of Roman 'consolations', telling her why she should not mourn excessively, he insists that she cannot invoke the excuse of womanly weakness because she has shown herself to be free of the feminine defects typical of her contemporaries. You, he says, have never displayed sexual immorality (*impudicitia*), the greatest scourge of the age; love of jewellery, wealth, susceptibility to bad examples, viewing fertility as an embarrassing admission of one's age and pregnancy as a deformity – *you* have never concealed your pregnant state or extinguished the hope of children already conceived within your body; you have not affected make-up or immodest fashions – your only adornment has been conspicuous respectability (*decus*) and chastity (*pudicitia*).[40]

This catalogue gives us the characteristics of the good woman we expect to find in a funeral *laudatio* and – in greater detail, as always – those of the bad woman we find in invective and satire. The bad woman (like the bad child or youth) is typical of the age and that makes the good woman stand out the more for her virtue.[41] It is also apparent from the moral homogeneity of Seneca's list that abortion is not considered an especially serious vice so much as an illustration of vanity (like wearing make-up) and sexual flightiness.

In the many literary variations on the theme of moral decline, the transgressive woman played a similar role. Some of her specified transgressions were more serious than others, some had greater narrative (or comic or shock) potential. Recurrent motifs, determined partly by *genre*, included adultery, plots to murder husbands or stepchildren, wearing transparent clothes and intruding in male spheres such as politics. On the literary scale of moral misbehaviour, abortion is moderately shocking but gains its impetus from its association with adultery, which has richer descriptive and narrative possibilities.

The use by scholars of such references is another matter again. Before social and demographic history came into its own from the 1960s on, it was the norm for those writing about Roman 'daily life' to repeat satiric and historiographic extravagances as factual.[42] Historical studies have diversified greatly in the last two generations and scholars specialising in population history or the history of western medicine have paid close attention to fertility management and women's health in classical antiquity. Their discussions of abortion, grounded in ancient medical writings, have thereby replicated the ancient division into moralising and factual/therapeutic discourse.[43]

Nardi's list (1971: 201-3) of scholarly opinions from 1743-1966 is eye-opening (and a source of great entertainment in itself). These opinions were based primarily on the small number of literary references to induced abortion. The process continues. Consider this extract from a 1995 commentary on Ovid's *Heroides* 11.39-44:

> The practice was a common means of limiting family size, and there is a good deal of literary evidence for abortion among upper-class women for cosmetic reasons.[44]

Such certainty is not shared by those writing about ancient demography, who may have different notions of what constitutes evidence.[45]

The theme of decline continues to have a strong narrative appeal to diverse audiences, scholars among them. Witness the title and structure of Gibbon's great *opus*, which has influenced the way in which nineteenth- and twentieth-century male scholars constructed the political events of ancient Rome and the moral climate in which they were embedded. Some have persisted in regarding women, particularly those of the imperial family, as providing variety and vicarious excitement in the essentially masculine narrative of wars and constitutional politics which was until the mid-twentieth century viewed as 'real history'.[46]

Sexual misbehaviour, a theme closely related to that of secret abortion, is another perennially interesting theme, and it is not surprising that Hollywood, Burbank and Cinecittà have seen fit to exploit the visual possibilities of Roman debauchery, symbolised by 'orgies'. One might have hoped for more judicious responses by scholars to widespread accusations of adultery and the few, very brief and mostly un-specific allegations of abortion in the élite of Roman Italy. But, just as German women symbolised the simple and admirable 'other' for Roman readers, so Roman women have found a place as the corrupt and exciting 'other' in the European tradition following the classical revival.

In the course of the twentieth century, abortion – once an open secret – achieved the status of political hot potato in some countries. For many, it is a more emotive topic than adultery and one with its own appeal. The vision of immoral, self-indulgent women in some decadent, over-privileged space in the past accords neatly with the casual recourse to a procedure condemned by the law and the religion of the historian's own society.[47] This heritage, in which abortion had much greater force for moral abhorrence, fuelled the uncritical use of throwaway lines by satirists as 'evidence' of widespread historical phenomena. An acknowledgement of the literary role of such claims within the Roman tradition of moral decline throws great doubt on the evidentiary value of such material and an appreciation of the emblematic purposes served by women, sex and the body in ancient literary and philosophical discourse. The Romans had one decline narrative and we have another.[48] In this case, they have been made to intersect.

III

Reading the Public Face

Legal and Economic Roles

Introduction

My longstanding interest in Roman women was sparked off many years ago by a paradox: the Roman citizen woman was legally constructed as a minor under 'lifelong guardianship', yet respectable women who feature in Roman law-court speeches and letters exhibit a degree of financial independence and social prominence which is historically unusual. To make the mix even more interesting, such independence seems on the whole to be taken for granted by élite male authors but, here and there, we find indications of a deep-seated unease cultural unease about female power.

In the three chapters of this part of the book, I take a close look at differing representations of women in legal, inscriptional and (to a lesser extent) papyrological sources. Such sources are commonly regarded as more reliable and objective than literary sources but I argue that they, too, draw on stock constructions of Woman (and of other rhetorical categories, e.g. Slave). In Chapter 6, 'Womanly weakness in Roman law', I re-visit my 1984 analysis of the legal construction of the Roman woman and its relation to various stereotypes of the feminine. In 63 BCE, in a masculine public space (the forum as law-court), Cicero invoked the stereotype that women's judgement had been deemed faulty by the revered ancestors, and thus set in train a reading which was to influence European-based legal systems for many centuries to come.

In Chapter 7, 'Profits and patronage', I contrast literary and inscriptional representations of female patronage and consider their relation to commerce. In contrast with the modern (notional) separation of the commercial from the personal, upper-class Romans preferred to view many of their business investments as acts of patronage which established continuing social relations with their 'inferiors' and distanced them from a direct, sordid involvement with commerce. Patronage was a vital institution which underpinned social and economic relations in the Roman world. The duties of patrons were stressed in Roman moral treatises. Yet favours could also be cast in a sinister light and, in the case of women, that often meant they were sexualised in hostile literary and forensic media.

Work, which has a high value in modern discourse, was not always seen as a good thing by the elite authors of classical antiquity. In Chapter 8, 'Women's work: perceptions of public and private', I consider how women's work was represented, especially in visual media. I pay particular attention to the way the same type of handiwork, namely cloth production, could be a symbol of feminine virtue (when performed or supervised by the *materfamilias* for her own household) and an earnest of low status when carried out by the contract weaver or domestic slave.

The inconsistency of many of the representations examined in this section of the book is an important caveat against ever taking a single *genre* as 'the' guide to ancient attitudes or taking any single stereotype as the key to cultural attitudes. The characterisation of work in different texts is a case in point. Cicero's much-quoted pronouncement on the despicable character of certain trades is belied by the visual messages of many monumental tombs which lined the approaches to Roman towns and proclaimed to posterity the livelihoods of successful businessmen and male artisans. But status and self-representation are complex matters. Self-made men like the prosperous imperial baker Eurysaces, happy to acknowledge the source of their wealth, nonetheless aspired to a gentlemanly image and typically represented their wives on these self-same tombs as leisured ladies (see Plates 3 and 4). Women's contributions to family businesses are sometimes noted explicitly in funerary inscriptions but more often suppressed in favour of emphasis on their family roles and generic female virtues.

We are reminded at every turn of how the content is affected by the purpose of the medium. The self-same women could be characterised in statues as gracious ladies bestowing largesse or, in satire and invective, as sex-crazed decadents buying sexual services (Chapter 7). The wives and mothers of exemplary industry lamented in epitaphs could collectively serve in literary sources as symbols of a luxurious and idle age (Chapter 8).

Changing fashions in scholarship and in social values have also generated conflicting visions of Roman women and their status in modern observers. It is now a truism that the respectable women of Roman Italy were not subject to the severe legal and social constraints associated wiith classical Athens.[1] There was no effective bar to their participation in the market-place or to their independent acquisition, exploitation and transmission of property and money. That does not mean that they were governed by the same conventions as their male peers, and I am not the first to be struck by the contrast between the active reality and the restrictive laws about women. Since those laws date from early Rome, probably preceding their expression in the Twelve Tables of the fifth century BCE, while most of our sources concern the period from the early second century BCE onwards, it has been tempting to see the contrast as evidence of change over time. But the women of the late Roman Republic and early Empire (say, second century BCE to second century CE) who invested in property, made wills, freed slaves, conducted business, initiated divorce and lent out money, operated under much the same restrictive laws as their ancestresses.

In the nineteenth and early twentieth centuries, many scholars, unduly influenced by the representation of women in certain literary *genres* as symbols of decline from a moral golden age, saw the remarkable freedom of Roman women as a disturbing historical fluke.[2] Others have not seen it at all. It is still possible to find text-books and global histories of women which present ancient Rome as an archetypal patriarchal society. Their authors do not always explain their reasoning, but they seem to believe that everyday family and marital relations and business dealings are somehow encapsulated in the extreme powers invested in the Roman husband/father (*paterfamilias*) by such institutions as *tutela mulierum perpetua* ('perpetual/lifelong guardianship of women'), *manus mariti* (literally 'hand of the husband', a special legal relationship resulting from certain forms of Roman marriage which had become unusual by the late Republic) and, above all, by *patria potestas* ('paternal power').

Such fallacies have been exposed in publications which demonstrate that Roman fathers did not, for example, regularly exercise their notorious power of life and death over their legitimate children (Dixon 1992a, Saller 1994). The notion of historical progression is also flawed (Dixon 1997). Roman laws bearing on the financial activities of women do not form a linear historical progress from suppression to liberty. We might discern such a trend over time, but it was not a process consciously fostered by the governing males. Putting the 'lifelong guardianship of women' (*tutela mulierum perpetua*) under the microscope (Chapter 6) makes this all too apparent. Tracking this institution bring us up against changes in Roman inheritance norms and Roman attitudes to their own imperfectly understood laws, a process aided by the occasional tendency of Roman jurists to embellish their decisions about real and imagined cases with brief elaborations of underlying principles.

The classical legacy of western civilisation has many facets, not all equally appealing. The representation of women in legal sources is an important element of our own inherited tradition. I am aware of the common aversion (shared by many classical scholars) to Roman law, but I hope readers will overcome it and brave Chapter 6. I hope that chapter will dispel at least some common delusions about Roman law, which is sometimes treated like a holy relic. Roman law is not a monolith. Our imperfect knowledge of the subject is pieced together from a jumble of sources: Justinian's *Digest* is a highly selective compilation from the sixth century CE of legal rulings (extracted from their original contexts) ranging over several centuries; the Theodosian and Justinianic *Codes* (*CTh*, 438 CE and *CJ*, 529 CE) record decisions (rescripts) by emperors in response to specific requests from subjects of all social groups from throughout the Roman Empire; papyri preserved by the sands of Egypt contain diverse legal documents from wills to local petitions, dating from the early to late imperial period; speeches delivered by Cicero in political assemblies or law-courts of the first century BCE, along with his letters and Pliny's (late first/early second century CE) contain legal references and information about financial activities in their own social circles. It is not surprising that there are so many gaps in our knowledge of the content of Roman laws, let alone of their rationale and development.

Views of Roman women through the ages have been dominated by the creations of literature – the boring and errant wives of Juvenal's sixth satire, Tacitus' scheming palace adulteresses, Livy's mythologised heroines of Rome's distant past. The women who emerge from the legal and inscriptional sources present us with other views, of women at work and at business, of women as patrons and petitioners, but constructed in each case according to codes and contexts. Some of these constructions represent women's actual behaviours (making wills or shoes, for example) but are not necessarily free from symbolism because of that. Women's voices might be embedded in the petitions they present to the emperor or in the inscriptions and depictions which they commission for their own shop-signs or in commemoration of their patrons and their dead or to dispose of their property. But they are still constructions, shaped by the conventions of each medium which determine how a woman presents herself to the world.

6

Womanly weakness in Roman law

Gender stereotypes, ancient and modern, are variable. They can be manipulated according to context or change over time. The little woman with no head for business co-exists in Roman culture (as in our own) with the grasping gold-digger. And both characters appear among the *dramatis personae* of Roman law, which is no more objective or reflective of reality than most of the other written sources created by members of the same social group and gender.

This chapter, reproduced here by kind permission of the editors of *Tijdschrift voor Rechtsgeschiedenis (Revue d'histoire du droit)*, first appeared in 1984 as '*Infirmitas sexus*: womanly weakness in Roman law' (vol. 52: 343-71) in response to a paper presented by J.A. Crook (then Professor of Ancient History at Cambridge University) at the first Roman Family Seminar in Canberra, 1981 and published in Rawson (1986).

I have heavily edited the extended jurisprudential and philosophic elements from my 1984 article, but retained most of the discussion of Roman female stereotypy which I marshalled to support my contention that *tutela mulierum perpetua* ('perpetual guardianship of women') was instituted to safeguard masculine control of family property, but rationalised by later generations as a safeguard of 'womanly weakness'. The concept of 'womanly weakness' was subsequently incorporated in other legal systems to justify restrictions of women's legal and financial activities until quite recently.

I have seen (and actively promoted) great changes in my lifetime to the legal bars affecting women and to the public representations of women's roles. I would like to think there has been some improvement (although Ally McBeal is not necessarily an advance on Mrs Cleaver). Unlike my mother in the 1950s and 1960s, I can now legally take out a loan without my husband's permission and men (even the most foolhardy) no longer make jokes in my presence about women drivers, rape or wife-bashing. But in the 1970s and 1980s, when I first presented in several countries the arguments which appear below, I regularly came up against the firm conviction that 'Romans' (i.e. Roman men) believed women could not and should not engage in business (and therefore benevolently protected them from themselves), and, indeed, that women *were* incapable of understanding business. So this chapter, like Chapter 4, has itself become part of an historical narrative of change.

I have done my best to make it more reader-friendly. I have cut back the legal element with that in mind. The full article can be consulted by those with serious legal interests. I have, however, retained some Latin terms in this version, preferring to use *tutela* and *tutor/tutores* rather than 'guardianship' and 'guardian(s)', which are not quite the same. In my analysis of Roman gender stereotypes, I have also retained conceptual words with obvious English parallels (*'infirmitas'* = infirmity, *'fragilitas'* = fragility etc.). I have explained all necessary terms and legal concepts in the chapter,[1] but the law-less reader will find additional help in Appendix 3, which has a glossary of legal terms. If that is not enough for comprehension or curiosity, I recommend chapter 4 of John Crook's excellent 1967 book or some of my earlier publications (e.g. 1988: 41-70; 1992a: 42-5), where the legal basics of Roman family relationships, marriage and inheritance are spelt out.

*

Lawyers and ladies

mulieres omnes propter infirmitatem consilii maiores in tutorum potestate esse voluerunt. (Cicero *Pro Murena* 27)

Our ancestors determined that, on account of the weakness of their judgement, all women should be in the power of their guardians (*tutores*).

This throw-away line of Cicero's before a jury of 63 BCE was to be very influential. It is one of a series of entertaining lawyer jokes – *academic lawyer* jokes – produced to divert the jury in every sense of the word. At his most flippant and flamboyant, Cicero piously tut-tuts about the smart-arse legal pedants who have contrived to subvert the revered ancestors' original aim of monitoring female economic activity. But Cicero's disingenuous reference to the lifelong 'guardianship' of legally independent (*sui iuris*) Roman women was itself a lawyer's trick. A barrister's smoke-screen. In defending his friend Murena, Cicero wisely avoided the substance of the charge of electoral bribery in favour of crowd-pleasing comic routines designed to undermine the prosecutors, including the jurist Servius Sulpicius, respected for his expert opinions on points of law.

This particular court-room joke had a long life. And the joke has been on the women hedged about with discriminatory laws in so many societies until the recent past, allegedly to protect them from their own weakness of judgement, particularly in money matters.

There was some truth in Cicero's claim. Every legitimate Roman citizen began life in the power (*potestas*) of his or her father (or the father's father)

74

and remained in it until the father's death, unless he chose to release them from his power by a specific legal procedure.[2] While in power, the 'child', of whatever age, was unable to inherit, make a will or own anything. On the father's death, all those in his power became independent (*sui iuris*) and normally inherited his estate in equal portions unless he had made some other provision in a will. But young children, though legal owners and heirs, had guardians (*tutores*) to safeguard their estate until puberty in the case of boys, who then took full control of their holdings. Girls, however, passed from one kind of guardian to another. The only real alternative for a woman (other than a Vestal) was to enter the 'hand' (*manus*) of a husband or father-in-law by a particular type of marriage which involved the transfer not only of her property but of herself to her husband's family. On her husband's death, the process was repeated. The widow inherited her share of her husband's estate along with her children and again acquired a *tutor* ('guardian'). It was true, then, in a sense, that the ancestors had arranged things so that a woman's property dealings could always be checked by a male, usually a relative by blood or marriage, even when she was technically independent.

It is not clear when these procedures had been established. They are referred to in the fifth century BCE Twelve Tables, which we know in fragmentary form (Table V.3 & 6).[3] By Cicero's day, these ancient provisions still applied but they seem to have had no impact on the exercise by women of their financial and legal independence. In court, playing – as we have seen – to the gallery – Cicero guesses at the reasoning behind the original institution of 'lifelong (*perpetua*) *tutela* of women' and half-seriously attributes it to an ancestral notion of female mental 'infirmity'. In this chapter, I trace the subsequent development of this idea and its association with measures restricting women's financial and legal activities. The gist of my argument is that *tutela mulierum perpetua* was instituted to safeguard family property, not people, and that adult women were subject to it because, unlike their brothers, they were likely to transfer their birth-right to a different family unit. Exogamous marriage, whereby women transfer themselves and their reproductive rights away from the family of their birth, is essential to the workings of patrilineal cultures (in which property, names and family membership pass through the male or agnatic line) but it often results in this kind of institutional suspicion of women, who constitute a dynamic and mobile element in a system which places great weight, economically and morally, on stability.

Tutela mulierum perpetua was clearly part of a land-based agnatic system of inheritance and marriage. Over time, Roman marriage preference changed and inheritance practices changed with it, until for many women and their male relations *tutela mulierum perpetua* had no significant relation to the direction of family property. The institution itself came to be perceived differently. It was weakened by successive amendments.

The identity of the *tutores* changed. Once 'guardians' of their own sister and her property – which would be theirs on her death – *tutores* were as likely to be compliant family friends or even freed slaves of the woman in question by the late Republic. But while the *tutela* of women declined, the *tutela* of children became more important and was increasingly constructed as a protective institution to safeguard youth against its own inexperience. This, I suggest, is why puzzled Roman observers increasingly associated *tutela mulierum perpetua* in its decline with the idea of female 'infirmity' or 'frailty' in a culture which did accept women's participation in business and loans.

An analysis of Roman gender stereotypes reveals that traditional misogyny attributed greed and cunning to women rather than financial helplessness. Any concern with keeping women out of masculine spheres was driven by the usual wish of insiders to keep the goodies to themselves, not by a paternalistic impulse to protect fuzzy-headed little dolls from the wicked world of business.

The argument which follows, though simplified from the original, is still complex and ranges over many centuries of legal and literary sayings. Eventually, the idea of 'womanly weakness' took on a life of its own in Roman legal thinking. It outlasted *tutela mulierum perpetua*, which had given rise to its expression. The concept was not consistently believed or applied, but it was invoked and ultimately had a great impact on European legal tradition. It is part of the history of western thought.

Two kinds of guardianship

As far as we can tell, in their original form, *tutela mulierum* (guardianship of women) and *tutela impuberum* (guardianship of children), were both likely to be administered by the heir(s) of the people in guardianship. By the mid-Republic, women were able to make wills, but in early Rome neither they nor children had that capacity.[4] A Roman *paterfamilias* did have the power to make a will disposing of his property as he wished (within the bounds of complex requirements) and appointing a *tutor* to the wife in his 'hand' or the children in his power and this became important to the historical development of the institutions, but the early scheme seems to have been based on the expectation that *tutores* normally had a personal interest in preserving the estate and other forms of *tutela* were almost treated as variants of that central notion. Women slaves who were freed and became Roman citizens passed into the *tutela* of their former male owners, who also stood to inherit from the women. This type of guardianship is not as far as we know mentioned in the Twelve Tables but, on the analogy of the guardianship of relatives in the male line (agnates), it, too, was styled 'statutory guardianship', *tutela legitima* (Gaius 1.165). All 'statutory' *tutores* of women and children therefore had a personal interest in seeing that the estate was not unnecessarily eroded (*Digest* 26.4.1 *pr.*, Ulpian 14 *ad Sabinum*). Their duties stressed this negative aspect. The permission ('authority', *auctoritas*) of a *tutor* was necessary to validate certain legal acts which might reduce the estate (Ulpian *Titles* 11.27).

Our information about the early institutions is meagre, so we cannot tell if the *tutela* of women originally operated in the same way as the *tutela* of young children, but by the early empire, there was a clear distinction. The *tutor* actually administered the estate of a ward (*pupillus/a*) until he or she attained puberty,[5] but an adult woman conducted her own affairs, calling on the *tutor(es)* to bestow his *auctoritas* for certain specified acts (most of them involving a legal ritual) which might reduce the estate drastically. This distinction was later summarised by Ulpian (late second century CE):

> *Tutores* of wards both conduct their business and grant their permission (*auctoritas*). But women's *tutores* only grant their permission.

This must have been the situation for centuries before Ulpian's statement. The literary evidence from the second century BCE onwards seems also to indicate that fatherless children's estates were managed *for* them, but that women managed their own, with major transfers of property subject to the veto of male relations. The fact that women customarily took their share of the family wealth in the form of dowry to a different family group was presumably a factor in the desire to limit their freedom. It remained necessary for a woman to secure the permission of her *tutor* before promising a dowry or contracting a marriage which would bring her into her husband's 'hand' and all her property under his ownership (or that of his father, if he were alive).

Two developments were to have a great impact on the meanings of *tutela mulierum perpetua*: the practice of women making wills and the change in marriage preference. The female capacity to make a will was not the same as the male equivalent. As well as requiring the prior permission of the *tutor(es)*, women had to undergo a formal ceremony, *coemptio*, which, like many Roman legal rituals, took the form of a symbolic sale. Like other significant Roman socio-legal developments, the shift in marriage style is essentially undateable. It had always been possible for a Roman woman to retain membership of her birth family after marriage (although she lived with her husband and their children were in the husband's power), and stratagems to avoid coming within a husband's 'hand' had been practised at least as early as the Twelve Tables, but in the early and mid-Republic it seems to have been the norm for a Roman wife to be in the *manus* of her husband. By the late Republic, that trend had been reversed until *manus* became an oddity, then probably disappeared in the early Empire (Watson 1967).

With all the qualifications which need to be built into such a generalisation, it is safe to state that from the second century BCE Roman women exercised greater economic independence apparently unhampered by the restrictions of *tutela mulierum*, which were whittled down by law and custom in the ensuing centuries.

We know that by 186 BCE (Livy 39.19.4) it was possible for a husband whose wife was in his 'hand' to grant her in his will the 'option of a *tutor*', the right to choose her own *tutor*. Cicero's allusion in the first century BCE to women who were able to exercise authority over their *tutores* probably refers to women who were in the *tutela* of a freed slave – either their own or their husband's. The Herculaneum Tablets and sundry inscriptions bear witness to the existence of such socially subordinate *tutores*.[6] The women of Cicero's letters and speeches – Sassia, Clodia and Terentia, to name only the most obvious – are seen as conducting their affairs independently, as if the permission of the *tutor(es)* were no practical bar.[7] This seems similar to the situation observed by the jurist Gaius two centuries later:

> For women who are of full age conduct their own business for themselves and in certain cases the *tutor* applies his permission (*auctoritas*) for form's sake. (Gaius 1.190)

Massive economic changes took place in Italy during the last two centuries of the Republic. The greater and more fluid wealth of the upper classes during this period probably underlay many of the changes in patterns of marriage and inheritance and, incidentally perhaps, the growing economic independence of Roman women. Yet these changes took place within a framework of legal stability – the laws on intestate succession changed little, while the practice seems to have developed separately.

In the Republic, such changes were very piecemeal. But with the change to a more centralised system, imperial legislation seemed to continue the same tendency, namely to weaken the impact of this institution on the lives of Roman citizen women. As part of his promotion of families, Augustus introduced the 'right of children' as an incentive to parenthood. It freed free-born women with three children or freed slave-women with four from *tutela*. This was the first of a series of legislative blows to the principle that all women should be subject for life to *tutela* (Gaius 1.145, 194). The emperor Claudius abolished the agnatic *tutela* of women, which meant that free-born women were henceforth liable to a less stringent form of *tutela*, not to 'statutory' *tutela*.[8] A *tutor* could, for example, be replaced in his absence by the praetor on the woman's application – and his permission could be compelled for a specific act if his refusal were deemed by the praetor to be unreasonable (Gaius 1.190).

78

In terms of the revered ancestors' intentions, a *tutor* who could be compelled to grant permission against his will was surely a contradiction in terms. And the 'option of a *tutor*' had apparently expanded some time between the early second century BCE to the second century CE, for Gaius mentions the possibility that deceased husbands could grant multiple options to their widows, who were thus able to appoint a *tutor* for a single transaction, then replace him at whim.[9] Claudius' abolition of agnatic *tutela* also struck at the heart of the original institution, which had been designed to serve the interests of the women's agnates.

The emperor Hadrian's abolition of the need for a testatrix to undergo a special ceremony before making a will marked a late stage in the separation of *tutela* from its origin in the early system of inheritance and its general deterioration (Gaius 1.115a). *Tutela mulierum* was maintained in form long after it had lost its teeth – even after Hadrian's reform, women who had a *tutor* still required his permission to make a will. The last recorded example of *tutela* was in conservative Roman Egypt, in 293-294 CE.[10] It finally expired from desuetude. It does not figure in the legal code of Theodosius (promulgated 438 CE).

The history of *tutela mulierum perpetua* was thus one of fairly steady decline. The development of *tutela impuberum*, the guardianship of minors, was otherwise. The institution which had originated as a private arrangement to safeguard family wealth gradually came to be viewed as a public concern, with the emphasis shifting to the interests of the ward (*pupillus/a*), though it remained the property rather than the personal welfare of the minor which was at issue. On reaching puberty, and therefore legal majority, a minor could bring a suit against a fraudulent *tutor*.[11] No such remedy was open to a woman *in tutela* because, as Gaius rightly observed (1.190-1), her *tutor*'s offices were of a rather formal character and he did not have the same access to her fortune.

Children and minors were increasingly viewed as in need of protection. A law of the early second century BCE, for example, extended the protection of the law to males over puberty but under twenty-five years, who claimed to have been defrauded by any person. They could claim an *exceptio* against pressing creditors, on the ground that their inexperience had been exploited.[12] By the very late Republic, when ethics and legal theory became the object of systematic study, the responsibility of a *tutor* was classed as a duty worthy of inclusion in moral taxonomies, likening the duties of a *tutor* to his ward to that of a patron to his client.[13]

When moralists or jurists of the late Republic or the imperial period spoke of *tutela*, it was of the 'guardianship' of children (*Noctes Atticae* 5.13.2.4). Where it does occur, the *tutela* of women is generally an afterthought, as in a learned dispute recorded by Aulus Gellius about moral priorities. One participant argues that a man's obligation to a ward should come before the obligation to a guest, which takes priority over obligation to a client, then to a relative, and finally to an in-law. The general rule, that obligations to women take precedence over those to men, those to children over those to women (*Noctes Atticae* 5.13.2.5), represents a hierarchy of need.[14]

This style of reasoning was characteristic of the rhetorical education of the late Republic. Determining the origin of *tutela* was an academic exercise for élite men with antiquarian interests. The connection between the *tutor* and the right of hereditary succession had been obscured over the centuries until it seemed reasonable to associate its origins with the anachronistic aim of protecting the interests of those too young to manage their own estates.[15]

The extension of this protective rationale to the original institution of the *tutela* of women would not stand much examination, as Gaius was later to point out, but it clearly made enough superficial sense to be used, as Cicero used it, in a passing appeal to jurors' prejudices and a popular notion of ancestral thinking.[16] Schulz (1951: 181) felt the concept of female 'infirmity of judgement' (*infirmitas consilii*) was conspicuously inappropriate in Roman society, where matrons had always occupied a position differing from that of women in the Greek-speaking world, and pointed to Cicero's knowledge of his own wife's business competence. It is, of course, possible for people to entertain such preconceptions in the face of factual evidence to the contrary, but in this case Cicero was surely presenting what he imagined (or pretended) to be a traditional belief about the nature of women. His point was that academic lawyers had thwarted the ancestral intention, which was posited on archaic reasoning.[17]

Gaius (1.144) also represented the reasoning as traditional:

> For the ancients wished women, even if they were of age, to be in *tutela*, on account of the levity of their nature (*propter animi levitatem*).

Ulpian (*fl. c.* 202-223 CE), elaborated slightly:

> *tutores* are appointed to males, too, before they attain puberty on account of the infirmity of their age, but to women before and after puberty both because of the infirmity of their sex (*propter sexus infirmitatem*) and because of their ignorance of legal matters. (*Titles* 11.1)

Tutela had greatly declined by the end of the second century CE. Gaius and Ulpian – more than Cicero – were explaining a vestigial institution in terms of its original formulation, as they imagined it to have been.

Tutela as duty

The divorce of female *tutela* from the *tutor*'s self-interest apparently reduced its appeal to *tutores*. Imperial statutes and judicial reasoning on the subject focus on acceptable pretexts for the release of *tutores* from this sacred trust.[18] The protective characterisation of *tutela* was belied by law which accrued around statutory *tutela* and acknowledged the interests of the statutory (*legitimus*) *tutor* as patron or parent, entitled to a prior right of succession to the person *in tutela*.[19] Agnatic *tutores* were apparently viewed by themselves and praetors as overly burdened by their lifelong obligation to female relatives as against the briefer obligation to the estates of children in their *tutela*. Unable to refuse the office outright, they were permitted to 'cede' it to another.[20] Claudius' abolition of agnatic *tutela* over women seems to reflect this official sympathy at a time when coercion was increasingly applied to *tutores* of children to perform their duty. While both forms of *tutela* were thought a nuisance, one was deemed essential and the other a puzzling anachronism (Ulpian 11.25, 27).

Patterns of inheritance had altered since the time of the Twelve Tables, though the rules of intestate succession had not. While patron *tutores* accepted the privileges and burdens of *tutela* over their former slave-women, agnatic *tutores* were more eager to evade the office because custom had deprived them of their traditional material advantage. Brothers no longer seem to have hoped to inherit from their sisters, who were now expected to name their children as heirs in their wills (Dixon 1988: 51-60). Under Hadrian, the long-standing rituals that a free-born woman must undergo before making a valid will were reduced.[21] A woman who had a *tutor* still required his permission to make a testament, but it was even possible for a will composed without such authorisation to be upheld.[22] *Tutela* had thus ceased from early in the second century CE to function even formally in the interests of the agnates, though it still protected the rights of fathers and patrons over a woman's estate unless the woman gained the 'right of children' which from the time of Augustus liberated her entirely from *tutela*.

Thus *tutela*, which had originated as a prerogative of male heirs, a matter to be arranged within the circle of family and friends, ended with the judicial and executive arm of government forcing the erstwhile 'privilege' on outsiders as a civic duty. The 'protective' conception of *tutela* gave rise incidentally to the doctrine of female 'infirmity' which took on a life of its own after the disappearance of the 'perpetual guardianship of women'. Neither the original function of *tutela* nor its later rationale could support its continued application to the women at the heart of the Empire. The latest recorded examples of *tutela mulierum* occurred in Roman Egypt, but it is impossible to tell whether that is because Egypt was more conservative, because records of that type survived better in that environment, or because *tutela mulierum* there operated as a variant on Hellenic (and Hellenistic) *kyria*, in which brothers and husbands were expected to act for women in financial matters (Sijpesteijn 1965: 174; Modrzejewski 1974: 292).

III. Reading the Public Face

Keeping the little woman out

The oddity is that the concept of female 'infirmity/fragility' (*infirmitas* and *fragilitas*) seemed to gain ground at just the time when the reason for the original institution of *tutela mulierum* had declined. The contradiction is embedded in Cicero's own rationalisation – he had, after all, invoked the presumed ancestral intention in order to point to its subsequent frustration by lawyers (*Pro Murena* 27) and Gaius' doubts about the usual rationale were based on its contradiction in everyday practice. Servius' definition – however mutilated – makes it clear that the usual juristic explanation of *tutela* was, by the very late Republic, in terms of the helplessness of the person *in tutela*.[23] This virtually necessitated a theory of female incapability on the juvenile model.

This presumptive feminine defectiveness became a literary commonplace – a characteristic of the sex which could be referred to in passing without explanation, as in Valerius Maximus 9.1.3 on the weakness (*imbecillitas*) of the female mind, which makes it rather difficult to pin down the precise nature of the well-known defect.[24] The assumption of physical inferiority seems to underlie extravagant praise of female courage for exceeding the expected standard, as in Lucretia's 'masculine spirit ... assigned by an evil error of fortune to a female body' (6.1.1).[25] This physical weakness is then generalised. Women were expected to be less restrained in mourning (Livy 3.48.8), naturally susceptible to flattery and persuasion rather than capable of regulating their own morality (Tacitus *Annals* 3.35), and easily tricked because of their gullibility (Gaius 1.196).

It seems fairly certain that educated opinion from the very late Republic onwards assumed a low *ancestral* estimate of female business sense; it is even probable that jurists endorsed this tradition, although there is evidence that some at least continued to appreciate the link between *tutela* and the succession rights of *tutores*. In trying to trace the development of such ideas and their legal application, it is particularly important to avoid the trap of inserting into Roman generalisations the prejudices of our own culture. It is also important to distinguish between statements made in a speech to a Republican jury, the considered definition of an academic lawyer and the legislative adoption of a line of reasoning.

Crook (1986b) held that the *senatus consultum Velleianum* passed under the emperor Claudius had been occasioned by the decline of *tutela mulierum* after Augustan legislation made it possible for women with the 'right of children' to have no *tutor*. His implication is that Roman women were not only perceived by the ancestral legislators to suffer from 'infirmity' but that they actually displayed this flaw – that in the absence of male guidance, legally independent women without effective *tutores* were being cheated. This clearly contradicts Gaius' own observation of second-century CE practice.

Cicero's suggestion that 'infirmity of judgement' underlay the institution of *tutela mulierum* (*Pro Murena* 27) is the first example of an attempt to link a legal construct with female incompetence. Later references from Gaius 1.144 and Ulpian 11.1 suggest that this connection had become a commonplace by the third century – to be repeated, if not wholly endorsed, by the jurists. Roman Republican authors and classical jurists agreed that it was more appropriate for women to be protected by men than vice versa (Paul at *Digest* 47.10.2). Women, though allowed to appear on their own behalf in court, were forbidden – probably from the early Empire – to appear for others (Ulpian 6 *ad edictum*, *Digest* 3.1.1.5), a principle upheld much later in the *Codex Iustinianus* (2.12.8). The prohibitions of the *senatus consultum Velleianum* seem to have been intended to keep women from intervening financially to relieve others, and this idea of women as properly needing rather than giving protection perhaps underlay the Severan confirmation that women could not exercise *tutela* over their own children.[26]

These imperial restrictions formalised a notion which had existed in Republican times.[27] In spite of exceptions and contradictions, the concept could be invoked as a rationalisation for a variety of legal measures. Sometimes the exclusion of women from certain spheres or offices rests on a tradition of gendered roles.[28] The jurist Paul points out that it is convention rather than nature which determines the exclusion of women and slaves from sitting in legal judgement.[29]

Earlier public statements about the exclusion of women from masculine spheres had sometimes been aggressive. Livy records a female demonstration of 195 BCE. The women had turned out to petition men attending the meeting to discuss the repeal of a sumptuary law under discussion that day in the male assembly. In his account, Cato the Elder (consul that year) appealed to traditional strictures on the female sex:

> Our ancestors decreed that women should not even conduct private business without the authority of a *tutor* but should be in the control of their fathers, brothers or husbands. But we – gods help us! – are now even allowing them to seize commonwealth business and to stick themselves into the approach to the forum and the public meetings and assemblies! (Livy 34.2.11)[30]

Gods help us, indeed. In Tacitus' account of a senatorial debate about the roles of provincial governors' wives more than two centuries later, a speaker argued that the husband was to blame if his wife exceeded the proper limits – in this case, by assuming masculine duties in the provinces, such as inspecting the troops or receiving influential petitioners.[31]

In his commentary on the praetor's edict, Ulpian explained the prohibition on female representation in court as having arisen historically from praetorian reaction to the disrespectful persistence of the unspeakable advocate Carfania.[32] The idea that modesty in public is proper for women is expressed in these statements, but it is not linked with female vulnerability or incapacity so much as an insistence on excluding from the public sphere women who are only too likely to force their way into it. As in the case of freed slaves, *nouveaux riches* and upstart provincials, a firm line was taken to maintain traditional distinctions. They are the remarks of a ruling group defending the bastions of privilege against real or anticipated assault.

The small surviving fragment of Cato the Elder's actual speech in favour of the Voconian Law of 169 BCE (limiting, among other things, the testamentary inheritance rights of women of the top property group) seems to take the line that women were already lording their economic independence over their husbands, and could not be allowed any more leeway (*Noctes Atticae* 17.6.1).[33] It is this argument which Livy uses to build up the portrait of Cato in the debate of 195 BCE. It can be associated with the idea of 'proper spheres' but at bottom it is exclusive. Ulpian, on the edict, says that women might not plead for others 'lest they involve themselves in the business/causes of other people contrary to the proper modesty of their sex, and lest women usurp the functions of men' (*Digest* 3.1.1). Both Tiberius and Nero demurred at their distinguished mothers' attempts to overstep the bounds of diplomatic propriety.[34] The idea was entrenched that women ought not to push themselves forward publicly.

This aggressive masculine exclusiveness differs in essence – if not in effect – from the argument that women, being in need of protection rather than able to provide it, should be *relieved* of certain masculine duties (or penalties), which seems to be the reasoning behind such rules as the praetorian dictum that a wife's honour is her husband's concern but an injury to his might not be prosecuted by her (*Digest* 47.10.2, Paul 50 *ad edictum*) and the confirmation by the senate *c.* 46 CE that a woman could not take on the debt of another 'because it is not reasonable (*aequum*) that women should perform masculine offices and be bound by obligations of that kind'.[35] Such obligations could have their advantages, as loan sharks through the ages have found, but the intention of the senate here, as of the emperors Augustus and Claudius, was seemingly to protect a woman from the danger of an open-ended obligation, particularly in favour of her husband.[36]

Does this mean that the assumption of womanly weakness – which Cicero had in the late Republic anachronistically attributed to the ancestors – actually became a factor in imperial policy-making? I think not. In the first place, it does not square with practice: for women *did* come to the rescue of men, in their capacity as patrons. Cicero sneered at Clodia and Sassia for hovering in the background of prosecutions, but deferred respectfully to Caecilia Metella, who virtually engaged him to defend her dependant, Roscius of Ameria (*Pro Roscio Amerino* 27). Women *did* lend money to men, and were legally free to do so, either as a favour or as a speculation, without the permission of a *tutor* (cf. *Pro Caelio* 31; Chapter 9 on Clodia Metelli). Sassia freed her slave doctor and set him up in a shopfront business (*Pro Cluentio* 178-9). Women such as Cicero's friend Caerellia and Pliny's mother-in-law Pompeia Celerina engaged in speculative buying and loans to build up their already considerable fortunes. Though barred for so long from being *tutores* to their own children, widows did bring them up and protect their economic interests.[37] Later imperial rulings acknowledged a number of female financial obligations to relations, both male and female – such as the one that a woman, though unable in general to bring a prosecution or defend another, could summon a defendant in the interests of a relation or pledge herself as surety to save her father from exile or provide a dowry for a daughter or dependant.[38] So, even given the general pronouncements made and reiterated over the generations about the proper limits to female activity, many of them were either disregarded in practice or inconsistently applied.

In the preamble to the *senatus consultum Velleianum*, Ulpian explains that, in response to an appeal by the consuls M. Silanus and Velleius Tutor, for clarification 'on the correct policy as to obligations undertaken by women on behalf of others', the senate ruled 'that the interpretation followed until now in the courts has been that no suit lies to creditors against women under that heading, on the ground that it is unreasonable that women should take on masculine functions and be bound by obligations of that nature'.

The *senatus consultum Velleianum* was thus a procedural measure to deal with an existing legal problem.[39] It needs to be distinguished from the interpretations, amendments and analyses which soon accrued about it.[40] The notion of female weakness soon plays its part in this later literature and was retrospectively attributed to the legislators, who were probably protecting women's property from their husband's creditors. By the late Republic, women were generally marrying without entering the husband's 'hand' (*manus*) and thereby kept their holdings distinct from those of the husband. The only exception to the longstanding principle banning substantial gifts between husband and wife under this regime was dowry, which was the husband's legal property for the duration of the marriage, but returnable on its dissolution by death or divorce.[41] Under Augustus, it became illegal for the husband to alienate or pledge dotal land without consulting his wife.[42] This would ensure the husband's ability to return the land or its cash value to the wife on the dissolution of the marriage.[43] Husband and wife were not responsible for each other's debts but if the husband were owner and administrator of the dowry it would in practice be fairly easy for him to pledge it as if it were his own – the Augustan rule and the praetorian interpretations of the early imperial period made it a little less easy.

A sixth-century Justinianic ruling preventing her from giving the husband permission to alienate dotal land certainly assumes her vulnerability: 'lest the fragility of the female sex might be exploited, to the detriment of their estates' (Justinian *Institutes* 11.8 *pr.*), but the Augustan legislation had assumed her rationality to the extent that her permission was a just ground for alienation. Justinian's concern, to help women in spite of themselves, post-dates the *senatus consultum Velleianum* by a good five hundred years, and even the juristic comments which viewed the *senatus consultum* as an antidote to female frailty are third century or later. The wish to preserve family holdings had not yet been quite as suffused with sentimental paternalism in the first century CE. There probably was a vague feeling that women would find excessive debt difficult – consider Pliny's sympathy with Calvina, who had entered on an encumbered inheritance which would have been burdensome 'even for a man' (*Letters* 2.4.1). But it was the vulnerability of the dowry and of the wife's personal fortune which inspired the legislation, not her gullibility. Though not liable at law for her husband's debts (*Digest* 1.5, 3-4), she might find the status of dowry in the event of his bankruptcy or *damnatio* to be more dubious, since the dowry was technically part of the husband's property for the duration of the marriage.[44] Perhaps it was this very dubiety which inspired the rulings, first applied to husbands, then extended to others – rulings which progressively became more protective of the woman's interest as such, though always considerate of the extreme claims of those whose interests were identified with hers – her father or daughter but emphatically not her husband.

Rationalising exclusion

A body of exceptions and explanations accumulated around the *senatus consultum Velleianum*, which later passed into various European codes and was only removed from the South African Roman-Dutch legal system in 1969.[45] This body of interpretation, which grew up over many years, has obscured the function of the original.[46]

If we look at the actual measure, we find that even after its passage through the senate women were still able (and expected) to promise dowry, to incur debts of other kinds on their own behalf, or to pay off the debt of another person who then became their debtor. Even later, when it was viewed as a means of protecting women from oppressive debt which they had taken on unwittingly, women were not permitted to invoke the *senatus consultum* willy-nilly to escape legitimate obligations, as minors could do. Ulpian recorded that Pius and Severus had disallowed the excuse if the woman concerned had set out to dupe a creditor – the ruling had been designed, they said, to help women who were deceived, not those who did the deceiving, and was inspired by woman's helplessness, not her cunning.[47]

6. Womanly weakness in Roman law

The argument that Claudius' abolition of agnatic *tutela* over women exposed them to the depredations of unscrupulous men and made it necessary to provide them with a general escape-clause (namely, the *senatus consultum Velleianum*) simply does not hold up. To my mind, Claudius' action actually shows how far *tutela mulierum* had declined by the first century CE. His abolition of this more demanding form of *tutela* was absolute, not a reward for some women (like Augustus' 'right of children'). It was surely a concession to male irritation rather than a surprise gift to Roman women.[48] By the same token, the *senatus consultum Velleianum* was introduced not in response to the new helplessness of women but to the separation of property within marriage. Goods, rather than people and their presumed inadequacies, were the concern of Roman law.

Roman concepts of feminine infirmity concerned physical, emotional and moral weakness.[49] The debate of 195 BCE (as passed on by Livy two centuries later) yielded two opposing arguments: that women, if unchecked, will simply hike up their outrageous demands until they are men's masters, versus the view that women – who *wish* to be governed by their male relations in personal matters – should be indulged by men in acknowledgement of their emotional vulnerability (Livy 34.7.7). Women, then, are emotional and more easily upset than men, they are not expected to be as brave as men, but there is no suggestion that they are witless with money or in need of masculine protection in business affairs: that is part of later western gender stereotypy and we must be careful about assuming it without sound evidence, or anticipating its appearance in Roman thought.

When a developed notion of female 'infirmity' surfaced, it was used both to justify the exclusion of women from certain spheres and to underline the need for protective measures. The former are often spheres which traditionally excluded women, and there were always dissenting voices (Gaius on 1.190, Paul on the edict, *Digest* 5.1.12.2), voices which at least suggest that these rulings were grounded in convention rather than posited wholly on a notion of female incompetence. The exclusion of women was the usual monopoly exercised by any ruling group. Feudalism, patronage and other forms of social and economic oppression commonly give rise to developed rationales about the incapacity of the oppressed group to exercise power, but it would be rather naive to read them literally.

Gradually, however, the notion of female incompetence crept into imperial judgements and – apparently – praetorian rulings (*CJ* 5.5.1 224 CE) and it is embedded in the legislation of Justinian (esp. *Institutes* 11.8 *pr.*). The exclusion seems to me to be grounded in traditional keep-'em-out misogyny. I suspect that the protective line, whether genuine or not, began to appear in juridic literature surrounding the *senatus consultum Velleianum* as awkward cases forced judges and commentators to speculate

87

more closely as to its function. Later commentators and the emperors themselves – doubtless acting on legal advice – interpreted the *senatus consultum Velleianum* in terms of their own perception of its rationale and contemporary ideas about women.[50]

Tutela of women had been severely eroded by common consent and by successive legislation at the time that expressions like 'infirmity of judgement' made their way finally into the juridic vocabulary. *Vatican Fragment* 325 (Diocletian and Constantius 293 CE) is the latest reference to the institution. The abolition in 410 CE of the 'right of children' (*Codex Theodosianus* 8.17.3) contains no specific reference to women. The institution seems to have survived longest in Roman Egypt, and even there women who ought to have been *in tutela* transacted business without a *tutor*.

The retention of the form of *tutela mulierum* is testimony to Roman conservatism. The ancient institution had a long existence, but it survived in very weakened form: The 'option of a *tutor*', compellable permission, the 'right of children', all contributed to this, but it was the abolition of agnatic *tutela* and the greater simplicity of female testamentary procedures, combined with a shift in marriage fashion, which stripped *tutela mulierum* of its very foundation. Roman reluctance to tamper with venerable institutions stopped short of outright abolition – the 'lifelong guardianship of women' was left to dwindle away from desuetude. It remains a legal curiosity that its decline should have coincided with the growing juridic respectability of a notion of feminine frailty.

7

Profits and patronage

Ladies, loans and largesse

Roman sexual activity receives more coverage in the surviving literary
sources than economic activity. Yet both had moral meanings for the
wealthy upper classes of Roman Italy on whom this chapter concentrates.
Following Rome's victory over Hannibal in 201 BCE and its subsequent
expansion into the Greek East, members of the ruling senatorial order
became the prime beneficiaries of the slaves and wealth which poured into
Italy, transforming social and economic structures and the range of status
markers (Hopkins 1978: 1-56). The new aristocratic taste for specialist
goods and Greek rhetoric and the visible proliferation of elaborate public
and private buildings provided the historical backdrop for recurrent literary laments about contemporary luxury and the perennial decline from
ancestral simplicity.[1] We have seen that élite women as a group were often
characterised as prime examples of these modern vices, yet the last two
centuries of the Republic, c. 201-27 BCE, also saw upper-class women
honoured with individual statues and inscriptions for their beneficence
and generosity, and in family tombs for their frugality and selflessness.[2]

The combination of investment and commercial speculation in the same
chapter with patronage might seem odd to the modern reader, but it
reflects the Roman conflation of social and economic categories. Loans
which yielded interest also extended patronage relations and were a form
of social investment. In a highly stratified society, kinship and patronage
were crucial safety nets and economic lubricants. Manumitted slaves
continued to show gratitude and deference to their former owners (masculine *patroni*, feminine *patronae*) and lifelong exchanges went in both
directions. It was in the interest of the *patrona* (f.) or *patronus* (m.) to lend
start-up capital to establish the former slave in a business based on skills
acquired in slavery. Such investment was profitable to the owner but its
characterisation as a 'favour' (*beneficium*) to the protégé(e) distanced the
superior party legally and morally from direct commercial involvement
(d'Arms 1977; Pleket 1984: 15). This distance was important to the self-
image of the upper classes (Wiseman 1971: 79). The fact that senatorials
are known to have exploited the system to maximise their own financial

benefit and protect themselves from losses does not invalidate its social importance to all parties.

Women's roles in business therefore reflect their social integration, as patrons and beneficiaries, in patronage networks. They were also subject to judgements based on gendered notions of propriety. It was deemed very suitable to the status and femininity of a prosperous woman to confer benefits on social inferiors but some kinds of favours could be wilfully misrepresented in hostile contexts as intrusion into a masculine sphere or even as compromising the woman's sexual reputation.

The revolution of the second century BCE introduced many of the leading families of Rome to land capitalism as well as Hellenistic culture. From at least this period until the early centuries CE, they diversified their interests. They invested in land and urban properties in different regions of Italy, sold or leased their properties for what we would regard as commercial and manufacturing ventures and produced goods (wine, olive oil, garum and Arretine pottery) for export. But the senatorial élite continued to construct itself as a landed aristocracy and expressed a distaste for trade which was reinforced by a statute of 218 BCE preventing senators and their sons from engaging in maritime commerce.[3]

Roman literary sources, designed for élite audiences, provide notoriously little hard information about the economy and a disproportionate amount of moralising about the uses of wealth, the sordidness of commerce and the vulgarity of work. Senatorials were not the only ones who prized land, which was generally perceived as the most stable and respectable basis of wealth.[4] But the inscriptions and iconographic representations in which petty traders and their ilk recorded their callings suggest that they did not share the contempt which the élite expressed for their sources of income. The *locus classicus* is Cicero's moral taxonomy:

> In the first place, those livelihoods which incur dislike – like those of customs agents or money-lenders – are disapproved of. The livelihoods of all journeymen whose labour is for hire (rather than their skills) are illiberal and low-grade ... And also those sources of profit which are marketed by petty traders are considered low-grade because they sell them on immediately ... All trades are considered a low category of skill. (*De officiis* 1.150)[5]

And so it goes on. Perfectly respectable lower-class trades and businesses are despicable.[6] But big business is (just) acceptable, perhaps because Cicero mingled on closer social terms with its proponents:

> If it is on a small scale, commerce should be considered base; but if it is grand and ample, transporting many goods from all over the world and passing them on to many recipients without flummery, it should not really be put down. (*De officiis* 151)

Small hucksters needed to lie (*De officiis* 150), but apparently large-scale importers could dispense with advertising hype (*vanitas*).

Such attitudes explain the virtual absence of commerce from most élite literature. Even the very wealthy equestrians who engaged in large-scale capitalist ventures and mixed socially with senatorials figure more as a political category in most of our sources. Some 'lower-class' traders and artisan shopkeepers appear on the comic stage and satire, which includes more everyday scenes, has some commercial detail, but it is hard for us to extract the information from the humour, which often hinges on finely-tuned social distinctions. Petronius' vivid portrait of the wealthy former slave Trimalchio and his circle is the perfect example. Trimalchio entertains his guests with an account of how he made his way up in the world (*Satyricon* 75-6). He tells them how he bought his wife Fortunata out of slavery, but also that she had subsequently staked him when he lost his first fortune (*Satyricon* 76.7). The details of his life are comically over-drawn, but it is tempting to associate the prosperous couple with examples from life, such as the baker Eurysaces and his wife Antistia, whose monument still stands outside the Porta maggiore in Rome (see Plates 3 and 4).

Legal sources are also skewed. Free workers and business-owners are of less interest to the authorities than slave and dependent (but freed) business managers and others involved in commercial activities which might incur liability for their owners or patrons (*Digest* 33.7). Women feature in jurists' examples and even more in imperial rescripts responding to petitioners from more humble backgrounds.[7] Such sources show that women played a greater role in business than the epitaphs and other funeral memorials of this social group would indicate, with their focus on women's family roles.

Wealth and its origins had little place in the elevated literary *genres* of history, epic and political speeches unless it was embedded in moral and rhetorical categories – set pieces on the growth of luxury, the disappearance of the free Italian peasant or the shameful decline of a once-proud family.[8] Letters – especially those of Cicero and of Pliny the Younger – and some forensic speeches contain more references to actual examples of élite acquisition, but we are indebted to non-literary sources for a wider picture of élite activity and particularly that of élite women. The imperial brick and amphora stamps analysed by modern archaeologists and epigraphers reveal the involvement of aristocratic imperial land-owners in the production, sale and export of primary commodities (especially wine) and manufactured goods (amphorae and bricks), construed by elite participants as natural extensions of agriculture and therefore honourable in a way that, say, banking was not (Bloch 1947-8: 1-2). Without these stamps and Cicero's letters, we would have a very different and more limited idea of female acquisition (Setälä 1977, Appendix 2).

Roman women of all social levels could engage in a range of what we would deem commercial activities suited to their means and station in life. But our records are strongly affected by entrenched values, particularly those of the dominant ruling class, towards profit. They are also affected by ideas of proper womanly behaviour, which are not particularly consistent. The Velleian senatorial decree of 46 CE forbidding women to assume liability for third parties and the Claudian statute rewarding freed women who engaged in grain import-export (enacted within years of each other), seem to reflect opposing ideologies of female financial capacity.[9] One has been seen as paternalistic protection for women's presumptive ignorance of business, while the other assumes and rewards female involvement in a high-risk, high-capital area of commerce. This review of women's business activities and the intersecting category of patronage shows up the flexibility of stereotypes and the ways that the same activity can be slanted by the source.

Profits

The more socially oriented areas of loans and patronage, dealt with in the later part of this chapter, overlapped considerably with modern financial categories. In this section, we focus on the roles and rules of status and gender bearing on women engaged – as owners, investors, employers – in business, an area identified by moderns as economic.

Given the general tendency to omit women from so many sources or to describe their roles from the masculine perspective, the range of business activities attested for women of the imperial period is impressive. Legal texts contribute odd pieces of the puzzle: a divorcing wife's entitlement to the products of a dotal orchard improved by her husband, a decision that a ruling about a slave manager (*institor*) in charge of a shop applies to a woman slave, or imperial rescripts responding expressly to female petitioners.[10] In Latin, women are the marked sex. Legal sources routinely use the masculine form to signify male *and* female actors, with explicit references to women only when there is a particular reason to note femaleness (Gardner 1995). Readers must therefore allow for the implicit inclusion of women in general categories – slaves, agents, owners, patrons – and for the absence of those who, like their male peers, seldom interest the lawmakers, such as free workers and tenants.

References in other sources are influenced by concepts of respectability and of appropriate feminine roles. The commemorative inscriptions of the small manufacturing-retail class (*tabernarii*) concentrated in the towns of Roman Italy in the first centuries of the Christian era tend to type the male owner/employer by his trade and the female owner/employer by her role as wife and mother, but both sexes are commemorated as patrons by their *familia* (slaves and freed slaves) (Joshel 1992a). Literary sources tend to focus on the land-owning senatorials of Roman Italy and are concentrated in the period c. 80 BCE – 120 CE. Those which provide the greatest detail of profit-oriented activity – Cicero's letters and speeches, Varro's agricultural hand-book and Pliny's letters – refer incidentally to the business affairs of élite women, which are seldom mentioned in inscriptions or depicted in iconographic memorials in the way women doctors, artisans and vendors are sometimes commemorated pictorially (Kampen 1981, 1982).

Unfortunately, the women's letters have not survived, just the records they have left on lead pipes and brick or amphora stamps, from which we can infer their land-ownership. Papyri from Roman Egypt provide census returns listing women's ownership of real property and documentary accounts of their involvement in law-suits, apprenticeships, dowry agreements and contracts of sale. Such 'hard' information, with concrete examples, considerably enhances our knowledge, but these documents seldom form a complete statistical record for any one period. Even in the papyri, mentions of women are always fewer for any given contractual category than for men and are more likely to be indirect. In her 1984a study, Hobson distinguishes three ways in which women figure in legal and financial records from Tebtunis: those women listed by name and acting in their own right, those named by acting with a male connection and those referred to in terms only of such a connection (e.g. wife/daughter etc. of 'x').[11] She finds that even when women act in their own right, it is often in connection with domestic roles, as in 'alimentary' contracts for spouse maintenance (Hobson 1984a: 378), and the number of women mentioned in the papyri is consistently lower than the number of men.

In such cases, we have to consider whether the record accurately reflects the number and types of female transactions or whether the record-format and social conventions governing male 'head of household' roles might overdetermine gendered divisions of work and economic responsibility. In other words, the ideology might determine the practice, or it might simply distort its formal representation in media for public consumption.[12] Collating and comparing fragmentary material, scattered over a wide chronological and geographic framework and shaped by diverse genres, is difficult whatever the topic. But it is not only the accidents of survival which affect the incidence and representation of female profit-making in the ancient world. The involvement itself or its recording had to conform to the requirements of specific genres and to more general notions of male/female roles.

The economic/social overlap is striking. Roman practice often seems to modern analysts a curious mixture of hard-edged economic rationalism and excessive attention to the claims of friendship, patronage and kinship. Land ownership was prized by the Roman élite not only for its perceived security but for its associated respectability, yet the land-owners of Roman

Italy were in many respects more profit-oriented than their noble mediaeval and early modern successors, who regarded land as an ancestral trust rather than a source of immediate enrichment.[13] Similarly, Romans of the highest social station who lent money at commercial rates to clients and friends regarded such arrangements as establishing or consolidating social relations which outlasted the term of the capital loan and its repayment with interest (Dixon 1993a, 1993b).

Such sentiments are to be found in many landed aristocracies. In the next chapter, we shall see that élite attitudes to work were not necessarily shared by non-senatorials, and the extent to which the upper class genuinely disdained commerce continues to be debated.[14] The landed aristocracy did not despise wealth itself – or profit, for that matter. It regarded usury as a low-status and rather disgraceful business but distinguished it from interest-bearing loans by ladies and gentlemen to their clients and friends (Pleket 1984), just as it distinguished large-scale business – morally and socially – from petty trading (Cicero *De officiis* 1.150). And there was no disgrace in selling on surplus agricultural profit, in producing bricks on rural land, in urban investment or even in commercial production from an elegant residential base.[15]

This chapter is not concerned primarily with the fine distinctions apparent to the Roman political élite as such, but they constitute a factor other than gender which might affect the source representation of élite women's profit-oriented activities. The apparent contradictions are another reminder that laws and social norms are seldom identical: senators who were forbidden from *c.* 218 BCE to engage in maritime trade seem somehow to have profited from it,[16] women restricted in theory by 'lifelong guardianship' appear to have transacted business freely (see Chapter 6). Men and women of the top census class not only managed to institute other women (their daughters) as heirs after the Voconian Law of 169 BCE forbade the practice, but considered it their duty to do so (Dixon 1985).

Public institutions and the mass media also mix up economic and moral assumptions in the modern world. Subsistence agriculture is not classified by UN agencies as productive activity, unpaid work is not counted in official GNP or OECD statistics, western statutes governing inheritance and matrimonial property frequently override the symbolic and cultural significance of the family farm. Economic rationalism, market forces and 'business' are concepts invoked with awe as if, like 'democracy' or 'motherhood', they embody immutable natural laws and moral imperatives. 'Business' and 'the market' held no such place in the consciousness or the material realities of the ancient world, in which the major means of acquiring or transferring wealth were inheritance and dowry, and grand entrepreneurs converted their fortunes to land-holdings.[17] Nor was profit (then or now) the only basis of 'economic' activity. Self-sufficiency (*autarchia*) was an ideal of the rich and a necessity for the peasantry (Veyne

1979). Some cloth production – a significant element of the ancient economy – was domestically based (Treggiari 1976: 99). Beneficence – whether conspicuous architectural donations to towns or the granting of loans and favours to peers and social inferiors – yielded social and political benefits prized as much as its material returns (Finley 1973: 53-5; Veyne 1990).

The landed élite does not figure as such in many legal sources – it is subsumed in the categories of slave-owners, testators, decurions and so on. The holdings and business activities of élite women – as distinct from their benefactions – are also unlikely to figure in inscriptions other than brick and amphora stamps. Women and economic activity are both topics incidental to the primary purposes of the literary sources which focus on the senatorial order of Roman Italy from the late Republic on. They provide us with isolated examples of extremely wealthy women who appear, on the whole, to acquire, administer and transmit their wealth in ways comparable with those of their male peers. Like their brothers, these women inherited their core wealth from their parents and supplemented it in their lifetime by means of non-kin inheritance and investment.[18] The closest we have to an ancient view of gender differential comes from that frustrating source, Plutarch's biography of Cato the Elder, which has Cato telling his son that it was the act of a widow simply to maintain inherited wealth and it was truly noble for a man to improve on his patrimony (Plutarch *Cato maior* 21.8).

The civil wars which led to the institution of the principate or empire took their toll on the fortunes of the ruling class. Surviving members of the losing side suffered wholesale confiscations and political penalties in the 40s and 30s BCE, as they had in the preceding generation. But the triumvirs of 43 – Octavian (Augustus), Antonius and Lepidus – anticipated significant revenues from a special tax on the wealthiest women of this order. It is only because those women took their resistance to the tax into the public sphere that the matter is recorded in Appian's history, chiefly given over to all-male military and political events.[19] Historians generally insert women in their narratives to make some political point.[20] We hear from Tacitus of the rich and distinguished Iunia, half-sister of Brutus, whose funeral was one of the great events of 22 CE (*Annals* 3.76), of Lollia Paulina, once married to the emperor Gaius (Caligula), left with a mere HS 5,000,000 from her vast wealth after a treason conviction (*Annals* 12.22), and of Iunia Silana whose wealth allegedly aroused the envy of the emperor's mother (*Annals* 13.19). In the Republic, women had been more quarantined from the loss of fortune through politically motivated prosecutions.

Pliny the Elder's *Natural History* cites women in different contexts which suit his Guinness Book of Records approach. His description of Lollia Paulina, decked out in gold, belongs with the moralising examples of Chapter 5, but also attests her wealth (*Natural History* 9.117-18). His

95

nephew, Pliny the Younger, published selected letters shaped by the conventions of the *genre* which had turned it into an essay-form by the late first/early second century and distinguished it from the more uninhibited and information-packed letters of Cicero. Pliny's report of his visits to the widespread estates of his mother-in-law Pompeia Celerina (*Letters* 1.4; 6.10) is designed to display his dutifulness. The fascinating account of a testamentary ceremony is part of an attack on his enemy Aquilius Regulus, whom he portrays as a legacy-hunter (*captator*) preying on the wealthy testatrix Aurelia.[21] His reference to the debt-laden patrimony of another woman 'which even a man would have found burdensome' serves to highlight Pliny's own beneficence – he forgives her debts to him which she has inherited from her father and informs her that he had also contributed to her dowry (*Letters* 2.4). Pliny's old family friend Corellia bought some estates from him at a very favourable rate. He represents the transaction as a favour to her, but with more than a hint that she was taking advantage of him (*Letters* 7.11).

These literary references, most incidental to the authors' primary purposes, give no sense of the typicality of the women mentioned (even for their class) and how they might compare with men in numbers and approaches to wealth. The authors assume rather than explain the acquisition and use of wealth, apparently on the basis that there was little significant difference in male and female practice, in spite of the lifelong 'guardianship' of women (Chapter 6). There is no indication that élite women sought the advice of peers or lower-class experts any more than their male counterparts. Certainly we owe much of our knowledge of their activities to male involvement, as in the references in the letters of Cicero and Pliny to the affairs of Terentia and Pomponia Celerina, but the women do not appear to have followed advice uncritically: Cicero's wife Terentia disregarded his pleas to keep her property intact during his exile (Cicero *Ad familiares* 14.1.5), Pompeia Celerina's approach to Pliny was the gracious but imperious use of his services.[22] In general, the upper class leaned on the informal advice of its social equals and the expertise of informed subordinates.[23] Terentia's employment of her freedman Philotimus is paralleled by Cicero's use of Eros.[24]

The Roman legal system, which had a weak concept of agency, imposed personal involvement for owners in many crucial transactions. This meant that Roman citizen women of differing social levels could not evade direct participation.[25] The Pompeian Umbricia Ianuaria – not a Terentia, but of some local standing and respectability – could entrust a man with the task of writing out her deposition but had to play an active role in auctioning her slave.[26] Clodia, in the agnatic *tutela* of her brothers, conducted her own affairs, negotiating the sale of her suburban estate and freeing slaves at will – and simply calling her relations in to authorise the necessary acts.[27] Typically, we learn of her financial activities because of Cicero's wish to misrepresent some of them in court (her loan to Caelius and her manumission of slaves) and, later, to acquire one of her properties.[28]

Mentions of agents or *tutores* are rare in literary accounts of women's acquisition, sale and profit-oriented use of land in the republican and imperial periods. Plutarch cites purchase by Sulla's daughter Cornelia Fausta of an estate at Baiae which had belonged to Marius as an instance of sharp dealing. She re-sold it for thirty times what she had paid for it.[29] Terentia seems to have treated her rural holdings in utilitarian fashion, with an eye to immediate profit (shades of Cato the Elder!). She owned woodlands and leased public land, probably for pasturage.[30] Varro's aunt had a small farm near Rome which catered to a specialist market.[31] The assumption behind these anecdotes is that women – far from being business innocents – had a good eye for a bargain. Indeed, women were popularly regarded as financially rapacious.[32] Paradoxically, they could also be represented as vulnerable because of their financial inexperience. Both stereotypes existed and could be exploited for rhetorical purposes.

Brick and amphora stamps – mostly from the second century CE onwards – provide a different kind of evidence for substantial female land-holding, viticulture and brick production. Amphorae were produced for storing and transporting wine and other produce. The stamps on the necks of amphorae have yielded the names of women, such as Calvia Crispinilla, engaged in wine-production (which required considerable initial investment) and possibly export.[33] Bricks were stamped from early imperial times with the name of the owner of the factory and sometimes of the manager, *officinator*. The stamps bear the names of a few female managers (*officinatrices*) and of many more female owners (*dominae*) of quarries and factories, some from the imperial family itself.[34] Setälä has calculated that of a total of 149 such land-owners with brick-factories on their property, 49 were women.

Inscriptions of another kind remind us of two means by which women who were not born to wealth could acquire it. Although Roman marriages were usually contracted between partners of equal wealth and status, Naevoleia Tyche, known to us through the expensive monument she erected to herself and her husband, might have gained admission to an established social position through her husband Munatius Faustus (Plate 1).[35] Nero's freed slave mistress Claudia Acte was not marriage material. She features in Tacitus' account of court intrigues and mother-son conflict, but it is characteristic that we learn of her extensive north African estates from inscriptional records.[36] Women in less spectacular situations might also have benefited materially from marriage to a former master. In many cases, the financial benefit would be mutual. Both men and women, mostly former slaves themselves, freed potential partners, who were usually practising the same business or trade as themselves and were already in a relationship with them. The law, however, focused on men manumitting women for the purpose of marriage.[37]

The upper classes hypothetically regarded urban investment as riskier – and therefore morally more dubious – than its rural equivalent, but diversified into both types of property (Garnsey 1976: 128 ff.). Terentia's dowry included an apartment-block in Rome which yielded rents (Cicero *Ad Atticum* 12.18a; 15.17). There are no indications of women outside the senatorial ranks having any qualms about exploiting urban properties. The splendid building of Iulia Felix in Pompeii – which appears to have been her own residence, *inter alia*, unashamedly carries a painted notice advertising up-market baths, residential shops and apartments for rent on the premises (*CIL* 4.1136). Iunia Libertas of Ostia bequeathed the income from her garden apartments and shops to her former slaves and their descendants in perpetuity.[38]

In ruling on the extension of a masculine form in the praetor's edict to women, Ulpian stated that 'there is no question that women can conduct business and be involved in litigation about it'.[39] And women are to be found in all types of enterprise. They were involved in maritime trade and in shipping loans, activities regarded by the élite as high-risk and questionable, but probably lacking any stigma for other social groups (Sirks 1980). Spanish inscriptions record women ship-owners engaged in the export of wine.[40]

Iconographic and written memorials depict women as saleswomen and artisan-producers in small shops and service businesses, such as bars and hairdressing establishments.[41] A certain disreputability attached to some of these businesses, but – as with men – the larger-scale enterprises seem to have been socially acceptable. Landladies of pubs and hot-food shops had a poor reputation, but wholesale dealers, *negotiatrices*, figure in legal writings as women of substance (Kampen 1981: 110-11). In the late Republic and early Empire, the term *negotiator* (and, by implication, the female form *negotiatrix*) implied greater social elevation than the more mundane *mercator*. The imperial jurist Paul refers (*Digest* 34.2.32.4) to merchandise disposed in the will of a female dealer (*negotiatrix*). The feminine ending *-trix* tells us her sex, where a more general ruling would have concealed it, but the scale and status of her dealings are obscured by our uncertainty about just when the term changed its significance.[42]

Jurists' rulings usually suppress gender and give only the bare-bones legal answer to problems. Their subsequent editing in the Justinianic corpus makes it difficult to contextualise them. The quote above, from Ulpian, refers to liability for administering the business affairs (*negotia*) of others and presupposes a degree of social or commercial responsibility on the part of the manager. The ruling might have been a pedantic response to a conventional surprise that the category included women, or a reproof to a canny businesswoman for attempting to escape the legal consequences of her actions.[43] Either reading would fit the case. Other references in the *Digest* title to women taking charge of the affairs of young relatives confirm that women had a grasp of finance but also imply that their official involvement was often determined by family relationships and perhaps the absence of a more obvious male administrator, which left a widowed grandmother as the protector of the family interests.[44]

The same question arises with small businesses apparently owned or managed by women. When a woman is recorded as sole artisan/owner, we are left wondering if that means that she is single.[45] Such businesses were often family concerns, and commemorative inscriptions sometimes indicate this.[46] Other inscriptions, however, name only the husband's role as artisan/businessman (Treggiari 1979: 79).[47] Even a woman commissioning such an inscription might characterise her husband and their *familia* by their connection with the business, but omit any explicit reference to her own position as co-owner/employer and fellow-worker (which can nonetheless be inferred from the context).[48] With such small numbers, there can be no definitive numerical demonstration of any trends but reading such inscriptions leaves an overall impression of a general tendency to suppress or re-form female involvement in public economic activities in favour of more 'womanly' characterisations.

This 'domestication' of female roles affects all the sources in slightly differing ways: the juristic references embody benevolent paternalistic assumptions about the need to protect women from their financial innocence and their own husbands. They also assume that certain tasks – notably, cloth production – are carried out by women under female supervision (by owner or fellow-slave) and that tolerance should be extended to women intruding in masculine spheres if they are doing so on behalf of male relations. The kind of papyri featuring women reinforce the impression that women should be characterised in public media by their family roles. Such assumptions affect the clustering of female references around certain topics in the Justinianic writings – dowry and other exchanges connected with marriage (and divorce), the maintenance of minors and the administration of their affairs – which consolidate this impression. But it is countered by opposing rulings on the capacities and liabilities of women in most legal and financial areas (Gardner 1995).

In all sources, the incidence of women's recorded economic activity is consistently lower than that of men and the range of tasks more limited. Traditionally, that has been taken to mean women were not as commercially active as men. The records found in the home of the Pompeian banker Caecilius Iucundus, for example, list only six women vendors and this has been read literally by scholars to mean there were few women vendors in Pompeii.[49]

But the consistency need not reflect reality. There are fewer references to women than to men even in sources dealing with cloth-production and dowry agreements, which necessarily involve women. References to slave-owners and slaves are predominantly to males, although we know women were well represented in both categories. The tendency to regard women as an afterthought and special 'marked' category in most discourse and the tendency to re-formulate female activities to suit notions of the feminine colours representations of women's economic behaviour in all *genres*, literary and non-literary. But the categories themselves are not consistent – women can be characterised, according to context, as in need of masculine guidance or protection, as safeguarding their family interests, as financially grasping or as operating on the same footing as male actors. Alternatively, they can be excluded altogether from most accounts or mentioned without reference to their economic activity in a world which did not draw hard and fast lines between the home and the market-place and had no particular regard for business as such but culturally valued the roles of wife and mother.

Patronage (i): loans, favours and investment

In modern egalitarian societies with a meritocratic ethos, patronage is a bad word and business a good one. In classical antiquity, patronage and friendship were sacred, pure commerce sordid. For this reason, references in our sources to commercial dealings are often suffused in (or disguised by) the language of patronage. Loans are favours, labour and repayments become duties (*officia, merita*), and acts of 'friendship' (*amicitia*) between social peers could encompass a range of services and commitments. In reality, things are always more complex than the dominant categories would suggest: many routine modern business practices can, when exposed publicly, erupt into political scandals. In Roman society, acts of friendship and patronage could also be transformed by hostile sources into undue influence or corruption and favours extended by women to individual men were particularly vulnerable to such interpretations.

Roman protocol required the beneficiary of any favour to acknowledge it publicly. The form of the acknowledgement varied according to the nature of the favour and the relative standing of the parties. Individuals might honour a socially superior patron with an inscription expressing gratitude for a loan, promotion, manumission or a job, or mention the patron's benevolence in a dutiful funerary commemoration. Such inscriptions, like honorific statues (with suitably inscribed bases) dedicated to the benefactor of a town, *collegium* (guild) or a needy group, typically record male and female generosity within the more public sphere and for relations between different status levels (i.e. vertical social relations).[50] Favours between near-equals were more likely to be acknowledged by visits (which leave no historical trace) and by personal letters. Many such favours are recorded in surviving letters written by the benefactors themselves, telling third parties about their own actions, or in the form of letters of commendation (Cotton 1981; Saller 1982: 108-10).

Yet again Cicero, Pliny, Seneca and Fronto are our sources for women's involvement in personal patronage within the élite. These men are naturally more inclined to advertise their own benevolence, and therefore to mention women chiefly as the objects of *their* generosity.[51] Their letters do, however, make it clear that both sexes were involved in extended social relations beyond the family. Women are included in the language of friendship. The social freedom of the Roman matron and its contrast with Greek custom was noted by contemporaries such as Cornelius Nepos:

> No Roman thinks it shameful to take his wife to a dinner party. As mistress of the household, the wife occupies the place of honour and, as hostess, presides over its social life. Things are very different in the Greek world, where the wife is never present at a dinner party unless it is a family occasion. (*Illustrious Lives*, preface)

The misogynist portraits of Juvenal's sixth satire support this observation, for the poet complains of women holding forth on politics and literature at mixed dinner parties, which they both host and attend as guests. This social interaction was invested with economic significance because of the role played by gifts, loans, favours and legacies in the Roman institutions of friendship (*amicitia*) and patronage.

Loans represent this intersection of social and economic relations. While professional usury was viewed by senatorials as an utterly dishonourable livelihood, loans were a respectable source of income and of political-social capital.[52] They were classed as favours and therefore acknowledged in inscriptional form, by personal attendance on the benefactor or by letter. Cicero and Seneca have both elaborated the protocols of such acknowledgement within the élite ranks in rather academic treatises which stress the disinterestedness of friendship and generosity over reciprocity. The examples they give in Cicero's *De officiis* (On Duties) and Seneca's *De beneficiis* (On Favours) are almost exclusively male, but their letters refer to contemporary women of their circles as debtors and creditors.

Cicero himself borrowed a large sum from Caerellia, an older woman of the senatorial order, in spite of hints from Atticus that this looked bad.[53] The wealthy Sassia of Larinum set her freedman doctor up in a shop with a capital loan (Cicero *Pro Cluentio* 178). A damaged funerary monument to the Ostian shoemaker Septimia Stratonice (see Plate 7) invokes the language of friendship and gratitude, possibly for a loan. The male commemorator describes her as his friend (*amica*) and refers to a *beneficium*.[54] All such loans would have elicited interest – probably on the usual days of repayment, 1 January and 1 July – but they would also have created or reinforced) a longstanding social relationship between benefactor and beneficiary, even within the same status group (Dixon 1993b: 458-9).

Disentangling the material, social, political and moral elements of 'friendship' for élite Romans is ultimately an artificial exercise, although that has not prevented ancient and modern commentators from trying.[55] The money Cicero owed to Ovia (*Ad Atticum* 12.21; 16.1.1) could have been for a share in an inheritance, or a loan. Pliny the Younger could borrow money from his wealthy former mother-in-law whenever he needed it (*Letters* 3.19.8).[56] But such arrangements were open to wilful misinterpretation. In a character assassination of Cicero in the senate, Mark Antony's supporter Fufius Calenus accused him of an illicit sexual relationship with Caerellia (Dio 46.18.4), and in court Cicero himself represented a loan by his enemy Clodia to his protégé Caelius as a sexual inducement (*Pro Caelio* 31.33). Yet Valerius Maximus records the case of a man who included his mistress in his will as a creditor, as if that were a more acceptable way to benefit her without revealing their sexual relationship. But when the man recovered and she sued him for the fictitious debt, the legal device – and the relationship – became common knowledge.[57] It is difficult to distinguish the finer points of the exchange and the sexual protocol, but it remains clear that the integration of women in the social/political relationships which bound élite men is expressed also in their material and financial exchanges, of which loans were an important element (Dixon 1993b).

Intercession by women to or on behalf of a relative was a longstanding tradition at Rome, enshrined in its history.[58] Excluded from political and military positions themselves, women could nonetheless help male connections secure such positions, often by woman-to-woman lobbying.[59] This was seen as perfectly proper behaviour for a mother, aunt or daughter.[60]

Like men, Roman women tended to accumulate wealth, prestige and social capital as they became older, and their connections could give them the power to confer favours. But the line between acceptable favours and corruption is seldom clear-cut. The same action, termed generous by a supporter, may be denounced by an enemy as a disgrace. Women's ability to confer favours was indirect – and therefore morally more ambiguous – because it was necessarily based not on their own formal position but on their influence with a husband or male relative. The blurred line between social (patronage and kin) and economic transactions heightened the ambiguity and therefore the possibilities of exploiting it for political purposes.

The perspectives vary by source. Vestals had always been uniquely distinguished and were by definition wealthy and influential. Beneficiaries of the third-century Vestal Campia Severina publicly expressed their gratitude to her for securing important civil and military jobs through her influence, and the Vestal Flavia Mamilla was similarly thanked by her nephews for their positions.[61] Inscriptions of the imperial era openly acknowledge women, usually married to provincial governors or senior military officers, for procuring jobs for the dedicator (or her relative). Vergilia and her consular husband Iulius Fortunatianus are both described by the grateful author of an inscription at Lambaesis as his *'patroni'*.[62]

But these same acts could be criticised. In the second century BCE, Cato the Elder had protested against the erection of honorific statues in the provinces to female members of Roman governors' families (Pliny *Natural History* 34.30-1). And Tacitus records a senatorial debate of CE 21 about the behaviour of governors' wives in the provinces, particularly their corrupt dispensation of favours (*Annals* 3.33-4). Neither objection seems to have been successful and both were probably driven by specific current political issues and alignments, but they show how much scope there was for reinterpretation of favours, even within a well-established social framework. By the standards of Transparency International (the modern transnational organisation), Roman provincial government was endemically corrupt. Trials of governors for extortion took place, but they were instigated for reasons of political vengeance and personal ambition and did not benefit the victims. The retinue of a provincial governor consisted of his relatives and the sons of friends, as well as selected slaves and freed slaves, all of whom were in a position to enrich themselves because of their presumed access to the leading official. Catullus complained, comically but without shame, that he was unable to make as much as he had hoped in service to the governor Memmius in Bithynia.[63]

Examples of female patronage in Roman political narratives are overwhelmingly unfavourable and, like attacks on women in Republican speeches, are a means of denouncing their male kin for failure to control them.[64] Tacitus' treatment of the power-struggle between the young emperor Nero and his mother Agrippina minor (*Annals* 13.2 ff.) exploits the Roman cliché of the political mother who is (properly) instrumental in her son's success but then oversteps the bounds in calling in her social debt once he is in a position to grant significant favours (Dixon 1988: 175-87). Seneca congratulated his own mother for avoiding this common female failing and thereby distinguishing herself from those women who, ineligible for office, exercised power by exploiting their sons' influence 'with female irresponsibility', *muliebri impotentia* (*Ad Helviam* 14.2). But Seneca's acknowledgement of the contribution of his mother Helvia and of his aunt Marcia (*Ad Helviam* 19.2) to his own career constitutes a public tribute to their political and social power, their tact and his gratitude. It is all a matter of perspective.

Political favours are a particular instance of the patronage mechanisms which pervaded Roman social and economic life. They are better attested in our literary sources which privilege political narratives, but there is no obvious distinction between the categories. The men who gained a position through the influence (*gratia*) of Livia or the *suffragium* of the Vestal Campia Severina benefited economically from their advancement. Women regularly held audiences of petitioners and participated in lobbying for appointments from Republican times.[65]

Women were also involved, as patrons and beneficiaries, in the patronage networks which affected many small businesses. The upper-class women who participated in the social-financial networks within their own stratum also extended patronage to lower social groups, notably to their own freed slaves. In a lawsuit of the late Republic, Cicero tells us how the wealthy municipal Italian widow Sassia had provided her former slave, a doctor, with shopfront premises from which to practise his profession.[66] In the terminology of Roman patronage, as expressed in custom and law, her capital loan or investment in the shop would – like the training and manumission of the slave in question – constitute a favour to him. In return, her former slave owed her cash repayments with interest, as well as services in kind, both classed as 'duties' (*officia*) and lifelong marks of respect and gratitude (*obsequium*).[67] This stress on patronal relations made such arrangements morally acceptable to the self-image of élite owners, with their professed distaste for petty commerce. The arrangements also distanced the creditor/patron from the economic consequences of financial failure.[68]

'Patron' (*patrona*) could be used as a general term for such a relationship of reciprocal but unequal benefit or, as in Sassia's case, would specifically denote a former owner. Even slaves bought for domestic use or the personal entertainment of the owner and trained in her establishment (or bought as skilled slaves), could be a source of income, as in the case of the largely female workforce of the Statilii Tauri (Treggiari 1976: 82). If freed, such slaves and possibly their own children were incorporated in the patronage network of the former owner.[69]

It is telling that a key literary example of such a common arrangement is grounded in lurid forensic accusations. Shops such as that of Sassia's doctor were everyday features of town life, but more likely to figure in legal and epigraphic sources than in élite literary *genres*. Inscriptions, chiefly epitaphs, commemorating the artisan-shopkeeper stratum – *tabernarii* – show a high incidence of freed slaves, particularly in the district around Rome, where the greatest number (still minute) of such references is found.[70] Their workshops faced on to the streets of Roman towns and their wares doubtless spilt out on them, much as they do in many Italian towns today. Artisan families and their dependants lived in such shops, which typically had an upper floor in the small premises, all part of larger Roman residential blocks of apartments of varying size and splendour, reached by separate entry-points (see Plates 12-14).

Such blocks were a popular form of investment, yielding rents from the commercial and residential tenants and providing the owner with a possible location for her slave and freed artisans in the shopfront premises. The resultant combination of commercial returns and extended patronal relations could survive death. The freed slaves of Iunia Libertas of Ostia continued to enjoy the revenues from her garden apartments and shops after her death, on the understanding that they and their descendants *and* their freed slaves and *their* descendants would continue to commemorate her. In her lifetime, they had probably managed the shops and occupied the attached residential areas.[71]

Inscriptions by the *tabernarii* shopkeeper-class themselves (or by *their* freed slaves), our main source, leave much to be desired as detailed economic records, but it may be that our wish to extract specific elements – such as loans and investment – from their social context and transform them into intelligible capitalist categories is misplaced. The main concern of the people who commissioned these inscriptions for a variety of monuments was to express particular attitudes and relationships, such as the celebration of a common skill or workplace (Joshel 1992a). Some were erected by workers to their husband-wife patrons. *CIL* 6.9375, a monument to the ivory carver (*eburarius*) Publius Clodius Bromius, former slave of Aulus Clodius and Clodia, his concubine Curiatia Arumnia and *their* jointly owned freed slave Publius Clodius Rufio, may represent husband-wife (Aulus Clodius and Clodia) investment in a slave (Bromius) and his training on the job, where he benefited the family business working alongside his owners until his manumission and partnering marked the repetition of the process.[72] The ambiguities of slavery are highlighted at this social level where slaves – legally classed as property – were incorporated in family life on near-equal terms, living and working with their owners, before being freed and then becoming quasi-kin, happy eventually to commemorate their former owners on a near-equal basis as friends and former workmates.

Some inscriptions use vocabulary with commercial and patronal overtones which might have held a specific meaning for contemporaries of the beneficiary's circle but are cryptic for a modern reader. The reference to a favour (*bene meritum*) in the commemorative inscription to the Ostian shoemaker Septimia Stratonice (Plate 7) probably indicates a loan she made to her friend and commemorator, M. Acilius Is—.[73] The monument to Aurelia Philematio (or Philematium) and her fellow freed slave (*collibertus*) husband Aurelius Hermia has her speak of helping her butcher-husband flourish by her '*officium*' and celebrates, among her many wifely virtues, her unceasing devotion to duty and lack of avarice. The long inscriptions stress the mutual affection and joint effort of the couple, but the repetition of '*officium*' implies a patronal element in the relationship which is reinforced by the visual emblem of her submissively kissing her husband's right hand. Unlike Claudia Prepontis in another monument from Rome, she does not describe her husband as her patron.[74]

Marital, kin, patronal and work-based relations and friendship merge in these lower-class commemorations, while upper-class literary references to favours, friendship and loans (Dixon 1993b) show a similar blurring of categories. Women's commercial and patronal roles are obscured in both cases by convention, by forgetfulness (by male authors) and by wilful distortion of common transactions for invective purposes. At all social levels and in all *genres*, women are likely to be located in a family or marital context or simply to be overlooked unless there is some particular reason for featuring them. The requirements of patronage constitute such a reason, and a slave trained and freed by a husband and wife will usually reveal this in his own epitaph by his nomenclature, as Bromius did.

Patronage (ii): benefactions

The legacy-hunter (*captator*) who cultivated a childless, wealthy patron was a stock figure in Roman satire. Such humour was also a way of asserting the 'proper' disposition of estates to family, rather than responding to the flattery of outsiders.[75] But public benefactions or foundations to benefit the *familia* or lower-class clients were never characterised as an improper diversion of family wealth. That is an index of the entrenched character of patronage in Roman culture. Nor did the moral ambivalence of personal favours to men outside their family extend to public liberality by women. Those women who dispensed largesse to groups – to towns, temples, *collegia* (guilds) or their own *familia* of slaves and former slaves – were typically acknowledged with statues and inscriptions which publicly proclaimed their generosity in much the same terms used for male donors (Forbis 1990).

Foundations which provided regular payments or distributions are also attested in legal and epigraphic sources (Andreau 1977). The funerary foundation was a common institution. Many such foundations were established in the lifetime of the patron or by testament to commemorate the patron herself (posthumously) or deceased relatives or members of the *familia* (i.e. manumitted slaves) who would bear the family name. Such funerary rites were important to the ancients and inclusion in them was a cause for gratitude.

Some foundations provided just enough to pay for commemoration on the customary days for remembering the dead (Dixon 1992a: 136). Others provided greater wherewithal for the general benefit of the former *familia*. The relatively lavish foundation of Iunia Libertas of Ostia gave all her slaves and former slaves the enjoyment of the revenue from her block of garden apartments and shops.[76] Juristic texts attest the practice – usually testamentary – of providing sustenance and shelter for former slaves who had been under the patronage of the testatrix in her lifetime. These are referred to as alimentary foundations (*alimenta*).[77]

Noblesse oblige: the élites of ancient towns were expected to build or repair public facilities such as temples, basilicas and theatres and to provide annual donatives of food in the form of dinners or distributions of bread and wine (*sportulae*).[78] The legal obligation for certain redistributions was linked to office-holding and therefore confined to men, but women of these élite families made donations in their own right or joined with husbands, fathers or sons.[79]

The priestess Eumachia, celebrated by a statue (Plate 5) and an inscription describing her as *patrona* of the fullers of Pompeii (Plate 6), had apparently donated a building to them.[80] She was clearly a citizen of some standing. We know of no women fullers and certainly the memberships of their influential guilds was not open to women in Pompeii, where cloth processing was a significant part of the economy.[81] Yet it was acceptable for a woman to be patron of this masculine association, just as it happened from time to time that a lady of the imperial family was called 'mother' of the military camps.[82] It was not seen as intrusion in a masculine sphere.

Different kinds of beneficence and patronage could be combined. An alimentary foundation was recorded in an inscription attached to a building constructed from a bequest in the will of C(G)aelia Macrina of Tarracina.[83] *Sportulae*, donations of food in various guises, were initiated by the women as well as the men of the wealthy classes, such as Corellia Gallia Papiana, who instituted foundations at Minturnae and Casinum for annual distributions of bread and wine on her birthday.[84] Such *sportulae* were sometimes commemorative, sometimes one-off celebrations of particular occasions, like the distribution by Apuleius' wife Pudentilla at Oea in north Africa on her younger son's coming of age and her elder son's marriage.[85] The Pompeian funeral monument to Naevoleia Tyche and Munatius Faustus depicts a distribution, which might have been a funeral commemoration (Plate 1).[86] Like other forms of gift-exchange, such *sportulae* constituted a material investment for a mixed return in the form of deference, political support, occasional gifts and labour and generalised obligation.[87]

Alimentary schemes targeting children were originally *ad hoc* charitable measures initiated by local notables, both men and women.[88] The emperor Trajan formally encouraged such schemes and many nobles, like Pliny the Younger, responded by including the schemes in the types of patronage which they extended to the area they lived in or their region of origin (in his case, Comum in northern Italy).[89] The rationale was that the schemes would assist the free poor of Roman Italy to rear their children. Official endorsement was expressed in coin issues of the second century CE and in their public association with women of the imperial family.[90] On the death of his wife Faustina the Elder, the emperor Pius established a foundation in her memory, the *puellae faustinianae*, which specifically benefited poor girls.[91] The empress Faustina the Younger supported another commemorative foundation for poor children (probably foundlings) from the estate she inherited from her aunt Matidia.[92] On Faustina's death, *her* widower, the emperor Marcus (Aurelius) dedicated an already established foundation to her memory.[93]

It was not only women from the imperial family who funded such schemes. Crispia Restituta of Beneventum offered her farms as security for loans to yield interest for one in 101 CE.[94] At about the same time, Caelia Macrina, mentioned above, established a fund for a monthly distribution to 100 boys and 100 girls of Tarracina.[95] At Ostia later in the same century Fabia Agrippina apparently contributed a million sesterces to an existing scheme to benefit one hundred girls, as a memorial to her mother.[96]

The recurrent association of women with schemes for children, especially girls, is interesting. Government alimentary schemes favoured boys and it has been suggested that private foundations for girls in Roman Italy were intended as 'top-ups' of imperial foundations.[97] This approach resembles modern charity. The testamentary grant by Matidia the Younger might have been a supplement to an existing private scheme.[98] Another scholar has concluded on the basis of the amounts involved that many so-called 'alimentary' foundations were too small to provide substantial contributions to children's upkeep and were more like the traditional annual donatives of food on festive occasions.[99]

Such disparities between the image of generosity projected by the donor and its practical effects are frequently noted by outsiders.[100] A marxist, a cynic or, indeed, most social scientists could justifiably point out that donations of perishable food are a classic example of redistribution which costs little to the donor, who gets a disproportionate return of prestige within the community at large and loyalty from the recipients.[101] Annual picnics for seasonal workers, in which they consume some of the products of their own labour as a gift from those who have exploited it, are common aristocratic institutions. But gift-giving is seldom amenable to a straightforward analysis.[102] Businesses confer Christmas presents with an eye to specific returns, and annual festivals around the world signal the exchange within families and among friends of presents which recipients could usually have afforded for themselves. The social meanings of such exchanges are not nullified by analysis of the specific benefit or the elements of self-interest in what purports to be generosity. Much depends on the perspective of the observer.

Whatever their specific use and purpose, we can say that alimentary donations were economically significant, involved women (although never as much as men), and indicate a readiness by wealthy women to extend substantial patronage. It was not uncommon to donate sums of one million sesterces.[103] Other donors provided land for its revenues from rents or mortgages. Both types of donation attest informed exploitation of their land-holdings by prosperous women and reinforce our impression that these women were a publicly visible part of the 'establishment' of local communities, maintaining (or creating) family status by such judicious gifts.

Women were also singled out at times as beneficiaries of female donors.[104] *ILS* 6583 records the expenditure of a husband and wife at Veii for a public feast. The inscription makes it clear that he gave the male feast and she gave one for the women.[105] In such cases, the recipients were themselves a select group, not the poor. The donations would secure political and social *kudos* for the benefactors. It is not quite clear how one Laberia Hostilia Crispina gained the soubriquet 'patron of the women of Trebulae', but the implication is that she benefited other women of her region in some way.[106] Elsewhere, *'patrona'* (like *'patronus'*, the masculine form) as an honorific title was conferred by towns and corporations in response to significant material donations and favours.[107]

The records of all such benefactions were 'public'. The display of the written texts and of statues in public spaces incorporated these distinguished women in the ranks of community benefactors. Tombs outside the town walls bearing references to donations to freed slaves (among others) would also contribute to this community image of beneficence and prosperity. It is typical of such public statements that they are wholly laudatory and fairly brief, with none of the overtones of many literary references to patronage. When we have both kinds of source referring to the same woman, the contrast is striking. In one of his letters, Pliny the Younger discusses the will of Ummidia Quadratilla, grandmother of his friend Ummidius, who had recently died at the age of 79. The letter is one of several he published to illustrate the idea that a good will can posthumously redeem a tarnished reputation.[108] In elaborating on the old lady's love of gambling and the popular theatre, which clearly made her relatives uneasy, he gives us a fascinating glimpse into the lifestyle of this social group. Under the cloak of respectful moralising, Pliny packs a great deal of innuendo into his description:

> She kept a troupe of pantomime actors and used to indulge them more freely than was suitable in a lady of rank ...
> When she was passing her grandson into my keeping for training, she told me herself that, as a woman of leisure, she was in the habit of relaxing with gambling games and that it was her practice to watch her own pantomime performers. (*Letters* 7.24.5)

Ummidia hailed from Casinum, and it so happens that an inscription records her gift to that town of an amphiteatre. She also donated a temple and probably restored a theatre which her father had built.[109] This suggests that, like Pliny, she accepted the obligations of her station to confer substantial benefits on her native region. Another inscription from Puteoli commemorates a pantomime artiste who may well have been one of the performers who caused such concern (ultimately unfounded) to those connections who feared for their inheritance.[110]

The typical literary characterisation went further than Pliny's innuendo. Cicero's reference to Sassia's common-or-garden patronage of her former slave is woven into a narrative of municipal murder and mayhem.[111] Routine examples of women's patronage had no place in historical narratives, but might be invoked as transgressive, or to illustrate palace power struggles. Tacitus, for example, reports a senatorial debate of 21 CE about the abuse of power by provincial governors' wives, the arrogant behaviour in 16 CE of Urgulania (who relied on the support of the empress Livia) and Nero's abolition in 56 CE of his mother's receptions of petitioners.[112] His favourable mentions of the protection afforded by such patronage are easily overlooked, because they are embedded in criticism of the emperor, like the claim that Nero dared not show savagery to his wife (and cousin) Octavia while his mother was still alive (Tacitus *Annals* 14.1). Since Tacitus constructed Livia as a vengeful stepmother (*Annals* 1.6), any acknowledgement of the protection and sustenance she provided for the exiled daughter of her own stepdaughter is grudging and qualified (*Annals* 4.71).

Livia's representations in the various media are interesting. She necessarily accumulated a significant following through her long life, and her public image set the style for subsequent celebrations of women of the imperial family.[113] Augustus had granted her even more titles and privileges than his half-sister Octavia and in his will he adopted her and conferred on her the title of Augusta.[114] As chief priest of his cult and daughter/widow of a god, she acquired even greater prestige, and was styled 'mother of the world' (*genetrix orbis*) in the provinces, where she was associated with goddesses.[115] She regularly received petitioners and extended largesse and personal favours to a broad social range of beneficiaries which included senatorial brides, the future emperors Galba and Otho and victims of fires in Rome.[116] Her active promotion of religious cults, particularly for women, included significant building at Rome and in the Greek east, where she also had extensive land-holdings and where honorific statues to her abounded.[117] The official thanksgiving on her recovery in 22 CE from a serious illness and repeated senatorial and provincial attempts to confer special titles on her in her lifetime (and after her death, Dio 58.2) indicate widespread affection for this grand old lady and are specifically linked in the sources to her liberality.[118] Yet literary depictions subordinate such elements to melodramatic narratives of mother-son conflict in the reign of Tiberius which reproduce the standard *topoi* of the undutiful emperor and the pushy political woman (Bartman

110

1999: 108). Characterising Tiberius as unfeeling, Suetonius groups his failure to return to Rome on his mother's death in 29 CE with similar derelictions towards other relatives (*Tiberius* 51-2; cf. *Nero* 35). The dramatic account of an argument between mother and son over a favour for one of Livia's protégés is used to explain Tiberius' withdrawal to Capri. It makes for great reading, but the parallels with Tacitus' version of conflict between Nero and *his* mother suggests that the narrative was a formula.[119]

Tacitus emphasises Tiberius' mean-minded resentment of his mother's popularity and power and gives examples of the emperor rejecting attempts to accord Livia special titles, but they seem to accord with Tiberius' general policy of catering to conservative senatorial standards by limiting extravagant honours to imperial family members, including himself.[120] Dio provides more detail about Livia's popularity and generosity, but maintains the themes of jealousy and conflict. All three authors portray a power struggle in which Livia, though overtly confining herself to the feminine sphere (never intruding on the army etc.), actually crossed the proper gender-lines.[121] To ancient readers, Tiberius' invocation of the limits of a woman's role (*Tiberius* 50) was part of a familiar literary tradition extending back to the *Odyssey*, where Telemachus told his mother Penelope that he would attend to men's business and she should get on with her work in the women's quarters (*Odyssey* 1.356-9). It is interesting that Suetonius chose a commonplace personal favour as the final straw in this mother-son story-line. Promotion of an individual by a higher-status woman is widely attested in inscriptions and does not seem to challenge convention in the least.[122] Mothers revered in Roman tradition had made much tougher demands on sons.[123] Elsewhere, Suetonius refers neutrally to the part Livia played in promoting the careers of Galba and Otho's grandfather (*Galba* 5, *Otho* 1). But here, Suetonius has Tiberius treat the request that a new citizen be included in the jury lists as a gross abuse of Livia's position. He says sarcastically that he will accede only if the paperwork carries the rider 'forced on the emperor by his mother', as if that would cause Livia embarrassment by exposing her undue pressure. Livia's power of patronage, a source of affection and regard for the empress, is thereby transformed into a sinister example of female presumption and an explanation for the emperor's withdrawal from the capital.

The reliance of Roman historians on ancient literary accounts has skewed modern perspectives on emperors and other members of the imperial family. Even more than the 'great men' of Republican political history, their characterisations have been driven by the personality-oriented accounts of authors like Suetonius, Tacitus and Dio, who draw on rhetorical and biographical clichés to flesh out the annalistic state records and the records in noble homes and imperial archives. In the case of Livia, an imperial woman, we have a countervailing mass not only of political propaganda such as coin issues and the Ara Pacis, but honorific statues and inscriptions from a wide geographic base which, like scattered references in the literature, reinforce the impression (equally manufactured) of a gracious lady bestowing largesse in the appropriate fashion to communities, social inferiors and fellow-women. Her building programme at Rome and apparently in Asia Minor is readily paralleled with examples of wealthy women throughout the empire. Her contributions to girls' dowries are akin to 'Turia's' contributions to the dowries of her more indigent female relations (*CIL* 6.1527). Her provision of a funerary monument for selected slaves and freed slaves of her *familia* is in keeping with élite practice by men and women alike.[124]

The sensitive politics of displaying the transcendence of the founding dynasty in what was nominally still an oligarchic republic imposed the need for tact. Livia had a very high profile when her son succeeded her husband and her public image and behaviour had to be manipulated to avoid too-obvious resemblances to Hellenistic monarchies. Tiberius' behaviour looks different once allowance is made for this situation.[125] Take Dio's allegation that Tiberius spitefully blocked her plans to give a commemorative dinner for senators and their families on Augustus' death. Tiberius' modification of her plans meant that, in the end, she entertained the senatorial women and he the men – which sounds in keeping with other such occasions within the élite of Roman Italian towns.[126]

Livia's religious activities and benefactions were seen as suitably feminine.[127] Her position was unique but its manifestations are really large-scale versions of appropriate and laudable public behaviour by distinguished women who were expected to play their role in lateral and vertical social relations by the dispersal of benefits and wealth. As we have seen, personal favours, particularly from women to men, were susceptible of distortion and sexualisation in hostile settings, but largesse to groups was acknowledged unequivocally as conforming to established status and gender expectations. In many respects, the obligations of patronage and kinship were similar for men and women of the same social standing, but there was a feeling that it was particularly appropriate for women to concern themselves with religion, children and other women. The domesticated public woman reassured everyone.

8

Women's work: perceptions of public and private

Real work

Now we have almost established, as far as trades and livelihoods are concerned, which ones are regarded as professional (*liberales*) and which low-grade (*sordidi*). In the first place, those jobs which arouse men's enmity – like those of toll-collectors and moneylenders – are looked down upon. And the livelihoods of all journeymen whose services are purchased rather than their skills are not professional but low-grade, for among them the payment itself is a source of servitude. Middlemen who buy from traders and immediately sell the goods on are considered low status, for they cannot further their business without lying ... All trades are considered low-grade skills for there can be nothing genteel about a workshop. And the trades held in least esteem are those which minister to pleasure: 'fishmongers, butchers, cooks, chicken vendors, fishermen', as Terence says. Add to this, if you wish, perfume sellers, dancers and the whole entertainment industry (*unguentarii, saltatores, totumque ludum talarium*). Those skills which display less triviality or have a degree of usefulness, like medicine, architecture or teaching of the liberal arts, are honourable for those of appropriate station ... And, indeed, of all sources of gain, none is better than agriculture, none more profitable, more agreeable, none more suited to a gentleman. (Cicero *De officiis* 1.150-1)[1]

You ask how I spend the day in summer at my Tuscan estate. I get up when I like, usually around the first hour, often before ...

Sometimes I hunt, but not without my writing tablets, so that I bring something back even if I have caught nothing. Time is also given to my tenants (not enough, they think) and their rustic complaints make my writing and these civilised studies appealing. (Pliny *Letters* 9.36)

In today's world, which equates 'real work' with paid work and stigmatises in various ways those who do not perform it, the job you do is a crucial part of your identity. To Romans, the morally loaded concept of 'work' was not interchangeable with 'job' and even those who claimed a job title had other ways of defining themselves socially. Women were praised for their domestic industry, but élite Greco-Roman authors such as Aristotle and Cicero notoriously scorned most manual labour, classing paid work as a kind of slavery.[2] Military, literary and political activity, supervisory care of landed estates and the duties of patronage were the proper business of an élite male. The tide has turned and to today's students Pliny the Younger's account of his typical day in Rome or on one of his estates is frivolous (if fascinating), and the idea that a wealthy senatorial woman with scores of slaves might actually have been as busy as a modern hotel manager running her primary residence and overseeing the management of her many estates seems a nonsense.[3]

Romans had many ways of constructing their social identity, according to context. Most studies of work in the Roman world have reflected modern thinking by concentrating on jobs specified in inscriptions – especially epitaphs and guild records – and the law, or depicted on funerary monuments and shop signs.[4] This chapter, while employing such sources, will draw on but not replicate existing overviews of identifiable occupations, to consider broader categories of paid and unpaid work, work done by slave and free women and the ways in which it was culturally valued (or not) and represented (or not) in diverse media. I am particularly interested in how gender and status affect perceptions of work. As we have already seen in connection with commerce, Cicero's well-known summary of élite attitudes did not necessarily reflect the views of the 'lower orders', who nonetheless imposed their own moral and social categories on representations of work.

The so-called 'occupational inscriptions' which figure largely in reconstructions of the Roman economy present methodological problems which are readily acknowledged (if variously interpreted) by those who work with them. They exemplify the skewings and exclusions which make majority history (i.e. the history of 'ordinary people') so difficult. Those most studied are inscriptions, particularly epitaphs, from Rome and its surrounds (*CIL* 6) which include job titles. The inscriptions constitute a fairly small sample, in which freed slaves and artisans are over-represented, a pattern which has been taken by some scholars to mean that only slaves performed such jobs and that women seldom had 'jobs' in this sense. But the exclusion of a category from a particular *genre* (or even from *all* records) does not necessarily mean the category did not exist in the 'real world'. Such reasoning would lead to the conclusion that there were no peasants in the ancient world and that children were restricted to very few regions.

We are continually brought back to issues of identity and context. The information contained in an inscription and the way it is slanted depends on the purpose of that inscription. Joshel (1992a) has focused on the solidarity shown by freed slaves to their co-workers, including their patrons (former owners), which transcends preoccupations with slave/free status. The 're-formation' of the self which she has highlighted in occupational inscriptions is one of many variations in representation. Gender is another. We saw in Chapter 7 how the same acts of patronage, performed

1. Inscription on a memorial erected by Naevoleia Tyche, a freed slave, to herself and her husband (an officer in the imperial cult at Pompeii) and to their freed slaves. Her portrait is at the top. In the inscription (*CIL* 10.1030), she has put her name before her husband's and in even larger letters. The scene below seems to depict a food distribution, which may indicate civic beneficence associated with her husband's funeral commemoration or some other occasion. The Street of Tombs, Pompeii, outside the Porta Ercolanea.

2. Inscription to a mother by a son (*CIL* 6.18920). Her name, Gavia Chrysis, makes it likely she was a freed slave. This simple type of tablet is the most common surviving form of commemoration. Its more expensive material, marble, made it more lasting than clay or wooden ones, which were probably the most frequent markers of cremated remains. Found originally in the vicinity of Rome.

3. The flamboyant tomb of the freed slave baker Publius Vergilius Eurysaces and his wife Antistia, outside the Porta Maggiore in Rome, celebrates his wealth and its source.

4. The tomb originally held these statues of Antistia and Eurysaces, in which they are portrayed as a dignified married couple in traditional élite style.

5. A copy of the statue erected by the fullers of Pompeii to their patron Eumachia (*CIL* 10.811). The original statue is in the Museo archeologico nazionale in Naples.

6. Inscription over the entry to the building Eumachia donated to the fullers (*CIL* 10.810).

7. Ostian relief of the shoemaker Septimia Stratonice, erected by a friend who commemorates the 'favour' she did him (*CIL* 14.supp.4698).

8. Funeral monument depicting a woman with a woolbasket signifying her feminine virtue and industry. From Gallignano (Ancona). The passer-by is addressed in the damaged inscription.

9. Relief from Rome showing a butcher's shop. The woman's dress gives no indication of her precise status or relation to the butcher at work. She may be a customer balancing her budget or the butcher's wife or owner, keeping the business accounts.

10. The barmaid depicted here is part of an Ostian relief showing a harbour scene. The low status and poor repute of barmaids were enshrined in Roman law.

11. A woman selling vegetables from a trestle table, Ostia.

12. Remains of a shop at Ostia. These small shops, found in all towns of Roman Italy, typically included an upper floor for the family and its dependants.

13. Shop-fronts opening on to a street in Ostia. My husband is standing at the separate entry-point to middle-grade apartments.

14. A Herculaneum street scene with a reconstructed balcony.

15. Mid-first-century CE stele of Menimani and Blussus, seated, with a bust of their son Primus between them, in the background (*CIL* 13.7067b). Menimani holds a distaff and a ball of wool. Blussus, a sailor, is holding a bag of money. From Weisenau (Mainz).

16. Third-century CE relief from the side of a sandstone monument, Neumagen-an-der-Mosel (*CIL* 13.4185). The seated woman is wearing the full dress of a Roman matron (*stola* and *palla*). Her exiguous hair is being dressed by a maid who, like the other (presumably slave) attendants, is wearing a simple long dress (tunic). This is a stock image of ladylike leisure and adornment, somewhat at odds with the written praise of feminine industry and simplicity.

by a distinguished woman, could be represented differently in the literary *genres* of speeches and letters and in the honorific inscriptional *genres*. The conventions loosely governing commemorative inscriptions allow the same man to be presented as former slave of his patron, as a husband, as a worker, as a fellow-freed slave, as an office-holder in an organisation. It will depend in part on who sets up the inscription and where it is placed. If his main purpose is to commemorate his patron, a worker is less likely to mention his own family roles.

Women can cover most of the same range, but are more likely, on the whole, to be commemorated for their family roles than for their job-titles.[5] This emphasis might reflect women's lower involvement in certain categories, but it might simply reflect the protocols of inscriptional representation. In the Roman context, as in many cultures, reference to a woman's work often amounted to a moral statement not only about the woman but about her husband – a factor which might influence a widower commissioning an epitaph, for it might suit his image of himself and their marriage to emphasise his wife's virtues as a mother and housekeeper but pass over her role in a family business, which he deemed inappropriate in such a memorial.

Perhaps women themselves valued the titles of wife and mother over explicit references to work they did within and outside the home to contribute to the family economy. Children seldom refer in epitaphs to their father's job and even more rarely to their mother's. Families of limited means might have seen no reason to celebrate typically lower-status jobs like contract weaving and street-selling (of which there are nonetheless a few examples).[6] The consequence is the near-impossibility of differentiating the 'occupations' of the mass of women. The quality of surviving memorials gives a rough guide to family wealth and status, but inscriptions describing women across the board as good wives and mothers are little help in distinguishing leisured ladies from active business-owners or moderately successful artisans for hire.

Some work – notably, that of child-nurses, midwives and doctors – was valued by their families and their owners or employers. Wet-nurses have a relatively high incidence of commemoration by their owners (or patrons) or former charges. A few nurses are commemorated with their occupational titles even by husbands or children.[7] Successful midwives and doctors also commissioned their own substantial monuments or left sufficient resources for their heirs to set them up.[8]

Other groups are remembered differently. The number of brothels in Pompeii has impressed visitors to the site for more than two centuries now. Even allowing for over-identification, the busy port did have a number of such places. Not surprisingly, the combination of poverty, low status and disreputability make family commemorations of prostitutes unlikely. They are, however, recorded – sometimes by name – as commodities, with prices, on brothel walls.[9] The brothels also feature wall paintings of sexual acts. Prostitutes may have posed for such paintings (which feature on the walls of apparently respectable residences as well), but they amount in this case to generic advertising rather than individual commemorations (Clarke 1998). If any such prostitutes were subsequently freed and eventually commemorated personally by family or friends, we cannot tell that from the epitaphs. The example of Vibia Calybene is unusual. She is actually commemorated as a *lena*, or madam, by her fellow freed slave Vibia Chresta. Perhaps this is an example of that general principle which favours the posterity of the managerial level in any group (Kampen 1981: 125). Chresta commemorates others, including her son, in the inscription (*CIL* 9.2029). Perhaps she was once herself a prostitute when still a slave (but that is entirely speculative). Workers in weaving shops were also named on walls, sometimes with work allocations or joking epithets. They were spinners and weavers, a much larger group than is evident from the occupational inscriptions, which are more likely to record the select group with its specialist tasks (von Petrikovits 1981).

The tendency to celebrate specific, honoured categories of work has been slightly subverted, then, by time and Vesuvius. Slave prostitutes and spinsters at the bottom of the social scale have emerged with names, if not personalities. Otherwise, women's work is largely subsumed in levelling commemorations of daughters, wives and mothers, just as élite men's work is submerged in their more general status characterisations as senators, decurions or equestrians. It is important for the reader to appreciate that occupational inscriptions – and occupational titles in general – are the exception. The mass of the population engaged in agricultural and pastoral production is virtually omitted from the historical record.

To evaluate Roman constructions of work, we may therefore need to set aside our own preconceptions. This involves thinking our way into an economy in which most people did not bear clear job-labels tied to cash payment. In the preceding chapter, we saw that the Roman élite regarded profitable brick production as a form of agriculture and perceived many kinds of commercial investment as 'favours' establishing long-term relationships within the patronage system. In this chapter, we may need a whole new language of self- and other-representation to read the relief sculptures, mosaics and inscriptions representing certain work categories and suppressing others. We must be prepared above all to argue from silence or to re-read the ancient images in the light of their symbolic value. Nowhere is this more evident than in cloth-production, a prime example of that eternal oddity whereby women's domestic work can be both idealised and forgotten.

8. Women's work: perceptions of public and private

Unravelling: representations of cloth production

Producing household cloth was a quintessentially female task in the ancient world. Girls of all stations learned at an early age how to spin, weave and sew. This domestically based work took on a moral significance associated with the good woman. In Livy's account of the founding myth of the Republic, the noble Lucretia's diligence in working after sunset with her female slaves is equated with her chastity, although the male onlookers in his account seem to draw no conclusions about the sexual virtue and allure of the slaves.[10]

The association of wifely virtue and handiwork was not confined to the nobility of the legendary Roman past. Wives continued to be described by their husbands on epitaphs as 'working wool' – *lanifica*, or its variants. The most famous example is the much-quoted second-century BCE commemoration of one Claudia:

> Stranger, my message is short: stop and read it.
> This is the unlovely tomb of a lovely woman.
> Her parents gave her the name Claudia.
> She loved her husband with her heart.
> She bore two sons, one of whom she left on earth, the other beneath it.
> She had a pleasing way of talking and walking.
> She looked after the house and worked wool.
> I have said my piece. Go your way.[11]

Less elaborate memorials echoed this theme, sometimes adding other housewifely virtues such as frugality.[12] It needs to be said that the most popular epithets for women were the same (with appropriate gender change) as those for men and are very general: *pia/piissima* (pious or 'good'), *bene merens / bene merita* or its abbreviation *bm* ('well-deserving') and *optima* ('excellent', 'very good'). But for those few dead women credited with specific virtues, *lanifica* and its cognates were invoked into imperial times. The adjective was applied to married women, usually by their husbands, to signify their role in household management. Indeed, Gordon Williams argued in 1958 that such epithets had by the late Republic become an anachronism, applied to women who did not produce cloth. By this reading, *lanifica* was the textual equivalent of a stylised or idealising relief on a tomb with no specific resemblance to the deceased.[13] His brief comment has acquired authority with repetitive citation since then, but the only ancient evidence to support his conclusion is Columella's claim that (wealthy) matrons had relegated this traditional task to their housekeepers, a claim which has the ring of the commonplace lament over the social decline which, as we have seen, is sometimes signified by the sluttishness of contemporary women.[14]

In fact, the evidence is equivocal. Roman brides continued to carry

spinning implements in the marriage ceremony and the wife of the triumvir Ledipus kept a loom in the household atrium as late as 43 BCE. In both
cases, the tools of cloth production served symbolic purposes. We hear of
the loom only because it was destroyed in a riot. The commentator Asconius says that it was a 'badge of virtue' (*signum pudicitiae*) and its
destruction underlines the shock-value of political violence intruding on
the domestic sphere.[15] The boast of the emperor Augustus, that he wore
only wool worked by the women of his family, is generally taken by scholars
as a consciously archaising assertion of old-fashioned values.[16] But even
so, one would expect well-born women to emulate the women of the
imperial family, much as they copied their hairstyles.

Testimony from non-literary sources is also ambiguous. Imperial jurists
assumed that the free-born mistress of the house (*materfamilias*) continued to supervise female slaves in the production of household cloth.[17]
Perhaps such statements were not intended to refer to the very wealthy
women of the upper classes who could delegate responsibility to the
slave-housekeepers (*vilicae*) on their various estates, but we should not
assume that wealth meant automatic renunciation of involvement in this
aspect of household production. It was, after all, an element of that
self-sufficiency which was a source of pride to the upper classes (Veyne
1979) and, as we have seen, it was an activity which reflected well on the
woman who undertook it and therefore on her husband. The famous
husbands of Lucretia and of the empress Livia derived greater moral
kudos from their industrious trophy wives than their modern counterparts
do by the acquisition of beautiful young women who display their wealth
in clothing and jewels.

Unfortunately, such considerations work both ways, for people are likely
to exaggerate the virtues valued by their culture. Few women in my own
society would openly admit to feeding their children on junk food as a
regular diet, even if they disclaimed any traditional or adventurous culi-
nary skills.

In her study of the gardens in the region of Pompeii and Herculaneum,
Jashemski found loom-weights in every garden she excavated. She concluded that weaving was a standard domestic activity and put down to
source-variation the low emphasis in written sources on this widespread,
commonplace activity (Jashemski 1979: 101-2). But scholars' views on the
subject have varied. Jongman (1988: 163) responded to Moeller's identification of loom-weights with specialist production by pointing out that their
numbers and distribution were consistent with small-scale production for
domestic consumption, and some have wondered if the numbers found at
Pompeii were insufficient even for that.[18]

These issues of scale and the organisation of production are germane to
continuing debates about the nature of the Roman economy. Those who
argue that it was 'rationally' organised have leaned heavily on references

in literature, but particularly in inscriptions, to specialised jobs such as those connected with the commercial production of cloth.[19] Such jobs are overwhelmingly male.[20] But the notion that, by Augustus' day, female domestic cloth production had become an archaism, is belied by the presumption in sources of the imperial era (not only epitaphs) that such production continued to be the responsibility of the *materfamilias*, the good housewife, in collaboration with the slave-women of her establishment, in the tradition of Lucretia. The jurist Pomponius ruled on this basis in connection with a matrimonial property dispute in the mid-second century CE (*Digest* 24.1.31 *pr.*).

A little later, the jurists Ulpian and Paul both referred to female slaves who produce clothing as part of the farm 'equipage', *instrumentum*, a collective noun which includes livestock and farm equipment.[21] Such dehumanising language is a far cry from the specialist job-terms for carders and fullers. Because they need to specify their tasks, the same jurists refer to the 'slave-girls (*ancillae*) who make the clothing for the farm workers' or the *lanificae* ('wool-working women') who clothe the rustic slaves (*familiam rusticam*). I include such detail to illustrate that language is used in complex and inconsistent ways – obviously the women themselves are part of the *familia rustica* and, presumably, of the *rustici* for whom they make clothing. The term *lanifica*, which takes on such strong moral connotations in literature and epitaphs, is a matter-of-fact reference to non-voluntary work when applied to slave-women. In both cases it is quite unspecific: although sometimes translated as 'spinners/spinsters', *lanificae* means only 'women who work wool'.[22] In this respect, it is like the term *lanarius*, which has no clear meaning, although some have assigned meanings to it.[23]

In fact, the terms '*lanarius*' (masculine) and '*lanifica*' (feminine) highlight our ignorance of Latin work terminology and the way we draw on uncritical assumptions to make up for it. '*Lanarius*', for example, could denote a specialist wool-worker, but might as readily describe someone who sells wool or woollen products. It is even possible that *lanarius*, always in the masculine -*us*(/*i* plural) form, was a convenient catch-all word like *lanifica* – a term always used in the feminine, and applicable to the lowly women of a *familia rustica* or a noble matron, according to the context.[24] In general, terms which end in *fic(i)us*/*(ficia)* or the feminine -*fex* are taken to mean someone who makes something, but the -*arius/a* ending can mean a producer or seller of the object. Only a context can clarify that and we frequently lack context for these work descriptors. There is a strong tendency for scholars to identify males as makers of products, especially those requiring heavy work, and women as sellers.[25] In her study of women's jobs mentioned in inscriptions from the area around Rome, LeGall (1970: 125) states that the *clavaria* Cornelia Venusta '*sans doute*' *sold* nails which her *clavarius* husband Publius

Aebutius made.[26] Yet English women of the 'Black Country' made nails at forges up until the early twentieth century.[27] Treggiari does translate *clavarii* as 'nail makers/sellers' (1979: 78), but translates *purpurarii* as 'sellers of purple' (p. 70) and treats most *-arii* as 'dealers' in goods. As always, the identification of female workers is made difficult by the Latin practice of putting male/female groups into the masculine.

When the ancient evidence is so sparse and equivocal, it is difficult for modern scholars to be consistent and free of assumptions, for they have to fall back on comparative studies and their own sense of probability. This sounds reasonable, but such speculative elements should be clearly identified and justified, for they are clearly open to contamination from cultural bias. It is true that in many societies artisan workshops function with the male as producer and his wife or daughter in the more social role of seller. Small modern bakeries frequently show this division of labour. But to assume that men dye or make nails, while women with the same title do quite a different job is a logical leap which should be acknowledged. The conventional wisdom that commercial weavers in Roman Italy were very low-status, probably servile workers is undermined by a single inscription commemorating a weaver who was triumvir, quaestor and tribune. The response of scholars is to conclude that these élite offices could not have been held by such a humble man and that they must refer instead to offices he held in a burial association.[28] But perhaps we should review our assumptions when they are out of kilter with ancient sources.

Gender categories often express cultural norms. In English, we assume that doctors are male and nurses female unless the speaker specifies otherwise ('lady/woman doctor', 'male nurse'). This is not a reflection of reality but of a certain view of the universe. In Latin inscriptions, no woman is commemorated specifically as a *lanaria* and the references in the plural are, in the usual Latin fashion, always masculine but it does not necessarily follow from this that the (unknown) work of *lanarii* was performed only by men.[29] Modern theorists have pointed to distortions in public records resulting from reading terms like 'peasants' and 'farmers' as exclusively male in many languages.[30]

Assumptions about gendered work pervade modern treatments of the Roman economy, which tend to polarise on whether it was essentially primitive or 'rational'.[31] A key factor in the debate is the extent to which manufacture was 'organised'. Job titles have been used as the basis of an argument that domestic production of cloth by the women of the household gave way historically to greater specialisation, which is associated with masculine, slave-based production for a market (Larsson Lovén 1998a).

Moeller's (1976) argument that Pompeii was a centre of industrial cloth production is based in part on the contention that men appropriated traditional female roles (Moeller 1969). Jongman, who refutes this characterisation of Pompeii, also associates domestic/female work without guild organisation with a less industrial style of production. This is most evident in his discussion of spinning:

> If a considerable number of these [specialist] processes was done in the countryside, or in the private urban household, then it will not really do to include these in the category 'urban crafts'. Of these, spinning was perhaps the most labour-intensive, a reason why in later times it was most prone to take place in rural districts, outside the control of urban crafts, and often done by women. (Jongman 1988: 162)

This female/domestic and male/commercial opposition is generally taken for granted, but some scholars explicitly argue a universal tendency for women to be excluded from manufacture as it becomes more organised and profitable.[32] One reasoned study of Bronze Age pottery production in the East Mediterranean acknowledges that the gender of potters and pot-painters cannot be assumed, that potting is a female task in many cultures and that such female production can be obscured by written records which attribute it in a blanket way to the male head-of-household who conducts public transactions.[33] But the study then goes on to claim that, even in an ancient economy, a distinction can ultimately be drawn between the sale of domestically produced goods surplus to household production and the more varied products of workshop industry resting on a more professional and technological base:

> In a workshop industry potting should be the most important source of livelihood, even if combined with farming or other work, and hence, according to Peacock, it is normally in the hands of men. It will be carried out for as much of the year as possible and will frequently involve the use of the wheel, a kiln and assistants.[34]

This is the most sophisticated statement I have seen of the principle elsewhere *assumed* to operate in the cloth 'industry' in the Roman world, particularly in Pompeii, but scrutiny exposes it as specious. Far from being a scientific observation of economic 'laws', it is a circular confirmation of existing prejudices about gender roles and an evolutionary view of economic history progressing along a standard track. Analogies can assist nuanced readings of ancient evidence, but they can never constitute evidence in themselves. Cross-cultural arguments go both ways. A countervailing and equally common phenomenon which affects the historical record is the tendency to discuss the domestic sector and the role of women in very general terms which stress their moral dimension and their relevance to masculine self-presentations, and obscure their material significance.[35] The ideal that a good woman keeps to the home is a recurrent one, found in the moral discourse of cultures as far removed as classical Athens, early modern England and contemporary Turkey, but

close studies suggest that a simplistic reading of such normative statements out of context would give a misleading view of the reality of such
women's lives, which quite routinely include a range of legitimate 'outside'
activities.[36]

In any case, this firm post-industrial distinction between the domestic
and commercial spheres is highly problematic in the Roman context,
whether we are talking of courtyard workshops (*textrinae*), slave (or freed)
dependents producing for high-status owner patrons, or small family
businesses operating out of residential shopfronts. The *monumentum
Statiliorum* (*CIL* 6.6213-6640), commemorating selected slaves and former slaves of the distinguished Statilii Tauri, lists a number of specialist
job titles connected with cloth production.[37] A comparable list includes the
slaves of the empress Livia.[38] Only a small proportion of each *familia*
figures in the monuments. Individual epitaphs were probably commissioned by fellow-slaves, but their owner (or agent) chose those who won the
posthumous favour of inclusion in the group memorial. They were therefore doubly selected. Although lower-status weavers and spinners,
elsewhere rarely commemorated, feature in these monuments, the epitaphs overall follow the usual pattern evident in so-called occupational
inscriptions, of featuring disproportionately the more prestigious jobs –
highly specialised categories, supervisors, and jobs which provided closer
contact with the free owners.[39] We cannot tell where the work was located
but the inclusion of specialist textile workers with bedroom attendants –
but not any of the estate workers – suggests these town-based workers
were notionally part of a total domestic establishment (however palatial)
serving the free family at its core and apparently producing as well for a
market.[40] Pompeian archaeological evidence confirms the likelihood that
comfortable residential spaces could also be commercial workplaces.[41]

The scale of production was never considerable by modern factory
standards. The weaving workshop (*textrina*) of M Terentius Eudoxus,
located in the peristyle of a large Pompeian house, apparently housed at
least nineteen slave workers.[42] Its function is declared not so much by the
ubiquitous loom-weights as by the walls, which bear graffiti listing eleven
women (Vitalis, Florentina, Amarylis, Ianuaria, Heraclea, Maria, Lalage,
Damalis, Servola, Baptis and Doris) as spinsters, with individual allocations of wool and naming eight men (Vebius, Tamudianus, Felix, Ephesus,
Xanthus, Successus, Faustus, Florus) generally assumed to be weavers
but not labelled as such.[43] In fact, there is no information about the men,
apart from their names, unless you count the obscenity attached to Ephesus (whose name is spelled phonetically as IIphisus).[44] There is no reason
to assume that the women assigned wool for spinning restricted themselves to that role. They are just as likely to have woven it, too. The space
would have been sufficient for a number of vertical looms, but it was not huge.
The production could well have been for both domestic and commercial

consumption. Nobody is characterised as *lanipendia*, although the supervisory role is implicit in the weights assigned to each of the women. Perhaps we should go back to the presumption of jurists long after the destruction of Pompeii in 79 CE, that it was the responsibility of the lady of the house (*materfamilias*) to supervise the slaves' production of cloth (e.g. Pomponius *Digest* 24.1.31 *pr.*). Graffiti and fifty loom-weights have also been found in the House of the Minucii.[45] The names of five men (Rarus, Rufus, Quietus, Onesimus and Primigenius) and two women (Gelaste and Savilla) are written on the wall.[46] In the absence of clear job titles, interpretations have varied. Della Corte (1954: 301) speculated on the basis of the loom-weights that the men and women were both weavers. Some find confirmation from graffiti in a neighbouring pub recording a joking exchange between two friends, one termed 'Sucessus textor'.[47] While we can rejoice that we have some names and remnants of workers at this under-recorded level of society, Jongman's merciless attack on Moeller's analysis of these and other weaving shops and dyeshops exposes the fragile character of any reconstruction of the workplace and its significance from these remains. It is certainly insufficient for forming any judgements about the relative contributions of male and female, slave and free, general and specialist workers to each enterprise.

Mixed house and apartment blocks in Rome, Ostia and the Vesuvian towns regularly had separate entrances for the more spacious internal residences and for the many small shops which faced out to the street and housed workers who lived, produced and traded from the one cramped location (Plates 12-14). These *tabernarii*, many of them part of that group of skilled slaves or freed slaves over-represented in the epitaphs of Rome, made a reasonable if not usually lavish living. They are the respectable lower to middling sector of the masses who probably enjoyed the patronage of former owners, perhaps even renting premises or getting start-up capital from them, as we saw in the previous chapter.[48] Roman society provides examples of former slaves, or their descendants, who rose from such origins to prosperity. One instance, from Rome, is of a few such people involved in luxury dyeing or selling of purple (possibly crimson) cloth – *purpurarii* – who bore the name Veturi-, presumably from some original family which had trained its domestic establishment in this specialist skill. Freed, they went into business and acquired slaves of their own, whom they trained and freed in their turn. This much is indicated by those inscriptions which include status and occupational information. Much, however, is excluded. Scholars are still trying to work out the general principles employed in these rare and usually brief tributes. Huttunen (1974) points to the rarity of finding more than one job title in the same inscription. If the occupation of the deceased is given, it is particularly unlikely that the dedicator's will also be included. Joshel (1992a) argues persuasively that occupational dedications stress shared work rather than the status or personal relationships of the people mentioned.[49]

Two examples from Rome illustrate some of the features of such inscriptions. One is a marble block, probably part of a larger sepulchral monument from the Via Praenestina, erected by Veturia Tryphera, freed slave of Decimus Veturius, 'in accordance with her judgement', to Decimus Veturius Atticus, purple dyer/dealer (*purpurarius*) from the Iugarian quarter, freed slave of another Decimus Veturius.[50] Tryphera – who takes up space (and expense) to let us know that it was her choice (ARBITRATV, l.4), not a testamentary obligation, to erect the monument, neglects to tell us her own occupation. She does not even tell us directly her relationship to Atticus, although we tend from analogy to assume that they are husband and wife, both former slaves (*colliberti*) of the same Decimus Veturius.

Another epitaph, erected by the freed slave Cameria Iarine, honours L. Camerius Thraso, her patron, *his* patron L. Camerius Alexander and her husband and freed slave L. Camerius Onesimus and all their descendants, whom she describes as 'fine tailors' (*vestiarii tenuarii*) in the Tuscan region of Rome.[51] In this case, she does feature her relationship with Onesimus, whom she had bought out of slavery and with Thraso, the owner who freed her, and his relationship with his former owner, as well as their common occupation. This seems to commemorate a workplace based on a family business. She excludes any reference to her own occupation, although it is likely that as a slave in this mini-community she was trained in the same craft which enabled her to buy her slave-husband. Her reference to *posteri*, descendants, is a general one and could be prospective, but the absence of specific reference to children (normally *sui*) need not mean that she and Onesimus were childless at the time she erected this memorial, but that its primary purpose was to express the ties, obligatory and sentimental, which bound this small circle of specialist workers. Romans erected memorials to themselves during their own lifetime and could include others who were still living.[52] On Tryphera's or Onesimus' death, the surviving spouse or children might well have commemorated them in their family roles, without any reference to the tailoring trade. The recorded epitaphs are not the only ones to the people named and, unfortunately, they are not always left in their original sites where their relationship to other memorials (or parts of the same memorial) is clear.

Such inscriptions, apparently simple, raise many questions. They reveal few specifics about jobs and their allocation, but they can help us move towards an understanding of the etiquette of their representation in this medium. In the various types of source, we seem repeatedly to come up against the same phenomenon, the relegation of women to the private and men to the public sphere. This may be more a matter of discourse than of practice, but the two can interact. Public aspects of life, coded as masculine – even if, as in marketplaces, many of the participants are actually female

– are typically represented in a more detailed way, less emblematic and morally charged than the female sphere. This brings us back to the principle we saw at the beginning of the chapter, whereby respectable womanly work is both idealised and rendered barely visible (Kampen 1981: 131-4). Given the great practical and economic importance of Roman cloth production, the familiarity of its many aspects to the ancients, its close association with women across the social spectrum and its moral connotations, it provides a supreme example of our difficulties in retrieving the most everyday aspects of women's lives.

Women on display: iconographic sources

Ancient visual representations of work fall into a few clear categories. Most studies of the Roman iconography of work have been catalogues of predominantly male artisans as they appear on funerary or shop reliefs.[53] Such representations are typically 'veristic', in the sense that they include likely detail of the tools and setting of each trade. The much smaller number of veristic reliefs featuring women workers generally show them in service roles which reflect commercial extensions of female domestic work – selling vegetables, serving wine in pubs, delivering or nursing babies. The inscriptional references to women's jobs also suggest a concentration in such areas, but they do attest a somewhat greater range of trades than do the visual sources: there were female goldsmiths, bakers, pearl-setters, dyers and one shoemaker.[54]

Before we conclude that women were 'employed' – as paid workers or slaves – primarily in service provision, we should review some of the ways in which the visual record definitely fails to reflect ancient realities. The most common categories of work – agricultural, pastoral and domestic labour – are likely to be represented, if at all, by mythological and allegorical figures on wall paintings and as sub-themes on sarcophagi. Winged *amoretti* perform the stages of fulling and dyeing on the walls of the House of the Vettii in Pompeii. A stylised goat-herd often sleeps or guards his charge on the ends of a sarcophagus relief. The peasant who – like the wool-working housewife – occupies a central place in Roman moral discourse – is, like her, absent from paintings and sculpture. If senatorial men are depicted on their funerary monuments in an active role, they are likely to be addressing troops rather than speaking in the Senate or inspecting tenants' returns or any of the many tasks which made up the 'work' of this class.[55] Many factors seem to operate in the emphases and exclusions – it is as if most everyday categories are too dull to be included in their own right.

Slave-women appear in attendance at the toilet of their upper-class mistresses but not engaged in outside farm work or the many kinds of domestic work, such as cloth production, which we know from other sources were part of their duties. Many women artisans, like the men, would have been trained in specialist tasks by their owners, but in the monuments commemorating the owner, it is *her* status and femininity which is stressed by having her hair done by attendants (see Plate 16).

That convention also seems to be at odds with the literary and inscriptional praise of women free from personal vanity who supervised or worked with their slave-women at producing cloth. Why shouldn't that be a dominant pictorial image on the tombs of slave-owning mistresses of households?

In her perceptive studies of Roman representations of work, Kampen (1981, 1982) has analysed the impact of status and gender. She has shown that the bulk of the population did not share the upper-class disdain so famously expressed by Cicero for most job categories.[56] Artisans and shop-owners are depicted at their trade and, while those who accumulated wealth from commerce certainly converted it into land, there is no sign that such people concealed the origins of their good fortune. There are, however, some conventional distinctions. Publius Vergilius Eurysaces erected a huge monument to himself and his wife Antistia which depicted the many stages of bread-making, the basis of his fortune, but he himself was shown in a large statue in full citizen dress, not in the tunic of the workers (Plates 3 and 4). Naturalistic scenes depicting textile shops also distinguish the owner, by dress and gesture, from his subordinate workers (Kampen 1981: 103-4), although many such owners would have had hands-on roles in the operation. Far from reflecting this differentiation, the inscriptions studied by Joshel (1992a) celebrate the common bond of work between employer/owner and freed slave.

Women who appear in shop-scenes feature almost exclusively as customers or their attendant slaves, although inscriptions suggest that there were women who produced, processed and sold cloth in such shops.[57] Kampen has suggested that even men who were content to be displayed in their own professional right preferred to have their wives depicted in postures of leisure imitating the iconographic conventions of upper-class women: in a dignified *pudicitia* (virtue) posture, wearing the matron's *stola*, or seated, attended by maids at her toilet (Kampen 1981: 92; 132-3). These passive images, not a very realistic or rounded picture of a businesswoman's (or busy housewife's) life, probably expressed the aspirations of her husband. It is not so long since men in the western world boasted that their wives 'did not need to work' as part of their own masculine image as providers. Unproductive wives and children, like ornamental gardens, are a recurrent badge of wealth across time and cultures.

Many well-attested categories, such as peasant-women and slave and free poor women who span for a living, are virtually absent from the record, presumably for reasons of poverty. Male peasants and weavers are also poorly represented in the inscriptional and iconographic record. We have seen that we owe to the eruption of Vesuvius the survival of otherwise ephemeral graffiti which offer us a rare glimpse into the lives of spinners, weavers and prostitutes. But one low-grade category does appear on shop-signs: the barmaid and landlady of the small pub. Archaeological remains suggest that some (slave) barmaids were expected to provide sexual services to patrons in small cubicles behind the public part of the business. It is likely that many such women were slaves, but the law included free barmaids in the limited category of women exempted by reason of the disreputability of their occupation from the penalties imposed from Augustan times on adultery and fornication.[58] The category also included actresses and registered prostitutes.

The complex links between status and sexuality have been noted by feminist scholars of different historical periods. Single female factory workers in early industrialised settings in northern England and in the United States were often stigmatised with assumptions about their sexual immorality and German sales assistants in the late nineteenth century suffered similar imputations. Sometimes such judgements were fairly consciously used by community figures and male trades unions to frighten fathers into keeping their daughters out of such jobs, but there are comparable contemporary myths which attribute sexual availability to women – particularly young, single women – whose jobs involve certain kinds of commercial service interactions with men. Air hostesses in the United States continue to be objects of male fantasy and jokes, in spite of their re-labelling as 'flight attendants'. Barmaids in Australia have also been suspected of being sexually 'loose' since they became a specific work category, but there was no such stigma when they were considered domestic servants, although female domestic servants have notoriously been subject to sexual exploitation by employers and family members.[59] The element of public display seems to be important in some of these sexual stereotypes: the saleswoman, the barmaid or the actress is seen to be offering her body to the male gaze.[60] Much modern visual advertising is based on the assumption that men interpret a range of female activity as a sexual presentation, while cultural systems which impose modest demeanours and strict dress codes on women appearing in public seem also to sexualise the male gaze in a very general way.[61]

Class and status play their part in such constructions. We have seen in Chapter 5 and will examine in the concluding chapter ways in which wealthy women as a group serve as fantasy-objects and moral signs for ordinary men. The converse is true, and élite men have often perceived lower-class women as fair game.[62] Roman slaves had no civil rights and there was no serious moral impediment to their sexual use by owners and even freed slaves, legally free to resist improper demands from former owners, were in practice probably vulnerable (Seneca *Controversiae* 4 *pr*. 10). D'Avino's judgement (1967: 16) about the disreputability of spinners was based on a workshop graffito describing one woman, Amaryllis, as *fellatrix* ('cock-sucker'). This in spite of the fact that one of the men (presumed to be a weaver) in the same workshop bears the epithet *fututor* ('fucker') – not, presumably, a job title.[63] I suggest that these references do not withstand the usual rules of rigorous source criticism. Such joking is not unknown in modern workplaces.[64] I do not believe we know enough (i.e., anything) to draw any conclusions about the sexual behaviour of Amaryllis or her workmates, any more than I am convinced by a graffito I once saw in a Sydney railway tunnel asserting that 'Janice sucks dead budgies' balls'. In both cases, I reserve judgement.

Such (ancient) graffiti are also insufficient indication of the sexual reputation of cloth-workers in general. The low status of slave and hired female cloth-producers is clear. Juvenal uses the contract-weaver from Trastevere as a symbol of a humble worker but Terence contrasts a poor woman's initial struggle to support herself with spinning as the virtuous alternative, which she abandoned by becoming a prostitute.[65] Both references suggest that spinning and weaving, while poorly remunerated and associated with very low status, were quite respectable occupations.

The situation of the pub landlady (*tabernaria*) raises interesting points about the intersection of status and sexuality.[66] She was also vulnerable to sexual slurs. On the same walls which bear prices and the accounts of regulars, the anonymous author of *CIL* 4.8442 claims to have had sex several times with the landlady (presumably on the premises where he recorded his boast).[67] But the Julian law on adultery distinguished definitively between the barmaid and the landlady of the same establishment. To put it simply, extramarital sex with the landlady *was* an offence.[68] She might work in a disreputable area, but her role as supervisor, employer, proprietor or businesswoman apparently elevated her legally. Is it significant that in shop-signs, she is shown behind the bar, and sometimes higher than the customers (Kampen 1981: fig. 34)? Or is it just our reading that assumes the woman depicted in this way must be the landlady rather than the barmaid?

So, even when they appear to be naturalistic, female representations in work settings raise many problems of reading. Unlike men, who wear tunics for more physical jobs, women are generally shown in long dresses whether they are shopping, being adorned in their bedrooms or working behind a counter, and their hairstyles do not significantly differ according to status. In stock depictions of the lady at her toilet, the slave-maids do not look significantly ill-dressed or unkempt. It is the fact that they stand and their gestures towards their seated mistress which mark their occupation and status.[69] The woman depicted in the relief of an Ostian butcher's shop (Plate 9) is a good example of the problems of reading images. The male butcher, in a short tunic, is standing and cutting meat while she is seated – normally the sign of higher status. She wears a long matron's dress and has a relatively elaborate hair-style and she holds some bound tablets, presumably account books. She could be a customer, the owner of the shop and of the butcher, or his wife. It's even possible that she is an accountant come to do his books for him. We have no inscriptional information to add to the picture and insufficient knowledge of Roman iconographic conventions to draw a definite conclusion.

Images of midwives and nurses are relatively straightforward. The activity and role of each figure is clear and usually accompanied by a written text (Dixon 1988: pl. 6, 9). But what of the Ostian vegetable vendor of Plate 11? She is clearly involved in the act of selling from a trestle table, apparently in the open market. Her gesture is the stock one of the subject about to speak – presumably to praise the quality of her merchandise. She, too, has her hair neatly done and wears a long dress. There is no way of telling whether she is slave or free and whether she grows her own produce or deals regularly from town as a retailer.

The painting on the garden wall of the Villa of Venus Marina shows a woman spinning. Jashemski comments (1979: 101-2) that this would have been a common sight in peristyles and courtyards, where women span and wove, and where she found many loom-weights. The woman is standing and wears dark clothing which might indicate servile or lower-class status, but, as elsewhere, the signs are not clearcut and certainly do little to inform economic speculation about whether commercial spinning was assigned to slaves and more likely to take place in the country, close to the source of wool, as some scholars assume. The painting stands out in its relatively realistic depiction of this everyday activity. Other examples of spinning and weaving are mythic or allegorical, like the fates in the background of a biographical sarcophagus or the frieze on the Forum Transitorium Temple of Minerva depicting the contest between Minerva and Arachne.[70]

The gendered skewing of representations is perhaps most marked in visual depictions, which proclaim generalised womanly virtues and social status rather than any distinctive features of the woman portrayed.[71] Visual representations of women's work cover a limited range of their known occupations, whether domestic or commercial/professional. Women in low-status jobs are sometimes depicted incidentally to the main purpose – as in the slaves attending a mistress at her toilet, or barmaids on a shop-sign or sarcophagus.[72] Midwives are depicted at work on tombstones commissioned by themselves or their families. In such depictions, it is the midwife's apprentice and the woman giving birth who are incidental. Wetnurses (slave or free) also appear with their charges on funerary reliefs which are probably commissioned by their husbands or families (Kampen 1981: figs 58-60). But overall, work is a rare theme of the many surviving funerary portraits of women, who are typically depicted in a few stylised ways which highlight their modesty or status in very general terms.

III. Reading the Public Face

Work and identity

The self is not fixed. People identify themselves and others by a range of factors according to context. 'My boss' can also be 'my neighbour' or 'my son's godmother'. Nowhere is this flexibility more evident than in ancient representations of work. This complexity is scarcely acknowledged in studies of the ancient economy which base conclusions about the extent of commercial production and of specialist slave labour on systematic studies of Roman job titles and veristic images of labour. Scholars necessarily bring to the task their own culturally determined constructions of work. These include their notions of how work intersects with class and gender. They automatically privilege certain activities as 'real work', preferably distinguished by a convenient job-title and performed by a hired worker or slave. This limited definition discounts altogether many élite pursuits vital to the self-image of the actors, and undervalues domestic production.

Behind such judgements lurk the post-industrial separation of domestic and commercial spheres and the association of women with domestic production and men with specialist, 'organised' production for the market. Yet such distinctions can be problematic even in modern economies. Women who work on family farms and small shops or keep accounts for a tradesman- or doctor-husband move between the domestic and commercial sectors in a way which confounds OECD statisticians. The so-called Information Revolution has re-united home and workplace for many who would describe themselves to market researchers and the tax office as 'graphic artists', 'systems analysts' or 'business managers'. In this they resemble the Pompeian banker Caecilius Secundus, who worked partly from home and had an occupational title. But consider Cicero's wealthy entrepreneurial friend Atticus. He was too elevated to describe himself by a job-title but many of his business affairs were conducted from his home(s) by means of his domestic staff who were more likely to be referred to as 'slaves', 'boys' or, collectively, Atticus' *familia* than by a single, distinguishing title. We know that from time to time Atticus pressed into his publishing business slaves who 'normally' performed quite different roles. This equates closely with English usage of the general word 'servant' even for specialist employees up to the early twentieth century.[73]

It is the modern reliance on job-titles as the basis for social identity which leads scholars to attach disproportionate significance to them and to overgeneralise from their absence, a practice with particular relevance to conclusions about women's work, which is less likely to be recorded by such titles. This chapter has stressed that job titles in the ancient world were not used in many media and that some of the most common occupations, with which people were strongly identified, were not included in the usual inscriptional sources used by scholars to reconstruct work categories. The Italian peasant was invoked in rhetorical and political discourse but not commemorated as such in surviving epitaphs. We have seen that Roman jobs took on different significance to élite observers and to those who performed them, who were not ashamed of working for a living but who nonetheless observed certain conventions and their sense of their own status in arranging visual depictions of their work.

Many jobs would have been performed by anyone available at times of seasonal or other pressure. Free women and their slaves are likely to have been multi-skilled and to have moved between tasks according to the needs – both domestic and commercial – of their household and estate. This would apply particularly to spinning, a task suited to being fitted in between other activities.[74] No scholar questions that women of most social stations could and did spin and, indeed, the uniform presumption is that spinsters were all female. The low incidence in epitaphs of commemorations of women described as spinners (*quasillariae*) is an irrelevance, readily explained by the extreme poverty and low status of professional spinners and the general preference for describing women in terms of their family roles or by generic virtues such as *lanifica* which *included* spinning.

We have seen repeatedly that context and *genre* determines what is expressed and what left out of any source. The patronal relationship is highlighted in a memorial to a former owner, work is depicted in a tradesman's shop-sign and emphasised in commemorations of colleagues from a workshop or slave *familia*. Even men who chose to be depicted for posterity at their trade or business were likely to immortalise their wives as ladies. We are still working out the conventions governing Roman epitaphs, let alone those in the small class which mention job titles. Artisanal trades are a sub-class of those. Inscriptions of any kind which mention women with job titles are a tinier sub-class and the range of jobs cited is tinier still. While women metalsmiths, dyers, teachers, actresses and one shoemaker are named, women figure more commonly as nurses, midwives, wool-weighers (i.e. supervisors of other women producing cloth) and hairdressers.[75] This concentration in 'female' service jobs conforms to familiar modern patterns and it could be that the Roman records reflect a similar reality, but we need to allow for factors which obscure certain activities. Barmaids, spinsters, prostitutes and peasant-women were certainly a feature of Roman society not apparent in inscriptions. Yet barmaids appear in shop-signs, bar graffiti and legal sources; prostitutes in legal and literary sources, brothel paintings and graffiti from brothels and public walls; spinsters appear in a few legal and literary references and in workshop graffiti but rarely in the iconography of Roman Italy. While the stigma attached to prostitution and bar-work and the poverty of the women involved provides a likely reason for their absence from epitaphs, there is often no obvious reason for the appearance of a job category in some media but not others. Nor has anybody ever come up with a conclusive explanation for the over-representation of slaves and freed slaves in the occupational epitaphs around Rome.

Throughout this work I have remarked on the tendency for male-oriented sources to focus on women's reproductive and sexual roles and on their moral elaborations. It is consistent with this that women are identified – and identify themselves – with their roles as mothers and wives and the mainstay of the family economy. If job titles are used and specialist training is provided, domestic production and processing and the physical nurture of household members translates into the roles of nurse, midwife, food saleswoman, barmaid and hairdresser. When women are commemorated as workers it is typically by or with fellow-workers in a commemoration based on the workplace, as in the many examples cited by Joshel (1992a) for small workshops around Rome or in large *monumenta* assigned by noble owner/patrons, such as those of Livia and the Statilii Tauri.

The kind of women's work valued by the culture (morally, that is – prostitution was more profitable than cloth production) was domestically based and therefore confined to certain kinds of celebration: primarily in epitaphs and in literature. Roman women were not frequently depicted at work, even the most exemplary work within the home. Some questions will always remain about their activities.

This is another way of saying that ancient references to work, status groups and specific jobs are determined by *genre* and ideology. Categories can be included or omitted from various sources for reasons quite unrelated to the actual work of the person or group cited. The *lanifica* matron's emblematic significance need not rule out the reality and economic importance of her work any more than the domestic emphasis of modern Mother's Day advertising precludes the economic contribution of mothers to the household from their outside paid work. By the standards of global capitalism, Roman production was relatively small-scale and the lines between domestic and commercial production were blurred. The preference for commemorating women as wives and mothers may simply reflect the value their husbands and families placed on those roles.

9

The allure of 'La dolce vita' in
Ancient Rome[1]

Any Roman woman will do

I began this book with a question: whether we can retrieve the lives of real women. I conclude it with a critical look at past and current readings of a Roman woman who once existed as a living human being and who lives on today in the writings of novelists and scholars as a vehicle for entrenched beliefs about ancient Rome and Roman women. I do not confine myself to cutting-edge scholarship on these readings, but include popular works and textual commentaries which, though outdated in their approaches, continue to be reprinted and to introduce new Classics students to Cicero and Catullus. My concern in this chapter is to explain why certain images and interpretations persist long after they have been debunked by experts and apparently outlived the social prejudices which made them plausible to earlier ages.

The way we 'read' depends ultimately on our own established beliefs. The ideas we accept most readily are those which reaffirm our own world-view.[2] The images which lodge most firmly in our consciousness are vivid artistic creations which tap into our imaginations and take on a tenacious sense of 'truth'.[3] As ancient propagandists and modern image-makers know, deeply-rooted beliefs and images are not easily dislodged by logical, factual refutations (Cicero *De oratore* 2.178). To someone convinced that the country (or neighbourhood or local club) is being taken over by immigrants, statistics and arguments are an irrelevance or a lie. Anyone who has taught Roman history will have encountered students who *know* that Livia poisoned her adult son Drusus and her 77-year-old husband Augustus because the image of Sian Phillips thoughtfully fingering the imperial fig-tree in the 1976 television version of *I, Claudius* – now an accessible video incorporated in the rituals of Classics departments around the world – has become part of their own visual memory.[4]

'Ancient Rome' as an *idea* has had many manifestations over the centuries. The 'decline' of the late Roman Empire was famously and evocatively mapped by Gibbon in the eighteenth century. He cast 'Rome' as a character in a narrative which culminated in the Christianisation of

133

European civilisation. 'Rome' therefore served by its moral bankruptcy to highlight the superiority of Christianity. The use of sexual licence (discreetly but pruriently conveyed) as the main sign of this moral/political decline was developed in nineteenth-century novels such as *The Last Days of Pompeii, Quo Vadis* and their equally popular twentieth-century film versions.[5] It was confirmed for the European élite by the discovery of Pompeian paintings and artefacts adjudged obscene by nineteenth-century gentlemen.[6] Academic and artistic representations alike drew on the Roman *topoi* of decline which we examined in Chapter 5, which foregrounded well-born women as vivid emblems of the decline, rather than those which focused on gourmet fads, personal ornamentation or youthful frivolity.[7]

Scholars and scholarship are not immune to the power of the image.[8] Long after Beryl Rawson's demonstration that those Romans able to marry did so, one can still encounter the odd reference to the licentious Roman preference for concubinage over marriage and its reform by Christian values.[9] Over the years, many well-regarded textual commentators, political historians and experts in Latin love poetry have blended the literary constructions of Catullus ('Lesbia') and of Cicero (the 'Clodia' of his *Pro Caelio*) and presented the resultant hybrid as a historicised woman with a specific personality and characteristics.[10] This historicised woman has become a third fiction, reappearing in much the same guise in modern novels and scholarship. She is beautiful, sophisticated to the point of decadence and sexually promiscuous, as befits the object of desire and hate depicted within Catullus' lyric poems and the object of ridicule venomously depicted in Cicero's speech in 56 BCE. The modern hybrid 'Clodia/Lesbia' is constituted rather selectively from these sources. Just how selectively is apparent from an analysis of ancient *genre* elements – the beloved of lyric poetry, the desiring woman of invective, the poisoning wife of folklore – and a discussion of why some have been taken up by scholars, while others have been played down in line with modern preconceptions.

Cicero's attack in the *Pro Caelio* on Clodia as an illegitimate force in élite power-games raises the issue of women's public roles and the public representations of their virtues and vices (Hillard 1989: 176). As we have seen throughout this book, the differing portrayals of individual women are largely determined by the stock qualities suited to the *genre* and purpose of the author (Richlin 1981). Some scholars have paid serious attention to historical reconstruction of Clodia Metelli from sources other than the *Pro Caelio* creation.[11] Skinner's resultant portrait (1983) of a formidable, independent *grande dame* did not require extensive reading against the text or between the spaces so much as a sober application of traditional methods of source criticism. In Cicero's letters, Clodia figures in the 50s BCE as a political enemy (like her brother Publius Clodius Pulcher), as a beauty Cicero dislikes and as a friend of Cicero's intimate,

Atticus. In the 40s she appears as part of the élite information network and as the savvy owner of a desirable property which interested Cicero.[12] The sum of the parts is relatively rich, as good as a Barbara Taylor Bradford heroine, but apparently too dull for general consumption, which seems to prefer a 'personality' manufactured like the public *persona* of a modern celebrity from do-it-yourself components which can be re-assembled at will (jolly, lovable Fergie turns overnight into loathsome fat-bum Fergie at the stroke of a Fleet Street keyboard). It is understandable that Clodia floats about in transparent clothing in Steven Saylor's novels, but it is discouraging that serious scholars continue to propagate the old stereotype without a pause for token critical review or, indeed, the most basic reality-check. The persistence of this tabloid image of a Roman woman in the face of careful scholarly revisions, the determination to roll together indiscriminately the 'evidence' of disparate *genres* and the continuing appeal of this sexualised figure to popular authors and their public illustrates the many levels at which we continue to read Roman women in the modern world. It would seem these women can still serve an emblematic Whiggish purpose, even when we believe that we are reading or discussing known facts about named, historically attested invididual women. The staying power and vividness of the Clodia/Lesbia characterisation remind us that popular and scholarly processes are not necessarily as far removed as we might like to believe.

The genesis of Clodia/Lesbia

In May 61 BCE, Cicero appeared as a witness for the prosecution of Publius Clodius (then Claudius) Pulcher, a member of a powerful and distinguished Roman family.[13] Clodius was acquitted but was henceforth a dangerous political enemy of Cicero. He succeeded in driving him into exile in March 58 BCE. Clodius had three sisters, each called Clodia in the usual Roman fashion, distinguished in discussion by their husband's names as the Clodia of Metellus (Clodia Metelli, widowed 59 BCE), the Clodia of Lucullus (Clodia Luculli, divorced 66) and the Clodia of Marcius (Clodia Marcii, widowed by 61).

Clodia Metelli and her biography are typically cast by scholars in a particular moral-psychological mode derived from the elegiac theme of betrayal (Catullus) and the forensic imputation of promiscuity (Cicero). There is in fact some mismatch of image between the exploitative Lesbia and the vindictive, ageing beauty of Cicero's speech. The two *genres*, equally malicious at times and both brilliantly executed, have quite different aims. Catullus' portrayal combines inherited elements into a loose, poetic pseudo-narrative of a love affair between the poetic 'I' and one 'Lesbia', identified by the second-century CE African intellectual Apuleius as a Claudia.[14] This identification, never hinted at by Cicero or his later scholiasts, is generally accepted by modern scholars, who associate her with the generation of the famous family active in Roman politics of the 60s and 50s BCE but differ on which of three Claudian sisters to highlight.[15] The temptation (which few resist) is to identify her with the wife of Quintus Metellus Celer, the woman vilified by Cicero in public discourse, private letters and the legal defence of Marcus Caelius Rufus (*Pro Caelio*), in the course of Cicero's decade-long political feud with her youngest brother P. Clodius Pulcher.[16] The focus depends on the orientation of the scholar, with literary experts invoking Clodia incidentally to throw light on Catullus' poetry and life and historians using Catullus as a supplement to their treatment of Clodia, who is usually a side issue to other topics. The narrative and moral parameters were established by the early twentieth century (Münzer 1900). Since then, dominant western attitudes to women and sexuality have purportedly changed radically. There have been equally significant changes in classical scholarship. Prosopography, the painstaking reconstruction of political careers from literary and inscriptional sources, dominated Roman history until the 1960s, when it was largely overtaken by interest in social structures. Modern critical theories have gradually rendered literal readings of classical literature obsolete. They have even influenced the way we read Roman historians and biographers. The typical article in journals of Roman history is no longer 'The forgotten Licinius' but 'Barbarians as "other" in Tacitus'. Yet 'Lesbia/Clodia' has survived *this* Roman revolution. Scrupulous studies which seriously undermine the more sensational elements of the favoured identification have not dislodged the image of the imperious, promiscuous aristocrat who gets her come-uppance from Cicero.

F. Warre Cornish's introduction to the Loeb Catullus, first published in 1913 and repeatedly reprinted ever since, is typical of earlier treatments:

> About 61 BC, when he was twenty-two, [Catullus] made the acquaintance of Clodia, wife of the consul Q. Metellus Celer, the most beautiful, powerful and abandoned woman in Rome, and the bulk of his poems is the history of his fatal love.

R.G. Austin's introduction to his commentary on the *Pro Caelio*, first published in 1933, also conflates the two constructs and assumes a firm knowledge of the alleged love affairs and Clodia's motivation:

> Just as she had broken Catullus, so she hoped to punish Caelius.

Both books are still reprinted, still to be found in libraries, and commonly used by students of Latin and of Roman history.[17] Subsequent treatments have purported to take a more reasoned approach, with some attention to method, but ultimately the hostile characterisation of the hybrid is constant, as is the repetition of gossip and invective as fact, e.g.

[Clodia's] affair with Catullus – the identification with Lesbia is widely admitted – began before the death of Metellus in 59, which Clodia was said to have caused by poison; by the end of that year M. Caelius Rufus was her lover. (*OCD* 1996: 350)[18]

Verdière (1977: 480) continued the Ciceronian tradition of witticisms at her expense, describing Clodia as 'cette ogresse, qui fut plus la mante que l'amante de Catulle'.[19] Even Wiseman, who has carefully revised so much of the biographic material on Clodia and is sceptical of the identification of Lesbia with Clodia Metelli (1969: 50-60; 1985: 136), infers the character of Lesbia from the poetry and clearly links it with his reading of Clodia Metelli's personality as a wilful, commanding aristocrat:

Everything we know about Clodia suggests a woman motivated by the love of pleasure and the love of sway.[20]

The remarkably consistent modern construction of this putatively historic figure, Clodia (Metelli), from selective use of Catullus and Cicero seems to be a product of moral and personal readings. To test this proposition, I shall consider the issue of poetic sincerity in Roman elegists and of truth and the politics of reputation in Roman law-courts, and analyse the figures employed by each author from his *genre*-stock and from the wider cultural pool of hostile stereotypes. But the modern hybrid is more than the sum of two ancient *genre*-parts. 'Rome' and 'Roman Woman' interact with inherited cultural images of Woman the Deceiver, the poet as romantic victim of the cold-hearted (Rich-)Bitch and – paradoxically, one might think – the Woman Scorned. Successive ages project their fantasies and prejudices on to a depressingly constant core image of Clodia/Lesbia.

The 'Lesbia' of Catullus

The small corpus of Catullus' surviving poems reveals his skill at adapting inherited Greek traditions and his innovative genius. He manipulated the lyric metres of Greek amorous poetry and its stock themes: love as a sickness, the beauty and faithlessness of the beloved. His most influential innovation was in addressing several poems to the same love-object, Lesbia, or writing about her to himself or the reader. Constructing the narrative of a love-affair, from initial euphoria, to doubt, to a climax of disillusionment and bitter vilification, involves re-arranging selected poems into an order different from that of the manuscripts in which they are preserved, ignoring poems to *other* named love-objects, and assuming that poems on an anonymous 'girl' (*puella*) must really be to or about Lesbia.[21] Not to mention the assumption that Catullus, the consummate artist, manipulator of Greek metres and themes, is artlessly autobiographical in his poetry, that *some* of his poems can be taken as utterly sincere and

137

literal records of his volatile emotions (unlike Petrarch, Rochester, Herrick, Bob Dylan and nameless troubadours and songwriters through the ages) and that his poetic perspective on the affair and his lover is the true, the only one.

Yet few scholars baulk at the exercise. The charming 1942 edition of Kinchin Smith & Melluish which constituted the introduction for many schoolchildren (including myself) to Catullus' poetry arranges selections under biographical headings, including 'Lesbia – Happiness'; 'Lesbia – Doubt'; 'Lesbia – Disillusionment',[22] prefaced with links reinforcing the impression of a biographical narrative wholly sympathetic to Catullus as victim, e.g.

> In Chapter II we read of Catullus in the very ecstasy of love. We do not know how long the period lasted when no thoughts of the future arose to disturb the two lovers ... In poem 30 we hear the first jarring note of a quarrel ...

> Catullus, however, did not find his love returned with the same constancy, and as time passes he is plunged into fits of increasing jealousy.
> (Kinchin Smith & Melluish 1942: 63)

More high-powered editions and literary analyses join the chorus. In his magisterial treatment of tradition and originality in classical poetry, Williams judges it extreme to question the essential reality of Catullus' affair with Clodia but classes the poems to boys as conventional. After token consideration of competing views, Quinn ends up endorsing the identification of Lesbia as Clodia Metelli and the Caelius of Catullus 58 as Cicero's protégé, M.Caelius Rufus.[23]

Let us consider the basis for some of these claims. There are 116 poems in Catullus' surviving *corpus*. Thirteen of these, 98 lines in all, explicitly refer to Lesbia.[24] About twelve others, invoking a 'girl' (*puella*) or love in general, are commonly taken to refer to her. They are 2, 8, 11, 36, 70, 76, 82, 85, 100, 104, 109, and sometimes 91.[25] Quinn (1970: xvi, 244) makes the basis of his judgement explicit, but most commentators tend to assume rather than justify their association of these poems with the Catullus-Lesbia love affair, so it is not always clear why they have made this identification.[26] As far as one can tell, the perceived intensity of emotion expressed and the themes of rejection, jealousy and betrayal of love and of friendship appear to be key criteria.[27] Sometimes it is a specific motif or theme – kissing, extravagant but worthless promises, faithlessness – which inspires the identification, but Catullus' poems on other love-objects, male and female, some of them also given names, exploit similar themes and even re-work specific devices and echo the wording of the Lesbia poems.[28] The pursuit of the boy Iuventius and 'Catullus'' lack of success in his suit is lamented in equally beautiful, tender terms, constituting another mini-narrative.[29]

Nor was Catullus always tender. He was a master of invective, turning out political and personal lampoons of magnificent vulgarity and hyperbole. He was also innovative in expanding the generic boundaries of lament and recrimination by the unhappy lover, equally skilled in elegiac and epigrammatic metres.[30] Love poets had always decried the mercenary and inconstant character of the beloved, but Catullus explored the love-object/hate-object equations with new elaborations of ambivalence and venom. Typically, 85 ('I hate and I love ...') is taken to be about Lesbia and paired with 75 to produce an image of the suffering poet, knowing prisoner of unworthy love.[31] The faithlessness of the beloved, a conventional theme of Greek love poetry, becomes the basis of vulgar accusations. Lesbia, named in other poems as of peerless beauty (86), as the object of the greatest love ever directed at a woman (87), is pictured in 58 as prowling the back-streets of Rome, committing unspeakable acts with all and sundry, like a low prostitute in common graffiti or later satires.[32]

In the manuscript, the poem follows one in which Catullus recounts an amusing (!) incident – the first-person poet-narrator had raped a boy whom he found masturbating – and another in which he denounces the *cinaedi* Mamurra and Caesar and their varied sexual behaviours with each other and a wider cast.[33] Elsewhere, Catullus sends a message to his unnamed 'girl' to enjoy her three hundred simultaneous lovers, breaking their pelvises.[34] This deliberately gross verse is followed by a tender and exquisite image of a bruised flower, which recalls classic references to defloration and is here equated with the poet's pure love which has been irretrievably – and carelessly – damaged by his sexually voracious, unnamed 'girl'.[35]

To concoct an emotional narrative in the modern style from such elements involves casting 'Catullus' as victim and 'Lesbia' as the exploiter and spoiler. The construction requires romantic elevation of his love as unique – which in turn involves ignoring or explaining away all poems to other love-objects (Iuventius, Ameana) or even poems referring to the poet's contemptuous sex with others of lesser status, such as Ipsitilla and the boy-slave. 'Lesbia' must be promiscuous, but 'Catullus' must not. She must be toying with him, he must be sincere. At least, about Lesbia.

It is no longer the fashion to treat the code-named mistresses of other Roman elegiac poets as 'real' (Wyke 1989: 35) but the desire to believe in Catullus' doomed passion for Lesbia is tenacious. Catullus 70, a stock lament (with a clear literary genealogy) of women's inconstancy, has been read as immediate and 'personal'.[36] Yet commentators point out that Catullus would hardly be a reliable source for Caesar or Memmius:

> We should bear in mind that abuse from the mouth of a hot-tempered poet ... should be heavily discounted. (Wheeler 1934: 103)[37]

Lee actually acknowledges – only to excuse – the apparent inconsistency in Catullus' own promiscuity:

> Does the *sanctae foedus amicitiae* [the pledge of sacred friendship] allow Catullus to have a bit on the side? Or is that unfair and does his placing imply that Lesbia failed him once more? (Lee 1990: 183, on poem 110)

But if we believe Catullus' testimony, the pledge (Fordyce's 'pure affection' destroyed by Lesbia's 'unfaithfulness', 1961: 362) was adulterous. Catullus gloats in 83 over their deception of Lesbia's husband. The identification of Lesbia with Clodia Metelli forces on Catullan fundamentalists the need to place the affair before the known date of Metellus Celer's death by March 59 BCE, and entails considerable biographic contortions. The Lesbia poems cannot easily be assigned to such an early date and it apparently disturbs the romantic illusion to have Catullus writing after the event.[38] The determination to see the Lesbia affair as serious necessitates finding true passion in 11 and 58, while reading 58b as showing a loss of interest in the Camerius of 55 (Lee 1990 *ad loc.*).

In Greco-Roman love poetry, as in the Blues, the ego-narrator is generically obliged to suffer at the hands of a cruel lover. Even with the innovation of a loose narrative featuring Lesbia, and Catullus' interesting introduction of new concepts of love, Lesbia does not emerge as a distinctive character.[39] Poems 5 and 7 are lively enough but in them she is a disembodied mouth to be kissed unendingly by the poetic *persona*, like the Iuventius to whom Catullus addresses similar sentiments (48). There are interesting variants in Catullus' poetic expression of them, but Lesbia's portrait is the usual template of unelaborated attributes: beauty, charm, wilfulness, faithlessness, cruelty.

When you add up the steps necessary to turn these poems into lifewriting, it begins to look as if Catullus is the only one in the process who is *not* driven by sentiment. For the narrative to work in the required way, Catullus' love must be unique. Lesbia must be the villain of the piece, who destroys something beautiful. Why, we are not told. Just because she's shallow and nasty, perhaps. But we don't need to know her motives any more than we need to know her body (Richlin 1983: 46-7) or her personality (Gold 1993: 87). The poems are about 'Catullus'' feelings. It is obviously spoiling things to suggest she has to be cruel to create a poetic narrative in the first place.[40]

The Clodia of Cicero's *Pro Caelio*

In April 56 BCE, Clodia Metelli appeared in court as a witness to debts which Caelius owed her, to rents he owed her brother and (possibly) to an attempt to poison her.[41] To deflect the interest of the jury from grave

140

charges of poisoning, sedition and murder against Caelius and to discredit her testimony, Cicero portrays her as, in effect, a high-class prostitute.[42] It worked, apparently. It still works.

The timing of the hearing to coincide with the Megalensian festival was exploited by Cicero as an opportunity to show off his histrionic talents. He acted out imaginary scenes between Clodia and others, including her revered ancestor Appius Claudius (§§33-5), and pursued entertaining theatrical imagery.[43] The speech is witty, colourful and virtually ignores the prosecution case, to paint a picture of a young man-about-town whose morals are somewhat lax, but who can hardly be blamed for taking up the opportunity of an affair with a disreputable widow. This line of argument is specifically designed to answer the prosecution's equally dramatic if less skilful attack on Caelius' character. Cicero has few things to say in his favour, if you look at the speech carefully. He purports to deal with two of the charges, but his account rests on confusion and hilarity.[44] In his handbook on oratory, Quintilian cites examples of wit from this rhetorical *tour de force* (e.g. *Institutio oratoria* 6.3.25; 8.6.53).

Cicero's employment of stock invective figures, which he inventively manipulates, produces a vivid cast of characters in keeping with his theatrical theme. Even without the benefit of his performance, the speech has had a huge impact on scholars. Possibly because they, too, are distracted by the theatricals, few scholars discuss in depth the charges against Caelius or even the attack on his character which Cicero rebuts in standard rhetorical-school terms.[45] Nor do they cavil at Cicero's entertaining evocation of the Palatine Medea, the aristocratic prostitute (*meretrix*), Clodia. While not informative to the modern reader (or to subsequent generations in antiquity), Cicero's allusive anecdotes about her fix in that reader's mind graphic images, however *ersatz*, like that of the lascivious widow eyeing naked young musclemen across the river (§36).[46]

Cicero was the last speaker on Caelius' behalf, with the task of restoring his character and rebutting two of the criminal charges. His speech, the only survivor of the original six (three for each side), follows the conventional pattern of introduction (*exordium* §§1-2), followed by a refutation of the prosecution case (*praemunitio* §§3-50), in which Cicero soon deviates from the expected account of the facts of the case (*narratio*). The refutation is rounded out by a defence of Caelius' morals, in which Cicero argues that Caelius is *not* dissolute, that young men are entitled to a bit of lee-way and that it's Clodia's fault anyway (§§43-50). The substantive part of the speech (the *argumentatio*, §§51-69) begins with the narrative of the charge about the gold, which is connected with the loan from Clodia and Dio's murder, then proceeds to the accusation of attempted poisoning (§§56-8), which Cicero counters with insinuations about the death of Clodia's husband Celer (§§59-60). §§61-9 contain a circumstantial analysis of how the poison was acquired and a very confused but hilarious account of some incident at the public baths (introduced by the prosecutors), before Cicero moves on to his peroration (§§70-80), which neatly balances his introduction.

Cicero cleverly shifts the jurors' focus to sex, hinting in his opening passage at a *secret influence* working behind the scenes against his upstanding client, who is besieged by the resources of a prostitute. This case, he tells them, is actually driven not by the perfectly proper filial feeling of the young prosecutor Atratinus (whose father had been convicted by Caelius) but female lust.[47] Repeating throughout that the charges against Caelius are without substance (thereby excusing orator and audience the tedium of dealing with them?), Cicero teases audience expectations by building up to his first mention of Clodia's name in §30.4 before pulling out all the stops in §31, then returning to the charge in his highly coloured description of goings-on in Clodia's suburban gardens in Trastevere and her villa at Baiae (§§36, 38, 47), adorned with the usual innuendo about brother-sister incest (§36; cf. *Ad Atticum* 2.2.5) until, finally, the pseudo-hypothetical portrait of an over-sophisticated society hostess gives way to open assertions that she is as good (or bad) as a prostitute.[48]

Now identified, this erstwhile hypothetical noblewoman is painted as the leader of a decadent set (§67). The accusation of husband-poisoning, a long-standing paranoid *topos* of Roman culture, is introduced §§59-60, and topped with cracks about her independence of all masculine authority (e.g. §68). This fits Cicero's characterisation of Clodia as unwomanly, a *dux femina* ('female general'), and his recurrent use of the language of unseemly warfare.[49] Such gender-inappropriateness has the dual benefit of being morally reprehensible and entertaining – a classic satiric combination.[50]

What we have here is an applied composite of hostile stereotypes of Roman women which taps into the tradition we have seen of using upper-class women as signs of contemporary moral failings. Clodia, who could have been (and presumably was, at the end of her life) characterised as an exemplary wife and mother, worthy descendant of a distinguished family, supporter of her brothers' political ambitions and benefactress of her social dependents, is here portrayed as the antonym of the traditional matronly virtues. Instead of being sober, industrious, homeloving and faithful, she is frivolous, luxurious, ambitious, a husband-killer and unchaste. In the peroration, as in the introduction, Cicero airily skates over the charges (§66), then precedes the usual closing appeal to the feelings of the defendant's poor parents (§§79-80) with one attack on the prosecution and another on the force *behind* the prosecution. For the jury's benefit, he invokes graphically the dangers of allowing feminine influence and lust to bring down civilisation as they know it (§78).

One would expect shifts in scholarly perspectives over the years to have affected attitudes to the parties to this case and there have been changes, but critical approaches again show inconsistencies. Caelius' portrayal – uniformly favourable – is based on this speech, fleshed out with references from his correspondence with Cicero and surviving fragments of his own speeches.[51] Few would now credit (as Münzer did) allegations that Publius Clodius Pulcher committed incest with all his sisters but his bad press has, like Clodia Metelli's, resisted scholarly restitution (Rundell 1979). He continues to be viewed in Cicero's terms, as a violent demagogue, although few classical scholars would now openly identify with Cicero's antipathy to the masses and to social remedies for their lot.[52]

Münzer (1900), Austin (1933) and Syme (1964: 25) accepted Clodia's crucial role in the prosecution and her feminised motivation – revenge for being dumped by Caelius Rufus. Note in passing that, while feminine vengefulness was intrinsically repugnant and trivial, revenge prosecutions by young nobles were admired.[53] Scholars now tend to reject any claims for Clodia's influence or political activity (Wiseman 1985; Hillard 1989, 1992), but many cling to her sexual characterisation as a high-born trollop with a taste for younger men, although that characterisation was linked to Cicero's assertion of her illegitimate female influence on the case and draws heavily on a literal reading of Catullus' poems about the sufferings of love. Cicero's allegations of unseemly female power are converted into the 'love of sway' even by Wiseman, who does not uncritically accept the identification of Clodia Metelli as Lesbia and who has taken the trouble to check the background of the 56 BCE prosecution of Caelius.[54]

Cicero's satiric image of an older woman preying on a younger man seems to colour reconstructions of Caelius' biography. Although by Cicero's account Caelius had held office as a decurion in his own municipality and supported Catilina in 64 and 63 BCE, Austin wants him to be 26, not 32 at the time of this case.[55] Even if we assume Clodia was the mother-in-law of the tribune L. Metellus in 49 (Cicero *Ad Atticum* 9.6.3; 9.9.2), that would be little help in reconstructing her date of birth or the date of her marriage to Celer, since both she and her daughter could, like Cicero's daughter, have been as young as thirteen at the time of their marriages.[56] It is Cicero's stereotypic narrative which requires her to be older than Caelius – whether she was two, five, or fifteen years older was irrelevant to his purpose.

The nature and role of Roman forensic invective are crucial to any assessment of the people and events represented in Cicero's speech, but, once again, we strike scholarly inconsistency in approaching the personalities of this case. Austin apparently accepted at face value Cicero's routine assertions that there was no substance to the charges against Caelius and his claim that Clodia was 'the real driving force behind [the prosecution]'. He went on to draw some odd conclusions about the consequences of Caelius' acquittal:

Clodia herself vanishes from sight, a fact which shows significantly enough the social importance of the trial. (Austin 1933: viii)

In the introduction to his commentary on Catullus' poetry, Fordyce creatively embellishes the emotional background before agreeing that the lady vanished:

Caelius had finally broken with her, to the relief of his friends, by 56, when she sought her revenge on him by engineering the charge of *vis* [violence] on which Cicero's ingenious advocacy secured his acquittal. The result of the trial seems to have been the end of Clodia's career and she is not heard of again. (Fordyce 1961: xv)

While it would be reasonable to argue that references to 'Clodia' in Cicero's later correspondence are to one of Clodia Metelli's sisters, advocates of the disappearance theory make no such attempt. They simply ignore references in Cicero's other writings.[57] And what if she *had* disappeared from the written record at this point? Many élite figures drop out of our imperfect records for no obvious reason. Prosopography would be much simpler if that were not the case. Our list of praetors would be complete, for a start, and we could fill out their careers (cf. Livy 8.40.3-5). And those of us who work so hard at digging out references to Roman women are all too conscious of just how rare they are in written sources other than epitaphs.[58] To suggest that public ridicule would turn a member of a leading noble family into a social pariah shows a very peculiar view of the force of abuse in Roman political life.[59] Losing a prosecution against a powerful enemy might force a young political hopeful out of Rome for a few years – Caesar's experience (Suetonius *Divius Iulius* 4) – but that does not seem to have happened to Atratinus.[60]

The classical critical faculty can apparently be flexible. The consensus since the 1950s has been that Cicero's allegation of influence behind the scenes of the prosecution was hollow invective and that Clodia was not so important.[61] The fashion now is to deny her political role but to retain the portrait of the promiscuous party-animal living it up on the Bay of Naples. Like others before and since, Austin was selective in his appreciation of rhetorical convention:

But lurid personalities were a feature of Roman public life, and were neither intended seriously nor taken so; no one would go to Catullus for a valid picture of Caesar. (1933: 52)

But perhaps for a valid picture of a society widow? Austin bases his confident knowledge of Clodia on Catullus and this speech, while Quinn (1973: 383) regarded the speech as 'unshakeable evidence' for Clodia's affair with Caelius, which Cicero deduced from the loan (*Pro Caelio* §36).

Cicero himself warned against believing all that you hear. He tells us not to credit the rumours and prosecution allegations about Caelius' morals because a good-looking young man always attracts malicious gossip (*Pro Caelio* §6). The rules of forensic invective, particularly their elaborations by Cicero and Quintilian, are well-known to classical scholars.[62] Several of Cicero's speeches exemplify the elements, which included fanciful attacks on the character and antecedents of their object and the fabrication of circumstantial anecdotes (*mendaciuncula*) which lent colour and veracity to the routine accusations (*De oratore* 2.240). The stories about Clodia's parties at Baiae and Trastevere fall into this mould and were obviously intended to balance similar stories about Caelius' nightlife. Contemporaries were no more likely to credit them than they were accounts of Piso stuffing his face and belching at dinner-parties, of Octavian prostituting himself to older men, of Cicero fornicating with his own daughter or of Caesar having oral sex with Mamurra.[63] Such allegations were made publicly and repeatedly, as if the offences were equally amusing and reprehensible. *Pace* Austin, gossip and the most public attributions of outrageous behaviour (including murder, incest and prostitution) were fairly routine in Roman public life and had no appreciable impact on the political careers of Piso, Caesar, Cicero or Octavian – to name but a few.[64]

When women were attacked in public, accusations were even more likely to concentrate on sexual transgressions. And charges of being unwomanly. The two could be combined, as in Cicero's attack on Clodia or Octavian's obscene poem to Fulvia, in which he claims she invited him to have sex with her or fight her and he found it more appealing to do battle with her – a political use of the stereotype of the desiring older woman rejected by the younger man.[65] Pompey's supporters in the amphitheatre countered the insults of Clodius' supporters with obscene chants about Clodius and his sister (Cicero *Ad Quintum fratrem* 2.3.2), just as Octavian's troops in the battle for Perugia inscribed bodily and sexual insults about Fulvia and Lucius Antonius on their bullets.[66] Political and social relations survived such public statements. Antonius (Mark Antony) married Octavian's sister (Plutarch *Antonius* 31). Cicero was reconciled to Piso after he had morally assassinated him in court and he had dealings with Clodia after his vile public accusations about her and her brother.[67]

Stalking the Roman woman: antique fictions and modern fantasies

Producing one 'real' woman, Clodia/Lesbia, from the disparate constructions of a lyric poet and a histrionic barrister is an awkward business. It defies logic, for one, to equate the 'girl' (*puella*) of Catullus' verses with the spurned older woman of Cicero's *Pro Caelio*. *Genre* dictates that the girl/Lesbia be desirable and reject the poet-narrator, but constructs the desiring older woman as an object of physical and moral disgust. By presenting Clodia's loan to Caelius as a bribe for sexual services, Cicero taps into the readymade stereotype of the older woman despised for wooing with presents and money and rejected by the poet/narrator who traditionally does the same without loss of face.[68] Assuming her sexual rejection (part of the invective package) enables Cicero to cast Clodia as the sinister female force driving the prosecution from behind the scenes. Such feminised motives were typically attributed to powerful women.[69]

We have seen that Lesbia, too, becomes a vehicle for the poet's invective skills. The epigrams are the only place for *her* body and *her* desire. *Genre* rules: elegiac woman is idealised, invective woman is abused. The distinction is partly metrical.[70] Like the 'Clodia' of the *Pro Caelio*, this Lesbia is Woman-as-desiring-subject, by definition a fitting object of vilification. Poet and orator variously explored *genre*-based themes we encountered in Chapter 4. The modern reception readily adopts the ancient authorial positions: scholars openly sympathise with the rejected Catullus and laugh at the rejected Clodia. Apparently the desiring woman still deserves humiliation, the desiring man deserves faithful adulterous love.

Not that the invective portraits are swallowed whole. Scholars now seem to accept that accusations of brother-sister incest and husband-poisoning were topical rather than factual. Accusations of murder, especially by poisoning, were readily inspired by any sudden death and suspicion of wives' powers to poison their husbands surfaces from time to time in Roman history and folk-lore.[71]

Skinner (1983) endorses the usual identification of Clodia Metelli with Lesbia but goes against the contemporary tide in suggesting Clodia was an actor in late Republican politics.[72] Skinner does believe that Clodia was a political force of her time. She argues that accusations of incest represent political combinations in Roman invective and suggests that Cicero's hostile portrait of Clodia in the *Pro Caelio* constitutes a form of punishment or social control of a woman who has ventured into a masculine realm.[73] Wiseman, who discounts her political significance, also relates Clodia's public vilification by Cicero to her independence, particularly her economic and sexual freedom:

> But independence has its price. To do without restrictions is also to do without protection. Clodia was vulnerable – to rude songs chanted about her in the Forum, to well-publicised gifts like the purseful of coppers or the perfume-jar filled with something unmentionable, and above all to the sort of treatment meted out to her at the trial of Caelius.[74]

There may be something in this. Savage public denunciations of women who step out of line are a phenomenon by no means confined to the ancient world. On the other hand, Cicero's attack on Clodia needs to be viewed in the context of Roman forensic invective, in which – as we have seen – men were routinely accused of extreme social and sexual transgression. The implication that Clodia's conduct of her finances was notably independent seems to me unwarranted. She was a member of a leading family, a prosperous widow probably in her thirties and managed her affairs, as far as one can judge, according to the expectations of her time.[75] Even being the force behind a law-suit was not intrinsically unsuitable for a great lady, as Cicero himself demonstrates with his many respectful references to his own engagement by Caecilia Metella to appear for the actor Roscius in a political *cause célèbre* of 70 BCE.[76]

But Clodia's actual role is ultimately irrelevant to her forensic *persona*. Cicero's strategy involved a vicious personal attack on her which he justified by his allegation that Clodia was the real force behind the prosecution of Caelius. Her influence is portrayed as illegitimate, motivated by uncontrollable female passions, particularly transgressive lust but also transgressive desire for power – *meretrix* and *dux femina*. Her passions are represented, rather paradoxically, as both ridiculous and dangerous.

Cicero was exploiting existing Roman stereotypes of women out of control. Such clichés were applied particularly to women perceived as intruding illegitimately in masculine domains or when the author/speaker wished to attack a man for failing to prevent such intrusion by his female connections, whether wives or sisters.[77] Within the setting of Roman vilification – forensic or literary – certain things (such as facts) became irrelevant or capable of transformation: the literal truth of an accusation, or the accepted norms of behaviour for élite women (political alliances with male kin, use of patronage to pursue interests in the court, retribution against family enemies).[78] Cicero's main aim was presumably to get Caelius off and to thwart his enemy Clodius rather than to harm Clodia, but his purpose was best served by representing the whole case as groundless, the ludicrous fantasy of an ageing libertine moved by sexual spite. Whether she was driving, navigating from the back seat, a passenger or an innocent bystander, Clodia had to be a casualty.

It has been suggested that Cicero's portrait of Clodia in the *Pro Caelio* became the basis of subsequent literary characterisations of errant women.[79] There are some parallels in Sallust's monograph on the Catilinarian conspiracy, published *c.* 42 BCE, some fourteen years after the delivery of the *Pro Caelio*.[80] Sallust describes the revolutionary Sempronia, driven to desperate measures by her moral and financial bankruptcy:

> Among them was Sempronia, who had on many occasions committed many misdeeds of a masculine audacity. This woman was quite blessed in her birth and beauty, and moreover in her husband and children; she was versed in Greek and Latin literature, she played the lyre and danced more elegantly than a decent woman needs to and had many other accomplishments which

are the accessories of decadence. But she always held her honour and chastity cheaper than anything else; you would have trouble working out whether she was more careless of her fortune or her good name. She was so oversexed that she went after men more frequently than she was pursued by them. Now she had frequently broken faith before this, she had repudiated her cumulative debt, she had been an accomplice in murder, and she had been made reckless by extravagance and impecuniousness. All the same, her natural abilities were by no means negligible: she could compose poetry, crack a witty joke, converse in a modest, beguiling or cheeky style; in short, she possessed great wit and great charm. (Sallust *Bellum Catilinae* 25)

This famous sketch elides Sempronia's dubious (but fascinating) sophistication, her shameless sexuality and her sedition. Sallust presents her, like Catiline, as an instance of outstanding qualities perverted to the wrong cause and, like other conspirators portrayed in more general terms (e.g. indebted youth), as a symbol of contemporary evils. In Chapter 5 we saw how Roman authors from many periods typically employed such figures to illustrate the decline of their own age from the standards of an imagined past, an ancient trope appropriated since Gibbon as an explanatory device to make the political/military disintegration of Rome consequent on its moral collapse (Johns 1982: 34). Since the nineteenth century, many artists and blurb-writers have pressed the connection, associating Rome's end indifferently with the late Republic (Clodia, Sempronia), the early Empire (*I, Claudius*, the *Satyricon*) or the second century CE (Juvenal's sixth satire) to create a dominant modern perception of an a-historic Rome teetering on the brink of ruin for several centuries. Ancient and modern clichés both invoke a transgressive upper-class woman to signify decline.

Clodia served no such emblematic purpose in the *Pro Caelio*, but a later scholiast on another of Cicero's speeches implies that by late antiquity Clodia's name had attracted stock negative qualities:

Ancient authors state that she had been enthused about dancing more expressively and immodestly than becomes a married lady.[81]

This in turn echoes Sallust's description of Sempronia, but a recurrent motif does not establish a firm line of transmission.[82] These prurient portraits of noble women gone wrong might owe their similarity to the re-formation of standard elements, the same process used to assemble other ancient stock portraits suited to the author's purpose, such as that of the virtuous wife or wicked tyrant/emperor.

The similarities of the female depictions might owe something to the fact that women were praised or blamed for a narrower range of qualities than men:

For these reasons, since the praise of all good women tends to be simple and standard because by maintaining their own sphere their innate good qualities

148

require no diversity of words and it is enough that they have all performed
the same actions meriting a good reputation and in that it is difficult for a
woman to earn novel praise since her life is marked by less significant
vicissitudes the celebration of their actions must necessarily be on a common
format, lest an omission on reasonable grounds vitiate the other qualities, ...

as a son has it in a turgid tribute to his dead mother, Murdia.[83] These
qualities tend to be related to women's sexual and reproductive roles – the
things of greatest significance to the dominant masculine gaze. Murdia's
son follows his pompous generalities with the conclusion that his beloved
mother *therefore* deserves all the more credit for the fact that her womanly
virtues were equal and similar to those of other good women: they included
modesty, uprightness, chastity, docility, wool-work, industry and faithfulness.[84]

The two sides of the feminine image are best illustrated by the women
of the imperial family. Conventions governing their representations on
coins and public statuary underwent significant changes from the time of
Augustus to the later Empire, but the emphasis on their exemplary
fertility and womanly virtue remained constant.[85] The fall from this
idealised position might mean condemnation not only to exile or death but
to widespread personal disrepute. Augustus' daughter Julia and Claudius'
wife Valeria Messalina both produced children with an important potential role in the imperial succession. Their virtues were publicly
advertised in dynastic sculpture and fawning provincial accolades. But
once condemned for adultery, both women became common discourse
property, and jokes and vulgar speculation circulated about them. The
details of their initial offences rapidly proliferated, so that later authors,
drawing on scandalous traditions, could present as history the assertion
that Augustus' daughter had copulated on the public speaking platform
in the forum and that Messalina turned the imperial palace into a
brothel.[86]

Jokes and extravagant anecdotes assigned suitable personalities to the
disgraced Julia and Messalina. Messalina was portrayed as cruel and
avaricious, her *muliebris impotentia* driving her to misuse her power over
her emperor-husband for wicked ends: murder, sexual gratification and
enrichment.[87] Her modern characterisation has shed these elements but
Messalina remains a by-word for epic sexual voracity.[88] For a long time,
art historians seeking Julia's portraits were misled by the insistence on
Julia's frivolity in the accretion of anecdotes which circulated long after
her fall. Surprise, surprise – it turned out she was depicted *not* as the
flighty girl of the gossipy jokes, but as a sober noble matron (Bartman
1999: 216). It was too easy to lose sight of the fact that while Messalina
was in her twenties when she was summarily executed for treason and
adultery, Julia was approaching middle-age when her sexual misbehaviour was publicly denounced by her own father in 2 CE, and that she had,

since her teens, been promoted as a role model for Roman womanhood.[89] The inference I would draw is that neither the fertile exemplar nor the frivolous wanton represented any real woman so much as a collection of qualities assembled for the particular purpose – to advertise the stability of a new régime or to have a good laugh (and to feel morally superior) about high jinks in high places.

In his book about Antonia, mother of the emperor Claudius, Kokkinos (1992) reconstructs her status and personal character from non-literary sources such as coins, inscriptions and sculptural portraits. But her image is identical with the image projected in those media for *all* the women at the heart of the imperial family. If we had no literary elaborations, we would construct identical portraits of Livia, Julia, Agrippina the Elder and Younger and Poppaea Sabina from similar sources.[90] Because women like Antonia, Matidia or Faustina the Elder figure so little in the literary tradition, historians have continued to characterise them in terms of the clichéd virtues, as exemplary Roman matrons who did not involve themselves in palace politics.[91]

The association of politics and sex is complex. In Chapter 4, we examined the link between concern for a 'pure' line of succession and social stress on female chastity, with its ramifications for masculine honour and the maintenance of high status in many social groups (Yalman 1963, Gilmore 1987). In the Roman Republic, politics was the province of a few leading families, who ruthlessly played to win. Young noblemen were praised for prosecuting senior statesmen who had done the same to their fathers: conviction meant exile. Speech was very free – at least, for the powerful and for anonymous pamphleteers, both of whom cheerfully accused opponents of a vivid range of vices (Syme 1939: 149-51). Censors had the power to expel enemies from the senate on moral grounds and the most distinguished women of all, the Vestals, were particularly vulnerable to attacks on their chastity.[92] If charges against them were upheld, Vestal and lover suffered a particularly unpleasant death and eternal disgrace.[93] Since Vestals came from the leading political families and could use their status to protect their connections, they were obvious political targets.[94] Gossip about married women from the political families could be exploited, as in the *Pro Caelio*, for political purposes. Hostile literary portraits of specific women are also underpinned by a conventional presumption that a woman who breaks some rules will break others – notably, the sexual rules. Sempronia committed treason and Clodia perhaps associated herself with her brother's populist political style. If we accept the argument that sexual insult was a form of social control used against women who stepped out of line, the sexual-political nexus becomes another side of the phenomenon we saw in Chapter 8, whereby a lower-class woman employed outside the home could be portrayed as sexually available.[95] The noble Clodia and the impoverished Pompeian spinner Amaryllis were exposed to similar impertinence. Being called a *meretrix* in a court or a *fellatrix* on a workshop wall amount to the same thing.[96]

The tradition of punishing female 'uppitiness' with sexual slander, like that of attacking male enemies through their female connections, runs deep, its ramifications including but extending beyond any one *genre*-based motif. Many of our most vivid and enduring images of political women in the Republican and imperial eras are ultimately based on hostile traditions which sexualise them. The process goes back to the moral and symbolic roles occupied by women in different Roman literary *genres*. If history, for example, is defined – as it was in Greco-Roman culture – as a chronicle of military and overt political events for moral edification, it is constructed from the outset as a masculine world.[97] The introduction of any individual woman or group of women into a political narrative is then an oddity, a literary device with a specific purpose. Roman historians occasionally cited a named woman as an exemplary icon – the classic case being that of Lucretia, which we examined in Chapter 4. More often, women highlight the deficiencies of their age, as in the account of the Bacchanalian persecutions of 186 BCE, or of their family, as in the legendary arrogance of the mid-Republican Claudia.[98] The very attempt by a woman to exert influence in the political sphere could be represented as a slur on her husband or male relations, who had thus failed to control her – consider the arguments put in the mouth of the disapproving Cato, faced on his way to the forum with a female demonstration, or the characterisation of M. Antonius and the emperor Claudius as dominated by their politically active wives.[99]

Nor were sex and politics distinct. Irregular unions as well as legitimate ones had an impact on political alliances. Syme's comment (1964: 25) on Republic politics, that 'marriage, divorce or adultery in the *nobilitas* seldom failed to be items of political consequence', was even truer of intrigue within the imperial family, where treason and adultery were linked (cf. Tacitus *Annals* 3.24). Augustus executed one of his daughter's lovers, Iullus Antonius, because he had been aiming to supplant the *princeps* and it was Messalina's ceremonial marriage to a high-born noble which sparked off her downfall.[100] A pretender's sexual alliance with a woman of impeccable lineage who had an established imperial image and children (or sons-in-law or grandchildren) with a claim to the throne could seriously threaten the empire's stability. Such women were typically accused of sexual crimes rather than conspiracy, but posterity has not always accepted the indictment: Nero's divorced wife Octavia (Messalina's daughter), accused of adultery and abortion, is represented by Tacitus as an innocent victim.[101] Tacitus also portrays as victims women of the dissident senatorial families who suffered under Tiberius and Nero. Charges of treason and adultery seem at times to have been almost interchangeable.[102] Such women, far from becoming the objects of coarse humour, were heroised as martyrs, cast in the mould of pitiable female victims of a tyrant's cruelty – a variant on the classic *topos* of the well-born girl or married woman victimised by the tyrant's lust (such as Verginia or Lucretia – Joshel 1992b).

The consequence is that named women figure in the literary political narrative as victim-heroines or as villains, and in the non-literary sources like epitaphs or imperial propaganda as impeccable models of female virtue. Tradition assigns to many of these women specific personalities – the spiteful Clodia, the dutiful Octavia (Augustus' sister), the frivolous Julia, the wanton Messalina – which are an amalgam of stereotypes. The good women like Lucretia, 'Turia' and the Stoic martyrs, are sexless, while the bad women (Sempronia, Clodia, Julia, Messalina) are virtually defined by their transgressive sexuality. In fact, the women of both groups were distinguished wives and mothers, many of whom showed extraordinary courage and judgement.[103] Some of these women – most famously, Cleopatra VII – have been taken up in subsequent works of imagination which have perpetuated their fabricated personalities. And their appeal. Many authors since Sallust have echoed his overt censure and his undertone of sexual fascination with a woman who did indeed exist but has since become the focus of fanciful projections, the academic equivalent of a modern celebrity stalked by deluded devotees who are convinced that they *know* the object of their passion. Now that Roman women are more often studied in their own right, revisionist histories veer between those which assert the women's political agency and those which class accusations of political ambition as vilification of the women and of their male connections.[104] The evidence can be read both ways. The collapsing of the political and the sexual in the case of women makes it particularly difficult for us to disentangle factual elements. All the more reason, one would imagine, to take particular care in assessing sexual accusations and imputations. Yet the theme of decline and its mediation through a vivid female portrait continues to exert a strong appeal. Skinner (1983: 274) points to Clodia Metelli's role in Balsdon's generally sympathetic characterisation of the so-called emancipated women of the late Republic. He classes her with

> other women – beautiful, intelligent and altogether immoral – who, without any interest at all in politics, set out to exploit their charm to the full, while that charm lasted. (Balsdon 1962: 53-4)

Balsdon argued that such lifestyles were in the Principate confined to the princesses of the imperial family:

> In that event their opportunities were greater than ever – so also, as Julia and Messalina both found, were the risks involved. (1962: 56)

Skinner believes that Balsdon's popular work had an impact on more high-powered proponents of Roman history, including Finley, whose 1965 essay, widely read in its reprinted versions, used to be a standard citation on Roman women before the subject attracted in-depth studies.[105] Balsdon and Finley wrote for different audiences but each reached an enormous public and therefore probably played their part in propagating the image of Roman woman, especially the élite woman, as modest home-body or flamboyant slut. But we have seen that the Clodia/Lesbia hybrid, an obvious example of the latter, was entrenched in popular literature and scholarly discourse before the publication of either work and has since survived great shifts in literary and historical viewpoints within Classics.

In novels, Clodia continues to break Catullus' heart and to gaze across the Tiber at muscle beach.[106] In commentaries, introductory disclaimers about the irrelevance of Lesbia's 'reality' are belied by references to her cruelty to Catullus and by attempts to glimpse the wicked Clodia within the poetry.[107] Austin's edition of the *Pro Caelio* continues to be the standard one and has been reprinted since 1988 in the OUP paperback version. Restrained by comparison with the blurb for Robert de Maria's novel, *Clodia* ('the siren, the conspirator, the most outrageous lover of ancient Rome'), the text on the back cover makes no concessions to scholarship since 1933:

> Clodia herself, fiercely resentful of her rejection, was closely involved with the case ... Cicero's speech ... also helps us reconstruct the 'social back-ground' of Catullus, and is of special interest to the literary historian.

Scholars in the vanguard of Catullan studies and Roman Republican politics might regard such views as amusingly outdated, but when they are challenged at conferences, classical colleagues react with shock and grief at the prospect of relinquishing the alluringly wicked Lesbia/Clodia.

The power of the image

How is it that conservative classical scholars, who normally stay within strict professional bounds, rarely veering between political history, lyric poetry and forensic oratory, have so readily accepted and combined the 'testimony' of Catullus the poet/lover and Cicero the forensic orator and disregarded other available constructions of the same woman? The answer lies in part in the artistic power of the portraits, in part in the under-standable desire to flesh out the characters we glimpse in one source with the yield of another, and in part in the fit between Roman and modern ideologies which lend plausibility and appeal to this wayward 'Les-bia/Clodia'.

Crossing and combining *genres* in search of the lived experience of historical women is a perfectly legitimate practice, one I support and advocate. But it demands critical appreciation of the purpose and traditions of each *genre*. Epitaphs, however sincere, are unlikely to describe the mixed realities of a long marriage but may express a cultural ideal and possibly a sincere belief that it has in some sense been achieved. Roman lawsuits, like our own, lock the parties into an extreme form of opposition. The discourse of the court invites moral posturing and invective which requires careful reading even to lay bare the norms allegedly breached or ostentatiously invoked.[108]

Dissecting the elements of Catullus' poetry and Cicero's *Pro Caelio*, the basis of the modern construct, demonstrates how the two authors each drew on and manipulated integral components of his chosen *genre*, with elaborations and additions of his own, and exploited available constructions of a more general kind pillorying transgressive female behaviours. If we wish to combine the yield of these disparate *genres*, we need to call on the full range of traditional classical skills of source and textual criticism and the self-critical awareness of modern theory. In the case of Catullus' poetry, we need to look at his whole surviving corpus and its Greek and Latin predecessors, to understand the elements of verse invective, erotic *topoi*, metrical virtuosity and, above all, the questions of how literally to take his construction of the first-person poetic *persona* and what has been read as a one-sided diarist's narrative of the vicissitudes of an adulterous love affair.[109] In the case of Cicero, we need to distinguish between the political and forensic expediencies, as well as the literary components of his speech, which was rightly held up as a model of its kind in later ages. We need to discriminate above all between the dominant morality espoused before a jury (that adult sons should live with their fathers; that widows who lend money to young men are sexually suspect), which – as in modern court cases – may not reflect Roman norms and realities or Cicero's own value systems (he does not usually subscribe to the view he adopts in the *Pro Caelio*, that boys will be boys).

We have seen throughout this work how our male-centred and male-authored texts from antiquity generally introduce women, like other non-dominant categories, for very specific purposes and in specific roles: the virtuous mother of epitaphs; the plebeian virgin who must be killed to thwart the lust of a tyrannical patrician; the propertied woman in need of legal monitoring; the wilful 'mistress' (*domina*) of love poetry, and so on. The emblematic role served by women in masculine discourse is apparent when groups of women are invoked in obviously moral contexts. When ancient authors referred to 'stepmothers' the term served as short-hand for neglect and murderous jealousy. Tacitus' account of German women implicitly contrasts their simplicity and chastity with the vices of the women (i.e. the élite women) of Rome. Individual women whom the authors cared for were not included in the unfavourable categories but, by implication, fell into the accepted range of female virtues: Pliny the Younger's friend Helvidia was admired for rearing her stepchildren, certainly not subject to the stereotype he happily invoked when attacking a stepmother in a celebrity inheritance suit.[110] Tacitus upheld his father-in-law's mother Iulia Procilla as a model of provincial virtue, a widowed mother who slotted into the litany of famous Roman mothers (all the others, incidentally, members of that élite, native Roman group elsewhere invoked as the embodiment of modern decadence).[111] But individual, named women could also embody unfavourable stereotypes. The empress Messallina, praised on public representations for her womanly virtues, became after her execution for adultery and conspiracy a fit vehicle for lurid and vulgar speculation. Her name is still invoked as a short-hand ribald joke in classical circles and beyond.

But the joke is on us if we take this kind of thing seriously. While ancient authors expressed ideologies in their writings, modern scholars bring their own to reading them. It is not a simple matter to retrieve even basic information about 'Clodia' – so easily elided with 'Lesbia', so effortlessly absorbed into respectable modern scholarly discourse as a historical personage about whom we know a number of 'facts', most of them highly dubious. And this is a woman (or women) known personally to Cicero, possibly to Catullus; a woman about whom we have a relative wealth of information, unlike so many others who figure only as 'wife of the consul' or a name and family role in a brief epitaph. We have seen that scrupulous scholarly reconstruction has not in any case shaken the preference for the lurid but largely fictitious creation.

Apparently Lesbia/Clodia the cruel slut still has more pulling power than a shadowy poetic device ('Lesbia') or a 'real' woman, Clodia Metelli, whose many conventional roles over the years encompassed those of wife, sister, widow, patron, witness, political campaigner and mediator, mother, acquaintance of Atticus, information-source, mother-in-law, property-owner. It is also much more difficult to fit such a mundane and human mix into a narrative of moral decline in which a named woman (embodying the well-known bundle of wink-wink-nudge-nudge qualities shared by 'Roman women' as a group) plays a starring role.

Modern readers have their own heritage of stereotypes which, if unexamined, might interact with those of this very different culture: Roman decadence, parasitic aristocrats, scheming Italians. Perhaps we can never quite shake them off. Readymade categories are comfortable, re-thinking the basis of each text and of our own responses to it is demanding and sometimes positively unsettling. Vivid images created by skilful artists, ancient and modern, become part of our picture of the ancient world, which we would like to know and understand well. Unfortunately, there is no short-cut.

In our quest for Roman women we need to keep in mind that the basic *modus operandi* should be the same whether the texts we are studying purport to describe particular, historic women or female types and female behaviour in general: we need in each case to assess scrupulously the particular purpose of the text, its codes, its emphases and exclusions. And to keep our brains switched on high and our fantasies on hold.

APPENDIX 1

ITALY AND ITS SURROUNDS
Late Republic/Early Empire

GALLIA CISALPINA

GALLIA NARBONENSIS

ILLYRICUM/
DALMATIA

Florence

Marseilles

LIGURIAN SEA

SPAIN

CORSICA

ITALIA

Rome

ADRIATIC SEA

Ostia

Naples

Herculaneum
Pompeii

GREECE

TYRRHENIAN SEA

SARDINIA

MEDITERRANEAN SEA

Lilybaeum
(Marsala)

SICILY

Carthage

Syracuse

NUMIDIA

AFRICA

MALTA

MEDITERRANEAN SEA

--- Approximate Provincial
Boundaries

LIBYA

0   200   400   600   800 Kilometers

Map drawn by D. Tully, The University of Queensland.

APPENDIX 2

Some Useful Dates

This is a very basic guide for the non-expert reader to the conventional divisions of Roman history. It will give some indication of where authors and characters fit in. People's names (Matidia, Naevoleia Tyche) are listed alphabetically in the General index, with brief identifying information, authors in the Index of ancient sources. Only a few are included in this Appendix.

THE REGAL PERIOD
conventionally dated 753-509 BCE

According to Roman tradition, **Lucretia**'s rape and suicide (Chapter 4) ushered in

THE REPUBLICAN PERIOD, 509-27 BCE

The Early Republic: 509-265 BCE
445 BCE: traditional dating of the *Twelve Tables*, at the time of conflict between patricians and plebeians, the setting of the **Verginia** story (Chapter 4).

The Mid-Republic: 264-134 BCE
The Punic Wars and the growth of Roman imperialism and wealth.
    Polybius wrote in the second century BCE.
    Cornelia, mother of the Gracchi, famous for her wealth and culture, lived in this period. Its end is marked by the tribunate of her elder son, Tiberius Sempronius Gracchus (133 BCE).

The Late Republic: 133-27 BCE
We have better sources from this period, e.g. Cicero and Sallust, who lived then. (The imperial authors Suetonius and Plutarch also wrote about this period).
    Some women from the period: **Clodia** Metelli (Chapter 9), **Sempronia** (briefly described by Sallust – Chapters 5, 9), **Fulvia** (Chapter 9).
    The **Hellenistic era** (dating from the death of Alexander the Great in 323 BCE) ended with the death of Cleopatra Ptolemy in 30 BCE.

THE IMPERIAL PERIOD

The Early Empire: 27 BCE - *c.* 192 CE
is also relatively rich in literary and material sources. (See Appendix 3 for information on 'Late Antiquity' and Byzantine emperors who are relevant to the legal Chapters, 4 and 6)

The Julio-Claudians: 27 BCE (Augustus) - 68 CE (Nero)
This period is also called the **Principate**, and the emperor the *princeps*.
    18 BCE and 9 CE: Augustan legislation on marriage, adultery, inheritance.

158

Appendix 2

Women of the imperial family were introduced into public propaganda and iconography (see Dixon 1988: 241-4 for relevant family trees). **Livia**, wife of Augustus, mother of Tiberius, is treated in Chapter 8. Those discussed in Chapter 9 include **Julia**, daughter of Augustus (Chapter 9); **Antonia**, mother of Claudius; **Messalina**, disgraced wife of Claudius; **Agrippina** the Younger (*minor*), sister of Gaius (Caligula), wife of Claudius, mother of Nero.

The Flavians (Vespasian, Titus, Domitian): 69-96 CE
79 CE: the eruption of Vesuvius buried the towns of Pompeii and Herculaneum on the Bay of Naples, thus preserving evidence of a different kind. See Chapters 7 and 8 on **Eumachia**, **Naevoleia Tyche**, **Julia Felix**, **Amaryllis** and others.

The Adoptive Emperors (Nerva, Trajan, Hadrian): 96-138 CE
Pliny the Younger and Tacitus both wrote under Trajan. Suetonius probably wrote a little later, under Hadrian. The alimentary schemes (Chapter 7) belong particularly to this period.
    Iunia Libertas (Chapter 7), the shoemaker **Septimia Stratonice** (Chapters 7 and 8) and the unnamed 'working women' of Ostia (Chapter 8) probably lived in this period.

The Antonines (Pius, Marcus, Commodus): 138-192 CE
Matidia (Elder and Younger) and **Faustina** (Elder and Younger) figure in imperial beneficence and propaganda (Chapter 7).

*

For later emperors see Appendix 3.ii.

APPENDIX 3

Legal Appendix

(i) Some Roman legal terms

auctoritas: the 'authority' of *tutores* was requisite for specified legal actions by a woman *in tutela*. Their presence as well as their permission was necessary.

filiafamilias: a girl or woman (of any age) in her father's power (*potestas*).

filiusfamilias: a boy or man (of any age) in his father's power (*potestas*).

manus: literally, 'hand'. Certain Roman marriage forms resulted in the wife coming into the husband's *manus*. She then joined his legal (agnatic) family instead of her own and ceded rights of property ownership and administration.

materfamilias: originally, a woman in the *manus* of her husband. The term came to indicate a respectable married woman.

paterfamilias: a Roman man *sui iuris* had the capacity to exercise *potestas* over others and was classed as a *paterfamilias* even if he was young and unmarried.

patria potestas: the special power a Roman father had over the person and property of his children as long as he lived (unless he agreed to a formal release, 'emancipation', or a legal transfer of a child to another *paterfamilias* through adoption or *manus* marriage).

sui iuris: independent (i.e. of paternal authority or husband's *manus*). All those heirs (*sui heredes*) in a man's *potestas* became *sui iuris* on his death (except his son's legitimate children, who passed into their father's *potestas*). A woman *sui iuris* would still be in the *tutela* of a man or several men. A child *sui iuris* also had a *tutor* or *tutores* until the age of twelve (girls) or fourteen (boys). See Chapter 6.

tutela: usually translated, rather misleadingly, as 'guardianship'. It was exercised over the holdings of Roman women and children who were *sui iuris* and therefore able to own property in their own right. Children's *tutores* (*tutores impuberum*) actually administered their estates and rendered an account when the children reached twelve (girls) or fourteen (boys). For women over twelve, *tutores* provided their *auctoritas* for specified legal transfers, e.g. manumission of slaves, sale of real estate, writing a will) but did not manage the property. Apart from Vestals, women remained *in tutela* for life until the imperial period. Hence the term 'perpetual guardianship of women' (*tutela mulierum perpetua*). Chapter 6.

(ii) Some jurists, some emperors and some dates for Section III

The emperors whose names appear below play little role in my text apart from legal citations in Part III, Reading the Public Face. For other emperors, see Appendix 2 and the General index.

Jurists and the Digest (Pandects): The *opinions* (*sententiae*) of jurists and the judgements of emperors are recorded in Justinian's *Digest*, compiled in Byzantium in the sixth century CE (See under Justinian below). References to the *Digest* therefore include the name of the jurist, e.g. *Digest* 33.7.1 (Paul).

Codices: The Theodosian Code (*CT* = *Codex Theodosianus*) and the Justinianic Code (*CJ* = *Codex Iustinianus*) record decisions made by emperors in response to appeals from subjects all over the empire.

See Crook 1967: 13-35 (esp. 25-7) on sources of Roman law.
Servius Sulpicius Rufus is the only Republican entry in this list.
All dates are CE (AD).

Alexander Severus: emperor 222-235.

Claudius: emperor 54-68.

Constantine: the first Christian emperor, ruled the western empire 312-337.

Gaius: a jurist and law lecturer, *fl*. 160-178. Author of the *Institutes*.

Hadrian: emperor 117-138.

Justinian: Byzantine emperor 527-565.

Justinian ordered a rationalised compilation of currently applicable law. The Justinianic *Codex* (*CJ*), which includes emperors' rulings in individual cases, was promulgated in April 529. An amended version, published in 534, has survived. The *Digest*, or *Pandects*, published in December 533, gives extracts from earlier jurists' authoritative opinions (for citation) arranged by subject in fifty books.

Marcus ('Aurelius'): emperor 161-180.

Modestinus: Herennius Modestinus, a jurist active in the early third century CE. He composed rescripts (responses to petitions) for Alexander Severus.

Paul: Iulius Paulus, *fl*. late second/early third century. He advised the emperors Septimius Severus and Alexander Severus.

Pius: Antoninus Pius, emperor 138-161.

Pomponius: Sextus Pomponius wrote books under Hadrian, Antoninus Pius and the emperor Marcus, but probably did not deliver authoritative 'opinions'.

Septimius Severus: emperor 193-211.

Servius Sulpicius Rufus: late Republican legal expert and author; an acquaintance of Cicero.

Theodosius: emperor 408-450, authorised the *Codex Theodosianus* (promulgated 438).

Ulpian: *fl*. mid to late second century. Author of the *Titles*. His opinions are cited extensively (as authoritative) in the *Digest*.

Notes

1. Re-readings: a partial survey of scholarship

1. Pomeroy 1975 is usually set in combination with the Roman source material in Lefkowitz & Fant's reader for students. English-speaking students now have the additional benefit of Fantham *et al*. 1994. Other countries have developed their own hand-books, e.g. Schuller 1987, Setälä 1994, Guiducci 1989, Fraschetti 1994a.

2. Reviews include Fantham 1986, Culham 1987, Skinner 1987b, Blok 1987, Clark 1989, Rabinowitz 1993, Sharrock 1997 and Scheer 2000 (which I have not been able to consult). For bibliographies, see Goodwater 1975 and Pomeroy 1984b. Gomme 1925, critical of scholarship on Athenian women, provides references to the subject from an earlier period. Most of the review articles cited in this note include useful bibliographies. Edited collections also provide good bibliographic starting-points, e.g. Rabinowitz & Richlin 1993, Walcot & McAuslan 1995. The on-line bibliography *Diotima* has become the supreme source:
http://www.stoa.org/diotima/

3. I am not playing down the importance of comparable publications in other countries, but the impact of the American studies lends them particular significance. Some, like Roberts 1977, were linked with International Women's Year, 1975 (which subsequently became the Decade).

4. This is particularly true of the older dissertations, many with promising titles, such as M. Thompson's *The Property Rights of Women in Ancient Greece* (unpublished. Yale, 1906). Some are in nineteenth-century journals which are difficult to acquire even in the country of origin, such as A. Desjardins 1865 'De la condition de la Femme dans le droit civil des Athéniens', *Mémoires lus à la Sorbonne dans les séances extraordinaires du Comité impérial des travaux historiques et des sociétés des savants*. In *Histoire, philologie et sciences morales*. 8: 616-18.

5. e.g. Boissier 1873. Cf. Balsdon: 'In a developing society, the history of women is the history of their increasing emancipation' (1962: 14). This reflects the 'status of women' criterion often associated with colonisation and apparent in many nineteenth-century ethnographic accounts and travellers' tales – Bashar 1984. A typical example is 'Like most other savages the Australian looks upon his wife as a slave' (Eyre 1845: 208). Cf. Blok 1987: 6-11 on nineteenth-century reductive views of 'The Woman Question' in academic discourse. Gomme 1925 and Just 1975 both provide surveys of earlier views of the seclusion of women in classical Athens and their relation to this concept. That the idea persists in non-academic circles is suggested by the tone of western tabloid references to Islamic cultures, and in equivalent Islamic attacks on the west.

6. Boissier 1873 presumes the gross social inferiority of Roman to contemporary Parisian women. In his witty 1925 essay reviewing the so-called scholarly

163

evidence for normative misogyny and the seclusion of women in classical Athens, Gomme provides a fascinating array of quotes from the nineteenth century to his own time. It is a very interesting example of 'Re-readings'. On the issue of excess, even the urbane and tolerant Balsdon concedes that Roman women went too far: 'They acquired liberty; then, with the late Republic and the Empire, they enjoyed unrestrained licence' (1962: 15). The intermittent modern *topos* of the 'well-known emancipation' of Roman women is dealt with in Chapter 9.

7. Until the 1970s most works which purported to treat the Roman family concentrated on father-son relations (Dixon 1988: 47). Exceptions to the rule include Corbett's 1930 book on marriage, which gave considerable space to legal questions involving women. Loane 1938 mentions women workers and property-owners and Syme always noted politically inclined Roman women. Lacey's 1968 discussion of the role of women in Greek families was unusually thoughtful.

8. This theory vacuum and the difficulties of attacking a complex subject in isolation are evident in Gomme's lively 1925 article on the alleged sequestering of Athenian women (which one could contrast with Cohen's sophisticated treatment of the same subject 1991: 147-63) and Schulz's discussion of the principle of 'womanly weakness' in Roman law. Both scholars adopted radical and relatively enlightened approaches, but they now seem paternalistic and naive. Witness Gomme's *extraordinary* summary of the plot of *Epitrepontes*, in which his only allusion to the rape is a reference to Athenian liberality in the attendance of the girl at 'one of those nocturnal festivals from which modern parents would be so careful to guard their daughters'. Schulz's faith in social evolution (a progressively 'humanising tendency' in Roman law 1951: 180-91) now seems reductive. But the prize goes to Kitto for: 'Women went to the theatre – often to see plays which we should not allow our women to see' (1951: 234). In classical circles this quote has become the equivalent of the notorious prosecution argument in the *Lady Chatter-ley* case (about the jurors controlling their maidservants' reading!). It is a pity, because Kitto also makes astute comments about sources and how to read them (1951: 219-36).

9. Consider Loane's assumption that female Spanish ship-owners 'had prob-ably inherited ships from fathers and husbands' (1938: 23). Like Helen's automatic agreement with Gummerus 1916 that Roman women took no part in the physical production of bricks (1975: 113), it was presented uncritically and without support-ing documentation, as self-evident. At least Moeller 1976: 8, 102-3 and Peacock 1982: 8-9 felt the need to provide a flimsy rationale for their equation of economic significance and specialisation with male-domination of a trade. More signifi-cantly, Setälä 1998: 100 has revised the views on the active participation of female landowners in brick production which she expressed in her 1977 dissertation.

10. Culham 1987: 15-16 reaffirms empiricist 'historical' values over literary phantoms.

11. The resistance was more evident in conversation (or simple sneering) than in print. Prof. Lefkowitz published her views in non-academic media such as *Atlantic Monthly*. See also Lefkowitz 1986: 9-14, a more reasoned approach than Fleming's 1986 no-holds-barred attack, to which Skinner 1987b responded.

12. In the USA, publication in the key periodicals has great career implica-tions. Rabinowitz 1993: 3-4 quotes from a statement of editorial policy issued in 1987 by the prestigious *American Journal of Philology* (vii-viii) in response to a number of explicit complaints about its conservative policies. In 2000, Barbara Gold became the first female editor of this 120-year-old journal. In the meantime,

Marilyn Skinner edited another prestigious American classical journal, *Transactions of the American Philological Association*.

13. The 1973 special issue of *Arethusa* (6.1) was immensely successful and was followed by another (11.1 & 2) in 1978, then reprinted with some changes in book form as Peradotto & Sullivan 1984. See Skinner 1987b: 70-1; Fantham 1986: 3.

14. The 1982 edition of Lefkowitz & Fant was called *Women's Life in Greece and Rome: A Source Book in Translation*. The same title has been retained in the most recent revised edition.

15. e.g. Roberts 1977; Foley 1981; Cameron & Kuhrt 1983; Levy 1983; Schmitt Pantel 1990; Blok & Mason 1987; Skinner 1987c, a special issue of a journal, was produced as a small book. In 1984, a special issue of the leading international journal for documentary sources, *Zeitschrift für Papyrologie und Epigrafik* (*ZPE*) 55 (1984), on men and women in Greek cults, was edited by S.G. Cole.

16. The 1981 collection edited by Foley in book form as *Images of Women in Antiquity* was reprinted from a special issue of the journal *Women's Studies* (8.1 & 2). In 1990, David Konstan edited a special issue of *differences* (2.1), on sexualities in the ancient world.

17. Relevant books include Schaps 1979; Kampen 1981; Loraux 1981; Hallett 1984; Peppe 1984; Pomeroy 1984a; Gardner 1986; Lefkowitz 1986; Dixon 1988.

18. This spirit is evident in collections such as Pomeroy 1991a, Richlin 1992a, Rabinowitz & Richlin 1993, and has affected the collections of the 1990s on sexualities and difference (Hallett & Skinner 1997, Kampen 1996). In 1983, Sarah Pomeroy initiated a co-operative project, supported by the National Endowment of the Humanities, to develop curriculum materials for teaching the new subject, Women in Antiquity, in schools and universities. What's more, she accepted the practical burden of supplying the materials to all who sought them, even if that meant sending them to Australia! She deserves credit as a founding mother of the new-look wave of scholarship.

19. See *Helios* 17 (1990): 161-70 (Culham); 171-4 (Gamel); 175-85 (Richlin). Cf. Gold's treatment of the debate (1993: 76-7) and her own engagement with it in subsequent pages.

20. Cf. Sharrock 1997. Americans often act as a bridge for the groundbreaking ideas of French theorists (Gold 1993), but so do British scholars (Henderson 1989a & b, Wyke 1987a & b).

21. Cf. Delia 1991, Boatwright 1991.

22. I should explain to those readers unfamiliar with feminist theory that there are now many brands of academic feminism. Tour guides to the ones of likely interest to readers can be found in fairly accessible form in Gold 1993 and Richlin 1992b, emphasising debates about the female voice and the politics of representations of the female and the sexual. Both provide substantial bibliographies. Brown 1997 has a useful survey of feminist approaches to archaeology and art history in the Classics.

23. See Rabinowitz, Haley and Hallett, all in Rabinowitz & Richlin 1993.

24. Gold 1993: 87; 94-5 (n.17) on possible approaches to androcentric texts; on high-status women, see Pomeroy 1991b: xii-xiii.

25. The book *Who Killed Homer?* does not seem to have had an impact outside the USA. Fleming's distinction between half-baked crazies and the sound feminist scholars who first prove their expertise in traditional techniques (1986: 74) is unsubstantiated. It is no easier to find grounds for Fantham's more mildly expressed fears about specialist scholars: 'out of concern for the Latinless and

Greekless in Civilisation and Women's Studies programmes, they may cease to research and write using the ancient languages' (1986: 2).

26. Skinner 1987a: 183, quoting Nimis 1984.

27. Pomeroy: 'That more pages are devoted to Greek than to Roman women is a reflection of the state of contemporary scholarship on women in antiquity' (1991b: xiii). The term gynocentric, woman-centred, is used by Gold 1993.

28. The introductory essays by Culham 1987 and Richlin 1992b reflect the Roman interests of the editors, Skinner and Richlin herself. Cf. the content of Larsson Lovén & Strömberg 1998.

29. Blok 1987: 35. In contrast with the preceding 35 pages on various approaches to 'women in antiquity' – i.e. to debates about the 'status' of the women of classical Athens, she gives the most cursory consideration to the issue of assessing sources on Roman women.

30. See Dixon 1992a: 4, 19-21, 90 and Rawson 1974 for a review of these earlier trends and their moralising tendencies. Westrup 1943 and de Zulueta 1953: 34-7 are typical of the early stress on social evolution and common Indo-European (sometimes Indo-Germanic) ritual origins.

31. e.g. Hecker 1910 which, like most such studies, deals with the imperial period (beginning with the age of Augustus).

32. The assumption that the situation was historically unusual was reasonable. Hopkins 1978: 88 links it with the legal rights of Roman women to own property independent of the husband's control and to initiate divorce, which 'induced a level of female emancipation in the Roman elite which has rarely been matched in human history'. He argued that these rights also made women actors in élite marriage arrangement. For a contrary view of women's roles in marriage, based on readings of Latin love elegy, see Hallett 1973 and Lyne 1980: 17.

33. Carcopino is a great example of this tendency and d'Avino 1967 an even more hilarious instance. Unfortunately, both works are very readable and still far more likely to be picked up by the general public than more sober examples. See also the earlier scholarship deplored by Rawson 1974 and Blok 1987: 36-7.

34. Balsdon 1962 (e.g. 14-15), Crook 1967 and Gardner 1986 all refer to this 'emancipation' (Crook: 'independence') as a well-known phenomenon. Crook was the first, to my knowledge, to approach the concept with scholarly scepticism (1967: 103). Even in the 1980s, the term was still invoked, albeit carefully, by Schuller 1987 (e.g. 54) and Gardner felt obliged to devote a chapter to the subject (1986: 257-66).

35. e.g. Kampen 1996, Hallett & Skinner 1997, Clarke 1998, Braund 1989a.

36. Examples of the incorporation of issues of gender in Roman studies include the volumes edited by Rawson 1986a and Rawson & Weaver 1991, 1997 on aspects of the Roman family, Garnsey & Saller 1987 on Roman social history, Andreau & Bruhns 1990 on the family in antiquity, Corbier 2000 on adoption and fostering.

37. But some maintain the bias towards men of the Rome-based élite. In contrast with other published work on the same subjects, Wiedemann's 1987 study of relations between Roman parents and children not only marginalises mothers but has little on the training and jobs of female slaves and virtually nothing on female child-care workers.

38. Dixon 1992a: 20, 30-1.

39. Blok's comment on this phenomenon (1987: 36) is regrettably brief but very penetrating: 'The intervention of women in this public, formal domain was usually felt to be a lamentable abuse of social spheres and, more precisely, as the intrusion of the dangerous and intangible force of feminine sexual power.' Cf. Dixon 1992b: 210-16, Joshel 1997.

40. e.g. Dixon 1983 on Republican women; Hallett 1984 for a detailed elaboration of the role of women in the key political families supporting the ambitions of their fathers and brothers; Delia 1991, Virlouvet 1994 asserting Fulvia's essential femininity against ancient accusations; Boatwright 1992 on Matidia (the younger).

41. But see Hillard 1992, Richlin 1992c; Woodcock 1999.

42. e.g. Treggiari 1976, 1979; LeGall 1970; Chastagnol 1979.

43. e.g. Kampen 1981, Hallett 1984, Gardner 1986 and Dixon 1988. Specialist books of high quality had, of course, been known before this – e.g. Gagé 1963.

44. Gardner's summaries of earlier scholarship are scattered under topic headings and are chiefly concerned with juristic questions rather than wider social-historical aspects. Her claims (1986: 1-2, 257-65) about the nature and timing of published work on Roman women are not well supported, e.g. 'Women's studies made a relatively belated appearance among the concerns of ancient historians and classicists' (p. 1) – easily refuted by the many examples of Goodwater 1975 and Pomeroy 1984b *passim*, or cited by Kampen 1981: 16, n. 16.

45. Compare Fantham's 1986 emphasis on understanding the features of different *genres* before citing examples from them to illustrate an argument.

46. The quality of such work has improved greatly since Giacosa 1977 (beautiful pictures of coins and ludicrous text). When I was writing *The Roman Mother* in 1982-6, the chapter in Grant's 1954 book was the best guide to analysing the imagery of imperial women. Standard coin catalogues were sketchy on the significance even of male political imagery.

47. Books by Hahn (1994), Rose (1997), Bartman (1999) and Wood (1999) greatly alter the availability of authoritative, thematic collections of images which include or concentrate on the women of the imperial families of the first and second centuries.

48. Rabinowitz & Richlin 1993 summarises and typifies these trends.

49. Wyke 1987a&b, Hallett 1989 & 1993, Henderson 1989a&b, Gold 1993.

50. Like Rabinowitz & Richlin 1993, the book provides an excellent guide to modern theories of representation and readings and suggestions about how they might be applied in modified form to classical texts, together with extensive bibliographies of relevant works from the 1980s and 1990s.

51. e.g. Hind 1972 on the theatrical elements in Tacitus's account of Nero's matricide; Kaplan 1979 on women in Tacitus.

52. Livy certainly regarded himself as writing literature (Henderson 1989c). See Culham 1987: 15-16, quoted below, on the misconception that the narratives of historians in the ancient world were somehow more 'factual' than other narratives. Cf. the examples and bibliography of Lindsay 1994: 73-5 on the history of the 'evil tyrant' imported from Greek originals into Roman biography.

53. For criticisms from within, see Haley 1993, Passman 1993. On the meanings attributed to 'Greek love' by nineteenth-century British homosexual men, see Blanshard 2000.

2. Reading the *genre*

1. Cf. Golden 1992: 7: 'We speak of "the history of childhood"; but what we usually mean is the history of adults; attitudes towards children and their treatment of them.'

2. Cameron 1989b reviews the implications for ancient history. On masculinity as a social and discourse construction, see Cornwall & Lindisfarne 1994, Gleason 1995, Foxhall & Salmon 1998 and 1999, Walters 1997 and Williams 1999.

3. Bradley 1986, Dixon 1988: 30-2, Parkin 1992: 129-32.

4. But see now Mustakallio 1999.

5. Kampen 1981: 69-72 on iconographic evidence and how to read it; 116-17 on written testimony.

6. See Étienne 1973, Rousselle 1988.

7. J. Mitford 1961: 41, 124 and N. Mitford 1988: 96-7.

8. Cf. N. Mitford 1988: 96-7 on Linda, based on Jessica Mitford. The upper-class protagonist of Scott Fitzgerald's novel *The Beautiful and the Damned* is confronted as a World War I conscript with ordinary men at a human level: 'For the first time in his life he was in constant personal contact with the waiters to whom he had given tips, the chauffeurs who had touched their hats to him, the carpenter, plumbers, barbers and farmers who had previously been remarkable only in the subservience of their professional genuflexions' (1966: 268). The Opies, who compiled classic studies of modern English children's games and rituals, were repeatedly told by *teachers* that children no longer played games in school play-grounds, yet these adults were standing as they spoke in the midst of traditional games, their observation apparently shaped by their preconceived ideas about inactive modern children and the decline of tradition (Opie & Opie 1969).

9. Ironically, our knowledge of childbirth ritual derives largely from male doctors – nearly always of non-Italian origin – who might have attended some élite women in childbirth but whose writings are directed in part to female midwives. Visual depictions of childbirth are to be found on midwives' memorials and follow standard formats (Kampen 1981: 70-1). It would be interesting to know if they were executed by male or female artisans and whether they were modelled on scenes they had witnessed.

10. e.g. Davis 1983: 62-81 fleshes out the account of a trial at Rieux.

11. Cf. Richlin 1992b: xi.

12. Contrast Sullivan 1984 with Dixon 1991.

13. The literary style of Cornelia (second century BCE), mother of the Gracchi, was much admired e.g. Quintilian *Institutio oratoria* 1.1.6. Letters allegedly by her circulated in antiquity (Cic. *Brutus* 211) and extracts have been preserved (fragment 59, Marshall 1977). We have some of Cicero's letters to and about his wife Terentia, but his devoted secretary Tiro did not publish hers. Nero's mother Agrippina (the Younger) wrote an autobiography (Bradley 1978: 49-50). There was more than one (woman) poet with the name Sulpicia, but we have only a few poems = Tibullus 3.13-18 (Parker 1992b and other articles in the 86.2 issue of *Classical World*, Skoie 1998).

14. See Gold 1993: 76-7 and the references she gives. Cf. Zetzel's criticism (1980: 60-1) of those who treat Horace's first person satiric narrative 'not – as poetry, but as diary' and that journals and autobiographies are themselves creative narrative constructions (1980: 74, n.9).

15. Male authors who put words in the mouths of famous women like Lucretia, Cornelia (mother of the Gracchi) and Hortensia stressed their conventional virtues and reticence as part of their exemplary role (Valerius Maximus 6.1.1; 8.4.3; Quintilian *Institutio oratoria* 1.6). Today, ladylike tones continue to be praised and ignored in the corridors of power, while female voices that insist on being heard are somehow 'shrill' and 'strident'. Gold (1993: 79-81) summarises theorists who have concluded that inherited language is so heavily 'phallogocentric' that women must eschew it altogether.

16. Compare the questions posed by Rabinowitz for literary texts: 'Our questions have much in common with those of other feminist scholars working outside the modern period. How can we get at women's subjective experience? Can we separate it out from the male literary record? What can we assume about women writers? Whose language and conventions do they use when they do manage to speak?' (Rabinowitz 1993: 9)

17. Richlin 1983 cites variations on invective themes in graffiti, priapic verse, political iambics, satire and oratory. Compare Dixon 1997: 152-3 on the cross-media re-cycling of villains such as the wicked stepmother, the profligate son and the silly old man.

Introduction to Part II

1. Johns 1982: 15-35

2. Less commonly, such passages might be rendered in Italian. Cf. Sullivan 1991: 185 n.2 on Martial. In my own undergraduate days, I was often called upon by students of Ancient History to translate Suetonius *Tiberius* 42-5 (on the emperor's alleged activities in Capri), because the Loeb English became Latin at that point.

3. The decision by the National Archaeological Museum of Naples to display in 2000 the objects relegated since 1819 to the not-so-secret cabinet is allegedly opposed by the Vatican (Palmer 2000).

4. In *Ad Atticum* 2.1.5, Cicero boasts of his sallies in the senate to his enemy Clodius (all word-plays about Clodius' putative incest with his sister Clodia). On this subject see further Richlin 1983: 96-102 and Chapter 9.

5. Suetonius *Divus Iulius* 49.4; 51.

6. As in the modern world, where women are typed as 'sensual', 'sexy', 'hot', or in Christian writings which depict women as wicked, in both cases because men reify the responses of their bodies to women. The protagonist of the Canadian television series 'More Tears' described a young woman as 'unconscious of her own sexuality', reifying in her a quality which was actually something about himself.

7. The many exciting books which have appeared in the last fifteen years on approaches to Roman material (there are far more on Greek sexualities) often have reviews of scholarship in the first chapter. A good sample includes Richlin 1992a (and the introduction to the 1992 reprint of her 1983 book), Hallett & Skinner 1997, Kampen 1996, Clarke 1998, Koloski-Ostrow & Lyons 1997. Many books on feminism, women and masculinities include important treatments of sex, the body and queer readings of classical texts.

8. Cf. the first chapters of Wiseman 1985, Clarke 1998.

9. Johns 1982: 115-42; Clarke 1998: 195-240, esp. on representations of copulation. Sculptured nudes were ubiquitous in public spaces and in homes, representing the classical association of nudity with divine and heroic representations; cf. Brown 1997: 14-18. In the modern west, by contrast, the naked human body is sexualised in almost every context.

10. Scholarly views are mixed on surviving statues of respectable matrons posing semi-draped as Venus, their heads realistically depicted with elaborate hairstyles, their bodies generic and youthful (d'Ambra 1993).

11. Masturbation does not figure at all in Australian teen soaps, which include sexualities and related issues (including many that deviate from so-called mainstream discourse) and terms like 'wanker' and 'tosser' are common insults, but it would be a mistake to conclude that masturbation is a particularly problematic category in adult or adolescent discourse.

3. Representations of female sexualities

1. The beloved has stock physical features – gleaming hair, expressive eyes, lovely arms – but even they are not described in recognisable detail – Richlin 1983: 45-7. Purists define the *genre* strictly by metre, not content (Parker 1992a: 91). Modern discussions of 'Latin love poetry' frequently include Catullus, who is credited with introducing a narrative and a regular love-object ('Lesbia'). His poetry and responses to it are discussed in some detail in Chapter 9. Quintilian ranked Tibullus, Propertius, Ovid and Gallus (whose work has not survived) as proponents of the *genre* – *Institutio oratoria* 10.1.98. Cf. Ovid *Amores* 3.9 on the death of Tibullus, *c.* 19 BCE.

2. Foucault himself has rightly been criticised for neglecting the female perspective of sexualities and for collapsing the whole of Greco-Roman culture into an oversimplified model – Richlin 1991, and see the introduction (esp. xiv-xvi) to the 1992 reprint of Richlin 1983; Skinner 1996.

3. e.g. *volgei nescia* (not knowing the crowd) of Aurelia Philematium, *CIL* 6.9499. See Lattimore 1942: 277-9, Williams 1958 for other motifs in epitaphs praising virtuous women.

4. See Chapters 5 and 9.

5. e.g. Cicero *Ad familiares* 8.7.2 (from Caelius); *Ad Atticum* 1.18.3. The more formal and guarded letters of Seneca and Pliny, intended for publication, are less fruitful sources of sexual gossip – and, of course, much less amusing. Cf. Richlin 1983: 84.

6. See Lefkowitz & Fant 1982, ch.11 for family inscriptions, ch.12 for inscriptions to benefactors and women with named occupations. Cf. Lattimore 1942, ch. 8. Women such as Statia and Petronia (*CIL* 4.3678, 3683) are mentioned respectfully in the political graffiti from Pompeii (Brion 1960: 139), but others very disrespectfully on the walls of workshops and pubs, e.g. *CIL* 4.8442; *CIL* 13.10018, no. 95 (Ostian pubs. Cf. Kampen 1981: 111 n). Cf. Richlin 1983: 82-3, d'Avino 1964: 16-19, 30-2, 41-59 (Pompeii).

7. Cf. Cicero's comment that producing legitimate children (i.e., having conjugal sex) is perfectly honourable, but it is not an acceptable topic of conversation – *Ad familiares* 9.2.2; *De officiis* 1.128.

8. Notably, Sullivan 1991, ch. 5 (esp. pp. 198-202) and Richlin 1983.

9. Cf. Rundell 1979, Skinner 1983 and see Chapter 9 below.

10. See Cicero *Brutus* 200, 290 for the excited anticipation of a noted orator's forensic appearance, *De oratore* 2.193-6 for a comparison of the actor and orator.

11. Richlin 1983: 96-104 on invective generally. See Geffcken 1973; Nisbet 1961: 192-7; Lenaghan 1969: 162 on Ciceronian invective techniques and *topoi* and cautions against believing it. Pliny *Letters* 6.33 describes an audience (many, he claims, with a personal interest in the controversial inheritance case) who gathered at one of his own appearances. The same letter reveals his use in the enclosed speech (now lost) of two stereotypes: the wicked stepmother and the silly old man (who falls in love with a gold-digger).

12. A successful Australian scriptwriter sparked off heated correspondence by quoting the dictum that 'nothing is more boring than a happy marriage' (D. Cox, November 1999, Sydney Morning Herald *Guide*). See below on conjugal sex.

13. Juvenal 6. 327-34 for abandonment – inflamed by wine and dancing – at the important all-female gathering to honour the Good Goddess (Bona Dea); 6.306-13, where women have sex and urinate (the two activities are almost equated) beside a statue of Pudicitia, the personification of female chastity and propriety. In both instances, Juvenal exploits the shock value of juxtaposing revered symbols of respectable female ideals with wanton behaviour (compare Early Modern claims that witches had sex on church altars or urinated in holy fonts).

14. Adams 1982, Richlin 1983. A glance at Richlin's critical bibliography of scholarly approaches to Roman satire (1983: 237-8 nn. 25-6), provides an amusing reminder of what has on occasion passed for social comment and literary analysis in the classics. By contrast, Sullivan's 1991 psychoanalytic reading of Martial's sexual attitudes (ch. 5) and Richlin (1983) combine a breadth of philological expertise with sophisticated application of modern theories.

15. Such readings, derived ultimately from the ideas of Jung, Freud and Frazer, have become entrenched in approaches to Greek myth. On the whole, Roman historians have taken a more empiricist approach, avoiding the analysis of symbolism and the unconscious. But see Africa 1978; Hallett 1984, 1989.

16. After Augustan legislation, adultery was strongly penalised – Edwards 1993: 34-62; Treggiari 1991: 60-80. Penetrative sex with free-born boys and young men had always been frowned on but legal penalties are not certain – Skinner 1997: 11. And see Chapter 4 below.

17. Valerius Maximus 6.1.13 and see above all Richlin 1981 for the most horrific self-help punishments and their analysis. Successive imperial legislation insisting on the prosecution of adulterous wives by husbands suggests that it was not an unforgivable offence – Ulpian (*Digest* 48.5.4 *pr.* 16 (15).5 and 2.3 for exceptions. Cf. Pliny *Letters* 6.31.4-6 and Sherwin-White 1966: 393-4.

18. Lesbia – Catullus 58.4-5; women having penetrative sex (apparently by means of an elongated clitoris!) with other women – Juvenal 6.307-311; Martial 1.90; 3.72.6; 7.67.2-3; the noble Eppia's elopement with a gladiator – Juvenal 6.103-113; older women soliciting younger lovers – Horace *Epodes* 8 & 12, Martial 3.32; 3.93; 10.90.

19. The legal status and social standing of the two women was, of course, very different. If convicted (we do not know whether she was), Neaira was liable to execution for passing herself and her daughter off as Athenian citizens (pseudo-Demosthenes 59). On claims that Clodia 'vanished' after the trial of 56, see Skinner 1983 esp. pp. 282-3, and Chapter 9 below.

20. See Plutarch *Cicero* 26.6. When badgered by the arrogant Metellus with the typical aristocratic taunt, 'Who is your father?' (cf. Horace *Sermones* 1.6.29), Cicero responded, 'In your case, your mother has made that a difficult question to answer.' His younger friend Licinius Crassus was 'Axios'. Cicero made a play on this term ('worthy') which depended on the assumption that Crassus was not his father's child – Plutarch *Cicero* 25.

21. Treggiari 1969: 211-12 on the law. Men might also be freed to marry their (female) owners. Literary references suggest that some male slaves could also profit from their sexual appeal to their owners – Petronius *Satyricon* 63.3, 69.2-75. Seneca, *Controversiae* 4 *per.* 10 implies that the sexual 'duties' might continue after manumission, in spite of the legal ruling e.g. Callistratus *Digest* 38.1.38 *pr.*

22. See Braund 1992 and note 35 below on the tradition of anti-marriage invective which, always presented in our surviving sources from the male perspective, amounts to anti-wife invective. That slippage was common in western popular culture (particularly US media) before the modern women's movement

171

had an impact on public media representations. Juvenal mentions unmarried girls incidentally, as potential wives, but generally Roman moral discourse ignores the young girl as a type and 'Roman women' equates with 'Roman matrons' for all practical purposes.

23. Juvenal 6.254 on the female gladiator; 6.349 on *libido* as driving the modern woman.

24. Cf. Hesiod, fragment 275, Ovid, *Metamorphoses* 3.316-38.

25. Geddes 1975; Dean-Jones 1992; Hanson 1992. Aristotle is the obvious reference-point for ideas about women's poorer self-control and weaker judgement e.g. *Politica* 1260a14, 1259b32. Cf. *De generatione animalium* 7650.

26. Rousselle 1988: 27-31.

27. *De Catilinae coniuratione* 24.3 See Chapter 9 below for a more detailed discussion of this passage.

28. As so often with Martial, one poem can be countered with another. In 11.50.11-12, the poet urges his mistress to comply with all his desires because he denies her nothing: *nil tibi, Phylli, nego; nil mihi, Phylli, nega.*

29. For example, Martial presents opposing views of the wife's duty to provide her anus to her husband in 11.104 and 12.96 on the superior attractions of boys (esp. lines 7 ff.), a stock theme in Greek love poetry.

30. Richlin 1983: 69. Cf. Martial 9.67 with Catullus 56 in which the poet comes upon a slave-boy masturbating and rapes him anally. Also meant to be a good joke.

31. Dio 60.22 (Messalina and Mnester); Horace *Epodes* 8; 12; Petronius *Satyricon* 134-8; Martial 3.32; 3.93; 9.37; 11.29 (desiring older women).

32. esp. Horace *Epodes* 8. Cf. Richlin 1983: 109-16; Sullivan 1991: 200-2.

33. Cf. Martial 10.90; *App. Vergil.* 83 (Bucheler, pp. 151-3 Oxford – text + trans. Richlin 1983: 115). It is normal in Greek and Latin lyric poetry for the male lover-poet to give presents to the male or female beloved for sexual favours and attention. Ovid's *Metamorphoses* is replete with rapes and attempted rapes of women by Apollo and Jupiter in particular (Richlin 1992d) and see again Catullus 56.

34. Sullivan employs a (pre-Kristeva) Freudian psychoanalytic reading. He relates it specifically to literary references to cunnilingus and to visual references to women climbing on top of men for sex. He also cites Martial's horror of older women e.g. Sullivan 1991: 202.

35. The play would have been performed in the late third or early second century BCE. Juvenal's sixth satire (early second century CE) begins with an adjuration to a friend not to marry, then proceeds to pillory different types of wives. The younger Seneca's attack on marriage has a similar, though less physically explicit, series of horror stories. Fragments have been preserved by St Jerome, who extracted quotes from it (along with other anti-marriage classical works) into a Christian diatribe, *Adversus Iovinianum*. On the Greco-Roman anti-marriage, anti-woman *genre*, particularly its rhetorical aspects, see Courtney 1980: 252 and his discussion of Seneca and Juvenal 6, pp. 259-62. A forthcoming collection, edited by W. Smith, explores the use of the theme in anti-marriage classical and mediaeval Latin texts.

36. According to Aulus Gellius *Noctes Attica* 1.6.2, it was Quintus Caecilius Metellus Numidicus, censor in 102 BCE, but it was probably Quintus Caecilius Metellus Macedonicus, censor 131 BCE and father of four sons, who gave the original speech (McDonnell 1987) which Augustus revived. Dio 56.8.2 has a slightly different version of Augustus' act.

37. Williams 1958: 24-5 on the compliant wife (= *morigera, obsequens* etc.).

38. Ovid, *Art of Love* 3.769-808 on showing off your best features, including

3.797-803 on faking it, all but completes the book devoted to amorous advice for women.

39. Fotis is forward but serves Lucius. On the compliant wife, see again Williams 1958: 24-5, 29; on mistresses and sexual demands, see Ovid *Amores* 3.14.17-26.

40. Hallett 1973 is one of the best elaborations of this theme.

41. Catullus wrote *c.* 58 BCE. Ovid was exiled under Augustus *c.* 8 CE at the age of 50 for an offence which in part concerned his poetry (*Tristia* 2.207, 211-12). Cf. *Amores* 3.9 (composed *c.* 19 BCE) and Quintilian *Institutio oratoria* 10.1.98 on the relative ages and status of the key elegiac love poets.

42. See above, at the beginning of '*Genre* and desire', for his description of Corinna's body *Amores* 1.5.13-26.

43. Cf. *Amores* 1.5.13-16; cf. *Met.* 17, where Photis covers her pubic area with her hand from form rather than modesty.

44. Cf. Richlin 1983: 47: 'It is as if there were a blank space in the middle of the woman.'

45. Significantly, Photis' lovely hair is the physical feature which receives most of Apuleius' attention – *Metamorphoses* 2.9,16. The narrator Lucius is a self-confessed hair freak (2.9), but in general the loosing of hair is a feature of many sexual scenes in literature (Morton 1999). I can find no correspondending dishevelment in visual depictions of copulation on wall-paintings and dinner-ware. In those, the woman's hair is done up and remains enviably neat and contained, however vigorous her activity.

46. In Catullus 61.97-106, the reference to the husband's eagerness for the bride's nubile nipples is paired with a sensuous image of his insinuating himself in her embrace, like a vine entwining a tree.

47. The wedding hymn concludes with the call to the bridesmaids to close the bedroom door on the newlyweds (Catullus 61.221-8).

48. Scholars who argue for the essentially cold character of Roman marriage include Lyne 1980, esp. 8-13, Hallett 1973, 1984, Bradley 1985, esp. 86-91.

49. Seneca *De matrimonio* 84-5. He elaborates 81-3 on the delusional/demented nature of physical passion and gives cautionary examples of husbands who were ludicrously attached to their wives; Tacitus *Annals* 15.63 for Seneca's love for his wife.

50. Cf. Cicero, *Ad familiares* 14.2.3, 14.3.5; Statius *Silvae* 3.5, e.g. 18-39 plots the course of his love for his wife, when his heart was transfixed by Venus. Ovid wrote from exile of hallucinating his wife's beloved image in illness – *Tristia* 3.3.

51. Sulpicia's extant poems are included in published versions of Tibullus, bk. 3. [4.], but editors differ on whether they classify only 3.13-18 [4.7-12] as being by her. See Treggiari 1991: 121-2, 302-3. Poem 3.12 [4.6] assumes marriage as the outcome of the love. Martial also refers (10.35.38) to a Sulpicia who wrote chaste verses, apparently about her husband, in the late first century CE, but they have not survived. For more on Sulpicia, see the special issue of *Classical World* 86.2 (1992) and Hallett 1992: 341, 349-53; Skoie 1998.

52. Ovid *Fasti* 4.1-164 is an elaborate aetiology. Only lines 133-56 detail the rituals – Fantham 1998: 115-23.

53. Valerius Maximus 2.1.6.

54. Catullus 23, 39, 71, 97; Martial 3.17, 3.98, 6.74, 6.93, 7.55 provide a random sample. Cf. Sullivan 1991: 200, 202, 209 (Martial on women and effete men), Richlin 1984 (women), Barrett 1984 (Martial on Jews): 42 & 45 on oral sex and smells. Individual satirists vary. Lucilius (second century BCE), the avowed model of Roman satirists, whose work survives only in fragments, appears to have concentrated on physical and political quirks. Horace and Persius, who feature physical and sexual oddities, supply less gruesome detail than Catullus, Juvenal or Martial (fewer exudations etc.).

55. Juvenal 6.431-3 (vomiting), 455-6 (correcting her husband), 306-12 (peeing and copulating by the shrine of Chastity).

56. This in spite of the conventional adoption of a fictive first-person persona in certain *genres*: the lyric poet typically represents himself as an impoverished bohemian who cannot match the gifts of a rich rival, the satirist is always at the mercy of patrons and the novelists seem to present themselves as shabby-genteel. Some argue that the love-poet persona is young. These conventions do not run deep: the dominant voice and perspective is consistently the one I have characterised.

57. Catullus varies this rule by naming a well-born boy-object of his erotic interests – Williams 1968: 554-6, Wiseman 1985: 130-1.

58. Richlin (1983: 69) would put it more strongly: 'The sexuality of the humorist constitutes the definition of normal sexuality; the sexuality of women and of adult male pathic homosexuals is by definition abnormal.'

4. Rape in Roman law and myth

1. Evans Grubbs 1989, Joshel 1992b, Beard 1999, Mustakallio 1999, Deacy & Pierce 1997, Dougherty 1998. This is by no means an exhaustive list of approaches and works since 1982. I have added few references to the original treatment, to preserve its own historical integrity. Unfortunately, I have had little difficulty updating the more depressing references to contemporary attitudes.

2. Joplin 1990: 52-3. And see d'Ambra 1993: 87-8.

3. Ogilvie 1965: 477 traces the development of this political aspect of the story, which was not embedded in the earliest versions.

4. A French soldier's disrespect (the actual offence varies in traditional accounts) towards a Palermo bride sparked the Sicilian revolt against Angevin rule in 1282. Stories abound about the evil tyrant/general etc. who does not honour the modesty of local (esp. noble) virgins and matrons: e.g. Herodotus 5.18-22 (Macedon). Cicero accused Verres of such behaviour in Asia Minor (Cicero *In verrem* II.1 26.65-7; cf. *De provinciis consularibus* 6, of Piso in Byzantium) and biographers regularly attributed it to emperors, e.g. Suetonius *Divus Augustus* 69, *Tiberius* 45. Cf. Cicero *De republica* 2.63, Diodorus 12.24 and see Ogilvie 1965: 477. On the 'wicked tyrant' theme in general, see Lindsay 1994.

5. Cf. Yalman 1963.

6. Plutarch *Solon* 23.1-2. Modern equivalents include the many Bengali women, raped during the war with Pakistan, who were subsequently repudiated by their husbands in accordance with local custom and Islamic law which stress the fact of adultery without making any allowance for circumstances such as the use of force or the woman's resistance. Such women may not remarry and, if they continue living, are outcasts, for society has no place for them. Mother Teresa succeeded in persuading some husbands to accept their despoiled wives regardless and described their grudging agreement as 'beautiful'. My own work with rape victims and wider reading makes it clear that women internalise such judgements even in 'sexually liberated' cultures and often conceal from husbands and family the fact that they have suffered rape.

7. Livy 1.58.7 (Lucretia) and 1.58.9 where the men echo her distinction between the fault of her body and her blameless mind.

8. Ogilvie 1965: 225.

9. In practice, such prosecutors were probably motivated by the hope of a share in the property which was confiscated by the state after the conviction of the person charged. For futher information on 'Augustan' legislation (inspired by him but sponsored also by others), see Treggiari 1991: 60-80:

10. Ulpian at *Digest* 48.5.30 (29).9; Modestinus at *Digest* 48.5.40 (39).

11. M. Hale: *Pleas of the Crown* I p. 629 (London 1778) On this, see Scutt 1976: 622-3. Compare the amendment to chapter 6 of the Swedish *Strafferetten*, cited therein.

12. Happily, this passage is now (2001) inaccurate. I leave it here to remind readers, especially those of the younger generation, that this was a battle we were still fighting in 1981 in Scandinavian and English-speaking jurisdictions. On a visit to Israel Dec./Jan. 1981/2, when religious reactionaries held the balance of power, and women had suffered significant consequences, I was impressed to learn that a scholar had unearthed an ancient ruling that the woman could control sexual intercourse within marriage because she knew when she was able to have it (an obvious reference to menstruation). As a result, Israeli men were actually in jail for raping their wives.

13. Plutarch *Cato maior* 21; 24 on his own visits to a female slave.

14. The references are all from later, imperial jurists: Marcianus *Digest* 48.6.3.4 and see Ulpian *Digest* 48.5.30.9, Paul *Digest* 2.26.12 and the Justinianic *Codex (CJ)* 9.20.1. Ulpian *Digest* 48.6.6 seems to imply the victim must be free-born. Cf. the literary reference to the law by the rhetorician Quintilian (*Institutio oratoria* 4.2.69) and see McGinn 1998.

15. Ulpian tells us at *Digest* 3.1.1.5 that the rule was formulated because a particularly bad (*improbissima*) woman, Carfania, had annoyed the praetor with her disrespectful interruptions in his court. See Chapter 6 below.

16. Justinian *Institutes* 4.4.9. It depended also on the position of the person who offered the insult, e.g. it was worse for a highly-born woman to be struck by a person of low station than by a social equal.

17. These notions are now familiar, although they are not necessarily incorporated in statutes. The 'Michigan model legislation' was much discussed at the time – Scutt 1976.

18. *Digest* 47.10.15. In the Republic, Cicero had trivialised his client's participation in the pack-rape of a pantomime actress *Pro Plancio* 30-1.

19. This severity was only slightly mitigated by subsequent rulings, e.g. an amendment of 349 CE introduced the possibility of loss of civil status and property as an alternative to death for the *raptor* – *Codex Theodosianus (CTh)* 9.24, which includes its 326 CE addition. In general, the terms were very harsh – slave offenders or accomplices were burnt to death.

20. Ulpian *Digest* 48.5.2 esp. 7 ff. (prosecution by an 'outsider', '*extraneus*'); *Digest* 48.5.30(29).5-8 (immunity from prosecution after five years).

21. *maxime cum virginitas vel castitas corrupta restitui non potest.* Justinianic *Codex (CJ)* 9.13.1. An Australian judge, defending a controversial sentence, explained judicial reasoning in terms of a hierarchy of harm to hypothetical rape victims and suggested the crime would not be as traumatic for a married woman as for a nun. The Almighty did not figure in his equation, but it is interesting that certain features recur. The voice of a radical nun was among the protests.

22. *Digest* 48.5 contains a number of quotations about the law. Papinian (48.5.6) lays out the definition clearly. See Treggiari 1991: 62-3.

23. Until recently, it was theoretically possible in common law countries for a man to sue someone who had seduced his wife, his daughter or his maidservant for the loss of domestic services – Winsmore v Greenbank (1745) Willes 577, 125 ER 1330. The object of such a suit was to claim monetary compensation for this 'loss'. Apparently a despoiled daughter or maid was so great a social outcast that she could not even perform household tasks – her productive labour was linked to her chastity.

24. See now Evans Grubbs 1989, who includes examples from modern societies.

25. *Codex Theodosianus* 9.24.1 (320-326 CE). Cf. n. 15 above and see Chapter 6.

26. 'Forcible and Statutory Rape', *Yale Law Journal* 1952: 76. Compare Scutt 1979.

27. See Hopkins 1965a, Shaw 1987 on the age of Roman girls at first marriage.

28. The Roman legal code was compiled in the sixth century CE under the emperor Justinian as the *Digest* or *Pandects*. In addition, the shorter and more accessible *Institutes* contained official prefaces to topic-headings, stating 'Justinianic' positions on certain issues, such as childbearing and adultery, which had been modified from their pre-Christian legacy.

29. Honorius and Theodosius, 420 CE – *Codex Theodosianus* 9.25.3 (trans. M. Pharr Davis/D. Pharr).

30. Hughes 1978.

31. Consider the provision that the children of an unlawful marriage contracted between a ravisher and his victim and kept secret for five years would be recognised as legitimate (*CTh* 9.24.3) and the exclusion (mentioned above) of some rape victims from succession (*CTh* 9.24.3).

32. Fortunately, we have won the major legal battles in many countries now. I have excised much of my original conclusion but am bound to admit with shame that an Australian feminist of my generation publicly used the 'asking for it' argument in relation to a controversial sexual harassment scandal and elaborated in print the principle that young women must take some responsibility for intrusive male responses to their dress. Victorian principles of female decorum and masculine *infirmatas sexus* can still be invoked in the most surprising quarters.

5. Woman as symbol of decadence

1. And compare lines 1-24.

2. See Dixon 1988: 30, 39 (n. 44), for a litany of famous mothers – Cornelia, mother of the Gracchi; Hortensia, daughter of the orator Hortensius; Aurelia, mother of Julius Caesar.

3. Suetonius *Divus Augustus* 34, Dio 56.1-10, who also provide some idea of the content of the legislation, probably the Julian laws on adultery and the Papian-Poppaean laws on marriage. Augustus was the force behind them and he claimed credit for them (*Res Gestae* 6, 8.5) as part of his programme of moral restoration. The laws rewarded marriage and parenthood and imposed certain inheritance restrictions on the childless and celibate. See Rotondi 1922: 445-6 for a collection of ancient sources, Csillag 1976 for an extended but flawed discussion, Gardner 1986: 127-32 for a summary.

4. Cf. Green 1967: 115, on Juvenal 4.153-4. Gold 1998 suggests that the whole satire is less about women than men and fears about boundaries.

5. Similarly, Pliny the Younger exploited the cultural stereotype of the wicked stepmother in court (*Letters* 6.33) but praised friends like Fannia, step-mother of Helvidius Priscus (*Letters* 9.13).

6. Pliny *Letters* 1.14.4, 6; Tacitus *Annals* 3.55; 16.5. And see Braund 1989c.

7. or 64 BCE to 12 CE, according to Syme 1964: 13-14.

8. Cf. Livy 39.6.7 and Pliny *Natural History* 34.14, based on L. Piso fragment 34 (Peter). Compare Walbank, 1979: 500 on Polybius 31.25.3.

9. e.g. Valerius Maximus 4.4. *passim*, esp. 4.4.9 on the Aemilii Tuberones. Cf. Plutarch *Aemilius Paulus* 5, who invokes this noble family as an example of brotherly harmony and altruism as well as simplicity and explicitly contrasts them with the acquisitive brothers of his own day.

10. Sallust *Bellum Iugurthinum* 84-5 *et passim*. Compare the portrait of the sluggish aristocrat Spurius Albinus, 44.

11. e.g. Tacitus *Annals* 1.2-4 on senatorial acquiescence. Cf. 3.55 on the century between Actium (31 BCE) and Galba (69 CE).

12. Lind 1979 esp. pp. 7-9 (n. 2) for examples. Lind set himself the difficult task of deciding *when* the decline took place – cf. pp. 10, 41! For a better discussion of the issues, see Edwards 1993.

13. On food, see e.g. Plutarch *Cato maior* 18-19; Pliny *Natural History* 10.71.139 ff.; Tacitus *Annals* 3.55; Juvenal *Satire* 11. Cf. Hudson 1989, Dupont 1990.

14. Tacitus' description of marriage customs 18-19 and the rearing of children (20) is pervaded with 'noble savage' imagery and the contrast with the decadent, sophisticated moral laxity of Rome. Cf. Juvenal's association of simplicity with goodness, 6.287-295.

15. The poetry of Burns is exceptional in this.

16. The nymph Thetis bore Achilles, the greatest warrior of the Greeks who besieged Troy. His killing of the opposing champion Hector spelt defeat for the Trojans. Venus was the mother of the Trojan Anchises and grandmother of Aeneas, who ultimately founded the site which became Rome.

17. Hallett 1973 first suggested that the elaborated use of this conceit by Roman love poets was a conscious subversion of the dominant spirit of the early principate. On interpretations of Juvenal's over-sophisticated evocation of the Golden Age, 6.1-20, see Anderson 1956, Mason 1963: 137-8. Singleton 1972: 165 sees 'a serious purpose behind the undoubted Juvenalian wit'. The jury is still out on precisely why Ovid was exiled in 8 CE, but by his own account poetry (generally thought to be the *Art of Love*) played its part – *Tristia* 2.207, 211-12. See Bauman 1992: 119-24, Fantham 1998: 38-42.

18. The cult of Venus Genetrix, ancestress of Augustus and of the Roman founders, was promoted by the first *princeps* (emperor). See Zanker 1988: 195-201. Vergil's *Aeneid*, which became Rome's prestigious answer to Homer's epics, charted the Odysseus-like wanderings of Aeneas and a group of fellow-Trojans from the Hellespont to Italy. Whenever Aeneas faltered, his divine mother Venus appeared to remind him of his destiny.

19. *Nux* ll. 23-4. The poem appears in G. Baligan's *Appendix Ovidiana* (Bari, 1955). See Nardi 1971: 232 for other editions.

20. *Heroides* 11.37-44.

21. Tacitus *Annals* 14.63. Cf. Gallivan 1974 for ways in which Tacitus emphasises the pathos and innocence of Claudia Octavia. It makes a nice counter to *Domitian* 22, where Suetonius reports the rumour (subsequently accepted as history by many scholars) that Flavia Julia died as the result of an abortion forced on her by her uncle, the emperor Domitian, to conceal their incestuous affair.

22. In a private communication, A.T. Dolan of LaSalle University has noted the connection in classical and early Christian writings between *'porneia'* (illicit sexual activity, especially adultery) and abortion.

23. Tacitus *Annals* 3.22. See Kleinfeller (1931), *RE* 7: 952 for later legislation on the subject.

24. See Sullivan 1984 on ancient misogyny, Cohen 1991: 138-43 for interesting examples from modern societies. Pliny the Elder's claim (*Natural History* 10.172) that, while men thought up lots of other wicked crimes, women invented abortion, has interesting parallels with the belief among some Mexican men that the women of their culture use an 'abortion tree' to limit childbearing – Browner 1986: 718-19. See Richlin 1997 on Pliny's inconsistent approach to abortifacients generally.

25. On women's life-chances in antiquity, see Salskov Roberts 1977, Parkin 1992: 15-17, 102-5.

26. Tacitus singled out for mention the fact that Germans did *not* expose children – *Germania* 19.5. Cf. *Historia* 5.5 on Jews. Although only Roman fathers had the legal right (which they did not commonly exercise in practice) to execute *adult* children, the paternal right to expose babies was standard in the Greek-speaking world – see Golden 1981. Tacitus' apparent surprise that the Jews did not practise infant exposure may imply that it was the Mediterranean norm.

27. e.g. Seneca *Ad Helviam* 16.3 (under Nero); Pliny *Letters* 4.15.3; Tacitus *Annals* 3.25-26 specifically on the 'avoidance' of parenthood in the late first and early second centuries CE. Horace *Odes* 3.6 speaks more generally of current immorality (more than a century earlier). All generalise about their contemporaries and elaborate on their selfishness.

28. Dixon 1992a: 119-23. See Hopkins 1965b (on methods of family limitation). On upper-class fertility, Hopkins 1966, Parkin 1992: 99, 115, 119-20.

29. Pliny *Letters* 8.10, 8.11 and 10.2.

30. Plutarch *Romulus* 22.3. The reference by Dionysius of Halicarnassus 2.25.6 to *'phthora somatos'* (defilement/destruction of the body) as a ground for divorce in early Rome has been interpreted variously to mean (the wife's) adultery or abortion.

31. Cicero *Pro Cluentio* 31-2.

32. Tryphoninus *Digest* 48.19.39. Cf. 47.11.4, recorded by Marcianus and referring to a rescript by Severus and Caracalla endorsing the decision by 'an official' (*praeses*).

33. *Digest* 47.11.4: 'for it would seem unworthy that she should have defrauded her husband of children without incurring a penalty' (*indignum enim videri potest impune eam maritum liberis fraudasse*).

34. Nardi 1971: 305-15. The first-century CE philosopher Musonius Rufus articulated Stoic reservations about abortion (as he did about infant exposure) and claimed that some Greek jurisdictions had legislated on the subject – Frag. 15a (Hense). See Hopkins 1965b.

35. See articles on this subject by Hopkins 1965b, Nardi 1971, Eyben 1980-1981, Clark and King 1994. Ancient failure to distinguish clearly between contraception and abortion does not help the population scholar. See Hopkins 1983a: 225-6, Parkin 1992: 119-33 on possible methods, including exposure.

36. Cf. *medicamenta*, Cicero *Pro Cluentio* 32.

37. Quintilian *Decl. min.* 327. The position is not helped by the highly improbable fictitious setting of this example from a rhetorical school of an unusually devoted stepmother who protects the rights of her stepchildren in this way. On the general vagueness about the contraceptive/abortive distinction, see Hopkins 1965b: 136.

38. e.g. 24.28, where he passes on 'what people say', that rubbing juice from the great cedrus (probably a kind of juniper) on the penis during intercourse but before ejaculation causes an 'abortive portent' (*portentum abortivum*). Courtney 1980: 341 (on Juvenal 6.595-7) points out that this passage is probably derived from Dioscorides 1.77.2.

39. Nardi 1971: 239-40 on the nurses, midwives and '*sagai*', healers with magical associations in certain cases. Some did write books on the subject of midwifery (which might have included associated subjects, like procured abortion or gynaecological ailments) – Parker 1992a. See e.g. Pliny *Natural History* 20.226, 28.81 on famous examples. Rousselle 1988: 24-6, Richlin 1997 stress women's roles in monitoring their own health.

40. Seneca *Ad Helviam* 16.2-3.

41. Seneca *Ad Helviam* 3: 'Brought up well in an old-fashioned, strict home, you were not influenced by the desire – which affects even good women – to copy the bad.' Upper-class men who choose in the early empire to have several children are also praised for standing out from the general practice of the age – e.g. Tacitus *Annals* 2.37 on Hortensius Hortalus; Pliny *Letters* 4.15.3 on Asinius Rufus. And cf. Polybius 31.25.2-3 on Scipio Aemilianus as a youth.

42. Cf. Sherwin-White 1966: 207, on Pliny *Letters* 3.1.5: 'Worthy wives were a feature of the times ... despite the strictures of Martial, and the suspicions of Carcopino, who takes the satirists at their face value, *Daily Life*, 84-100'. I would argue that the 'worthy wives' are equally skewed by *genre*.

43. See esp. Dean-Jones 1994, King 1993, 1998. Ancient medical works were not value-free (Rousselle 1988: 44-5 on Soranus and Galen makes *that* clear enough), but their treatment-orientation distinguishes them from the incidental references by poets and historians to the body as an emblem of contemporary decline.

44. Knox 1995: 266. The example he cites of the literary evidence is *Nux* 23.

45. Neither Nardi (1971: 199-201) nor Hopkins endorses such silliness, but even Hopkins accepts the improbable notion (which has no evidentiary basis) that married women at Rome (rather than their husbands) determined their own fertility: 'Some upper class women had children; others restricted their fertility' (1983a: 95). Cf. Dixon 1988: 91-5. Rousselle 1988: 44-5 seems to accept ancient moralising as evidence of women's behaviour. Cf. Parkin 1992: 127-8, Richlin 1997.

46. Syme's ironic comment 1986: 168 ('Women have their uses for historians') was read as offensively misogynist by most US participants in an electronic discussion on the ANAHITA network in December 1995. The context was his analysis of certain books in Tacitus' annalistic account of imperial history: '[Women] offer relief from warfare, legislation and the history of ideas; and they enrich the central theme of social history, if and when enough evidence is available.'

47. See again Nardi's collection of scholarly opinions (1971: 201-3).

48. See Johns 1982: 15-35 for an excellent discussion of the nineteenth-century reception of 'sexual' paintings and artefacts from Pompeii, particularly in Britain.

Introduction to Part III

1. Classical Athens continues to be invoked as the extreme of female seclusion, although that stereotype might also bear modification (Cohen 1991) and should not in any case be extended uncritically to Greek women from other places and times. Cf. Schaps 1979, Pomeroy 1984a.

2. See Chapters 5 and 9 for more detail.

6. Womanly weakness in Roman law

1. I owe particular thanks to Susanna Braund and Rob Wills for their suggestions about making this chapter more comprehensible and palatable to the lay reader.

2. Such as 'emancipation' or adoption. As we shall see, the most common method was the transfer of a daughter to the 'hand' (*manus*) of her husband or father-in-law.

3. *Institutes* 3.3 gives a detailed guide to the principles of intestate succession. For a clear and accessible summary, see Crook 1986a.

4. Vestals were the exception – e.g. Tables V.1; Gaius 1.144-5, 1.130; Aulus Gellius *Noctes Atticae* 1.12.1, 18.

5. Reckoned at twelve years in the case of girls, fourteen (or puberty as revealed by inspection) in the case of boys, Gaius 1.196, *Institutes* 1.22 *pr.*, *CJ* 5.60.3.

6. e.g. Calatoria Themis, whose *tutor* Petronius Telesphorus (Herc.Tab. XIII, XIV) had been a freed slave of her deceased husband Petronius Stephanus (Herc.Tab. XIII/pag. 5; Pugliese Carratelli 1948). Cf. *CIL* VI.2650, *CIL* VI.7468.

7. *Pro Cluentio* 178, 179, 181 (Sassia); *Pro Caelio* 31, 68, *Ad Atticum* 12. 44.2; 12. 32.2 (Clodia), *Ad Atticum* 2.4.5; 2.15.4, *Ad familiares* 14.1.5 (Terentia). Some of the transactions listed in these sources formally required the permission of the women's *tutores*, while others did not (Ulpian has a list at 11.27). In both cases, the women, not the *tutores*, seem to have made the decisions. The tacit assumption appears to be that their compliance could be taken for granted by these financially active matrons.

8. Gaius 1.171; 157; Ulpian 11.8; Gaius 1.165, 192

9. Gaius 1.150-4; i.e. husbands whose wives had been in their 'hand' (*in manu*). Whether there were still such husbands in Gaius' day is moot. As elsewhere, he might be referring to an earlier practice with no contemporary application. Fathers could also appoint *tutores* to daughters in their wills.

10. *Vatican Fragment* 325. And see Modrzejewski 1974: 292.

11. This action dated back to the Twelve Tables *FIRA*. I: 61: Justinian *Institutes* 1.26 *pr.*; Cicero *De officiis* 3.15.6.

12. This was the *lex (P)Laetoria*, introduced some time before 186 BCE – Rotondi 1966: 271-2. Cf. Watson 1971: 42. See the original 1984 article for more detail about the extension of this law to women and the development of *curatela*.

13. e.g. *Noctes Atticae* 5.13.2.5, where the second century CE scholar Aulus Gellius cites a speech of Cato the elder (second century BCE) about traditional moral emphasis. Given the strong cultural value on ancestral virtue, this in effect located *tutela* in a kind of moral genealogy. Cf. Cicero *De officiis* 1.25.85.

14. Cf. the definition of *tutela* in terms of need, originating with Cicero's contemporary, the jurist Servius Sulpicius, and passed on (certainly with changes), via imperial jurists at *Digest* 26.1.1 (Paul 38 *ad edictum*). See also *Institutes* 1.13.1.

15. Cf. the jurist Paul's wording at *Digest* 26.1.1: 'for the protection of one who is unable to defend himself at law by his own effort' (or 'will' = *sua sponte*).

16. See Dixon 1984: 351-3 for discussion of Schulz's suggestion that Cicero was echoing Aristotle *Politics* 1260a.

17. On this, compare Zannini 1976: 64. On pp. 63ff., he gives other instances of Cicero's reasoning in *De republica* 3.10.17; 4.6.6, to show that Cicero's expressed views were not elsewhere contemptuous of women's rights to economic equity or dignity.

18. Modestinus composed six volumes on excuses for evading *tutela* (*Digest* 27.1).

19. Gaius 1.165-6; 192; Ulpian 11.3-5; *Digest* 26.4 and esp. 5 (= Ulpian *ad edictum*); Inst. 1.17, 18

20. Gaius 1.168. And compare Ulpian 11.8.

21. Gaius 1.112, 115a. See Dixon 1984: 354 on the implications for agnatic rights. Cf. Gaius 3.21.

22. Gaius 2.118-19, 121-2.

23. *Digest* 26.1.1 and *Institutes* 1.13.2. Cf. Arangio-Ruiz 1954: 495-6 and Watson 1967: 102.

24. Valerius Maximus compiled a ready reference, classified by topic, to outstanding examples of good and bad behaviour, for orators to use in speeches. His sources were clearly varied and must have included word-of-mouth. The collection is colourful and often bizarre, not unlike modern 'strange but true' TV shows (with talk-show moralising). While not always reliable as history, it provides interesting insights into Romans' ideas about their own past. Literary references to female 'weakness' listed by Beaucamp 1976: 485-509, Schulz 1951: 182, Zannini 1976: 65-6; Arangio-Ruiz 1954: 495-6 refer chiefly to physical weakness.

25. Valerius Maximus 6.1.1. Cf. Seneca *Ad Marciam* 1.1.

26. *Digest* 16.1.1; *Codex Iustinianus* (*CJ*) 5.35.1 (Alexander Severus). There was a later form of maternal *tutela*, but it was very specialised – *Codex Theodosianus* (*CTh*) 3.17.4; *CJ* 5.35.2, 3.

27. Consider Cicero's scornful reference to the influence of women behind the scenes of the trials of Cluentius and Clodius respectively – *Pro Cluentio* 169, 192; *Pro Caelio* 1, 39. See Chapter 9.

28. *Digest* 16.1.1 (Paul 30 *ad edictum*); *Digest* 50.17.2 (Ulpian 1 *ad Sabinum*)

29. As *iudices*, not equivalent to English 'judges' – *Digest* 5.1.12.2 (Paul 17 *ad edictum*).

30. The law, passed during the war with Hannibal, limited luxurious display. It was repealed on this occasion.

31. Tacitus *Annals* 3.34. Livy's Cato had also taken the view that the individual husbands had fallen down on the job by allowing their wives to crowd the entries to the forum.

32. *Digest* 3.1.1.5 – probably the same woman whom Valerius Maximus calls Caia Afrania 8.3.2.

33. Cf. Gide 1885.

34. Suetonius *Tiberius* 50, Tacitus *Annals* 13.5.

35. Ulpian, 29 *ad edictum* (*Digest* 16.1.2.1), quoting the words of the senatorial decree passed under Claudius or Nero (i.e. the *senatus consultum Velleianum*).

36. The *senatus consultum Velleianum* prevented women from acting as loan agents unless they actually paid the debt and tied the original debtor to their own debt. Simple transfer of the debt without an intervening payment was not possible.

37. Cf. Cicero *In Verrem* II.1 105. And see Dixon 1988: 47-51, Ulpian *Digest* 38.17.2.25.

38. *Digest* 43.29.3.11; 4.4.12; 16.1.25 *pr.*; 16.1.2.3, 30; *CJ* 4.29.22-5; Novel 13.4.8 – these necessarily postdate the *senatus consultum Velleianum*, and reflect the thinking of an age which increasingly referred to female inadequacy and helplessness, but which nonetheless admitted certain socially acceptable exceptions.

39. *Digest* 16.1.2 and Crook's (1986) summary of the function of the *senatus consultum Velleianum* to confirm magistrates' response to existing practice.

40. Cf. speculation about the Voconian law, which puzzled subsequent generations of Romans – Dixon 1985.

41. *Digest* 24.1.1 (Ulpian 32 *ad Sabinum*) – the rationale being that spouses might be led by their mutual affection to erode their respective estates. See Thayer 1929.

42. *Institutes* 2.8 *pr.*; Gaius 2.63.

43. See Jolowicz 1972: 246-8.

44. *Digest* 24.3.66.1 (Javolenus citing P. Mucius Scaevola) and see Daube 1965, Waldstein 1972 and Dixon 1986 for the status of the dowry of Terentia and Fausta.

45. Thomas 1976: 243 n. 47.

46. *Digest* 16.1.1 (Paul 30 *ad edictum)* seems to represent the *senatus consultum* of his day.

47. *Digest* 16.1.2.3 (Ulpian *ad edictum*). Cf. Alexander Severus, *CJ* 4.29.5, 224 CE). The decision is at *CJ* 8.27.11 (Diocletian).

48. Cf. Gaius 1.168 on the agnatic *tutela* of children.

49. Such as the expectation that female mourning was more abandoned than its male equivalent (Livy 3.48.8).

50. Cf. *CTh* 9.24.1 *pr.* (320 CE).

7. Profits and patronage

1. Polybius 31.25.2. and Plutarch *Cato minor* 17-19 record some colourful contemporary complaints by Cato the Elder (as censor 185 BCE) which could have set the tone for subsequent denunciations (cf. Liv. 39.6.7), but he might not have been the first.

2. Pliny *Natural History* 34.30-1, Forbis 1990 on public statues (but see Forbis 1990: 493 on private terms of praise); Lattimore 1942: 295-9 and Larsson Lovén & Strömberg 1998 for the stock of womanly virtues, especially those listed in epitaphs.

3. The *Lex Claudia (/Flaminia)*, c. 218 BCE – Livy 21.63.2, Cicero *In Verrem* II.5.18, 45. It remained technically in force until at least the first century BCE.

4. Cicero *De officiis* 2.87, Cato *De agricultura* pref. i-ii on the respectability of land. Cf. Horace's retired gladiator, *Letters* 1.1.5.

5. Cf. Cicero *Paradoxa Stoicorum* 43.

6. Attitudes to jobs are examined in more detail in Chapter 8. They are included here because the category of tradespeople overlaps with that of small shopkeepers (*tabernarii*).

7. Some jurists' examples were taken from actual cases, some were hypothetical. It is not always obvious which is which. Imperial rescripts were decisions handed down by emperors in response to petitions from subjects all over the empire. Crook 1967: 13-33 has an accessible treatment of the sources of law and their authority.

8. Appian *Bella civilia* 1.1.7, Plutarch *Tiberius Gracchus* 8-9 on the plight of the peasantry; Tacitus *Annals* 4.13 on the imperial Sempronius Gracchus who so disgracefully travelled on ships with his own cargo.

9. See Chapter 6 on the *sc Velleianum*, its rationale and its possible consequences; Suetonius *Claudius* 18.2, 19 for the privileges granted to freed-women ship-builders in the grain trade.

10. *Digest* 14.3.7 (Ulpian), *Digest* 7.1.58 (Scaevola) on women managers; Huchthausen 1974, 1976 on women petitioners in rescripts. And see Gardner 1986.

11. Hobson 1984a: 377. In this study, Hobson succeeds in assembling a good body of examples from the early imperial period, 45-46 CE, roughly contemporaneous with the Velleian and Claudian statutes limiting female guarantors and encouraging female ship-owners.

12. Cf. Cohen 1991: 166-7 on such discrepancies in modern settings. I could add my own experience as a child, trained to lie to school and other authorities about my mother's employment and to the family about the fact that we kept a boarding-house.

13. See E. Rawson 1976 (*pace* Treggiari 1979) and consider Pliny's surprise (*Letters* 10.54) that Bithynian land did not change hands by purchase. Romans bought and sold rural land at a rate unknown to the later Italian or English aristocracy, but it could also be retained and its produce consumed by the owner or sold for profit.

14. See Wiseman 1971: 77-89, Huttunen 1974: 127-8, d'Arms 1981, Hopkins 1983b.

15. On the residential/commercial combination in Pompeii, see Brion 1960: 132-3. On brick production, see Helen 1975, Setälä 1977.Wealthy landowners took pride in supplying food for their households from their own estates (e.g. Petronius *Satyricon* 48; Horace *Letters* 2.2.160), as well as making the most of specialist crops and related manufacture. See also Finley 1973: 35-7, Veyne 1979.

16. Possibly through slave or freedman agents from whom they distanced themselves, while retaining access to the profits available from this high-risk area which was formally regarded as 'sordid' and inappropriate to the landed aristocrats of the governing senatorial order. Plutarch's account of the elder Cato's activity in the second century BCE (*Cato maior* 19-21) leaves open the question of how typical his practice might have been. On the continuing debate about senatorial involvement in commercial shipping and in commerce generally in the mid-to-late Republic, see d'Arms 1981, Pleket 1984.

17. See Finley 1973: 17-34 for the insight that there was no concept in antiquity of 'the market' – or, indeed, of 'the economy' – as a distinct entity.

18. Setälä 1977: 250-7 (on Arruntia Camilla) traces a typical example of land transmission over four generations. Even female scholars treat businesswomen as oddities. Loane (1938: 23) took for granted that Spanish women who ran export businesses (*CIL* 15.3691, 3729) had inherited the ships and the businesses from fathers and husbands. Quite likely. Most such wealth was inherited, but she never sees the need to discuss the origins of male wealth in that way.

19. Cf. Livy's apologetic rationale for recounting the female demonstration of 195 BCE against the sumptuary Oppian Law (Livia 34.1). The equally pedigreed demonstrators of 43 BCE, led by Hortensia, daughter of the famous orator, first approached the wives of the triumvirs. Rebuffed, they then ventured into the masculine sphere, appearing publicly before the triumvirs themselves, where Hortensia delivered a speech against the measure (Appian *Bella civilia* 4.32-4).

20. Or, occasionally, a military one. Cf. Busa of Canusium, who equipped and fed Roman citizen-soldiers after the battle of Cannae, 216 BCE (Livy 22.57.2-3).

21. Pliny *Letters* 2.20.10 on the will ceremony. Sherwin-White's rather confused note on this subject includes the comment 'But in practice [women] did what they liked, as always.' Sherwin-White 1966: 204.

22. Pliny *Letters* 1.4 on Pompeia Celerina; cf. *Letters* 7.11 on his mother's old friend Corellia, discussed below.

23. Brick stamps and documentation for Egyptian land holdings in the early empire furnish us with the names of some agents – Crawford 1976: 44-5. The examples are biased towards the women of the imperial family, but probably illustrate the trend, supported by legal developments, of using social inferiors to manage estates and transact some business without the owners apparently relinquishing control – *Digest* 3.3.1 (Ulpian).

24. e.g. Cicero *Ad Atticum* 11.19; *Ad familiares* 14.24; *Ad Atticum* 12.21.4. Cf. Shatzman 1975: 422-4. Cicero's complaints about Terentia's freedman Philotimus perfectly parallel those about his brother's freed slave Sestius.

25. Cicero *Ad Atticum* 12.21 indicates upper-class uncertainty about the legalities of delegation. See Schulz 1951: 438-41; Asser 1971, Fabré 1981.

26. *Tabulae Pompeianae* 25 p.5 = *CIL* 4 supp.1: pp. 308-10.

27. Cicero *Pro Caelio* 31; 68; *Ad Atticum* 12.32.2; 12.44.2 on Clodia's transactions. It is particularly significant that even this, the strongest, most traditional type of *tutela* seems not to have limited her financial independence.

28. Or those of her sister of the same name. It makes no difference to this argument. On his vilification of her in the speech *Pro Caelio*, see Chapter 9.

29. Plutarch *Marius* 34.2 See Münzer 'Cornelia' *RE* 4.1596 (no. 412); d'Arms 1970: 26-9.

30. Cicero *Ad Atticum* 2.45; 2.15.4. Cf. Plutarch *Cato maior* 21.

31. Varro *De re rustica* 3.2.14-15. The farm bred birds for special festive occasions in Rome (like modern turkey farms geared to the Christmas market).

32. e.g. Tacitus *Annals* 13.19; Aulus Gellius *Noctes Atticae* 17.6.2-3.

33. Duncan-Jones 1974: 34-5 on the need for substantial start-up capital for viticulture. Calvia Crispinilla's involvement is recorded in *ILS* 8574a + b; *CIL* 6.3.12020.7; 14371-7. See Manacorda 1975, Paterson 1982 on wine export and the evidence of amphora stamps in general.

34. Owners from the imperial family include the two Domitiae Lucillae (mother-in-law and mother of the emperor Marcus Aurelius) See Setälä 1977: 107-9; 147-9, Setälä 1998: 101-6 for an analysis of female owners.

35. The monument was erected by Naevoleia Tyche in her lifetime. Plate 1 shows a close-up of one side of the relief, with Naevoleia's portrait at the top and her name, as dedicator, in the first line of the inscription, *CIL* 10.1030, in larger letters than the name of her husband in the following line. See the preface for my discussion of Koortbojian's 1996 interpretation of the monument.

36. On Claudia Acte's estates, see *ILS* 1742; *CIL* 6.6.15027; Tacitus *Annals* 13.12; 13.46; 14.2 for her role in court intrigues; Suetonius *Nero* 50 for her faithful attention to Nero's funeral rites. Petronius *Satyricon* 75-6 reminds us – with the rather extravagant example of Trimalchio – that male slaves could also base their fortunes on their sexual appeal to an owner.

37. Both men and women from the slave class freed their partners and are commemorated by the surviving spouse as *patrona* or *patronus*. Rawson 1966, 1974 has inscriptional examples. On manumissions of *female* slaves for the purpose of marriage, Ulpian *Digest* 40.2.13. Marriages to former slaves were more likely to occur between people of comparable status – in particular, those who had been slaves in the same *familia* – Flory 1978. A few examples from *CIL* 6 include

3593, 14014 (wife as manumitting *patrona*); 7788, 13332, 1833 (husband as manumitting *patronus*).

38. Calza 1939 on Iunia Libertas of Ostia. Cf. Garnsey 1976: 129 on provincial and municipal towns.

39. *Digest* 3.5.3.1. See Will 1979 for material evidence from Pompeii of women's commercial activities.

40. *CIL* 15.3691, 3729, 3845-7.

41. Cf. the women's jobs listed by Treggiari 1976; Kampen 1981: esp. 126-7, 1982.

42. On the later use of *negotiator*, see the examples in Greene 1986: 166-7.

43. Cf. *Digest* 16.1.2.3 (Ulpian) and *Codex Iustinianus* 4.29.5 for the ruling that the Velleian excuse had been formulated to protect feminine vulnerability, not to shield female cunning.

44. Cf. *Digest* 3.5.33 (Paul) on the probably hypothetical but clearly plausible grandmother-manager; 3.5.30.6 (Papinian) on the mother-manager acting on the father's wishes for their common child.

45. Cf. Treggiari 1979: 76-8 on possible widows in *CIL* 6.

46. e.g. *NS* 1922,144 refers to a husband and wife shop in the Vicus Iugarius of Rome. The husband-wife relationship is sometimes inferred from other elements in an inscription, e.g. *CIL* 6.9489. Treggiari 1976: 86 n. 48 lists husband and wife with a job in common, e.g. *brattiarius* and *brattiaria CIL* 6.6939, 9211; *furnaria* and *furnarius*, *CIL* 8.24678.

47. See Treggiari's excellent discussion of these issues 1979: 76, 79.

48. The context of *CIL* 14.2433 strongly suggests that Plutia Auge was, like her fellow freed slave Plutus Eros, a dyer or cloth-seller in the Tuscan quarter of Rome.

49. Jongman 1988: 223, Andreau 1977: 114.

50. The donor would actually provide funds for this purpose. Duncan-Jones 1974: 302 gives examples of statues erected to benefactors by the urban proletariat of Rome (n. 5), members of the same *familia* (n. 7), and even agricultural labourers to their overseer (n. 8), as well as dedications to members of the imperial family by children who benefited from the public *alimenta* schemes (pp. 301-2). Cf. Veyne 1990: 127-9 on the Greek world. Sometimes statues might be erected, e.g. by a town, in the *hope* of receiving such largesse from an important figure like a provincial governor or member of the imperial family.

51. Even when some of Cicero's and Pliny's letters are addressed to women involved in lobbying and patronage (such as Caerellia, Terentia, or Pompeia Celerina), the absence of the women's correspondence affects our understanding of the relationships. In *Letters* 4.17, Pliny not only points out his own deserts as the recipient of a favour, but explains why he is therefore obliged to appear in court for Corellia, the daughter of his now deceased benefactor.

52. In letters and other literary *genres*, loans were termed *beneficia* or *bene merita*, like material gifts or personal favours. Legal terms such as *faenerator* (moneylender) or *aes alienum* (debt) carried more negative connotations in élite usage. *Debita* was a more general word, quite suited to obligations of a more personal and honourable kind. Cf. Skydsgaard 1976; Saller 1982: 20-1; Forbis 1990: 500-1.

53. Cicero responded that borrowing money from a woman was less disgraceful than being unable to pay other debts (*Ad Atticum* 12.51.3).

54. The word is not complete in the fragment – *CIL* 14. supp. 4698; Kampen

1981: 64-9. In love elegy, 'amica' tends to mean 'girlfriend' but its use is wider in other media.

55. Cicero and Seneca take a very high-minded view of 'favours' and disinterested acts of friendship which are necessarily at odds with their own practice and even the normative morality they follow – e.g. see Rawson 1978: 3-9.

56. On senatorial loans in general see Shatzman 1975: 74-9; Wiseman 1971: 78-81.

57. Valerius Maximus 8.2.2. The device would also have circumvented Augustan limitations on legacies to non-kin.

58. e.g. Plutarch *Coriolanus* 37, Valerius Maximus 5.4.1 on Volumnia. For more examples, see Fischler 1994: 131.

59. Dixon 1983: 96-7 (Republican examples), Saller 1982: 162 (early Empire).

60. Cf. Seneca *Ad Helviam* 14.2-3 and 19.2, discussed below, on the resources (apparently both money and patronage) Seneca's mother and aunt contributed to his career.

61. *ILS* 4928/2929 = *CIL* 6.2132/2131 and *CIL* 6.2133. Saller 1982: 64 nn.

62. *AE* 1917-1918, 52. Other instances of North African patronage are listed by Saller 1982: 195-9. Only five out of 53 are to women patrons.

63. Catullus 10, esp. 9-13. Cf. 7. Finley argued (1973: 55) that such oppression should not be described by modern commentators as corrupt because it was structural.

64. Saller 1982: 161-2 has a collection of moralising literary references to women exercising patronage in an allegedly corrupt or improper way.

65. Saller 1982: 11, 61-2 on audiences of petitioners; on women and political lobbying in the Republic, Dixon 1983; on political mothers in biography, Dixon 1988: 168-209.

66. *Pro Cluentio* 178. Cicero blows this patronal act out of all proportion for the purposes of the case, which was part of a very nasty family feud. He represented Sassia's son, Cluentius.

67. See also Skydsgaard 1976, esp. p. 46 on the social and economic meanings of such arrangements. There were legal means of enforcing the social requirements of respect. In extreme cases, freed slaves could lose their liberty – *Digest* 1.16.9.3 (Ulpian); 25.3.6.1 (Modestinus). See *Digest* 37.15, 38.1.

68. As notoriously practised by Cato the Elder, according to Plutarch *Cato maior* 21. Cf. Pleket 1984: 7. In modern transactions, too, a partner or investor assumes liabilities from which a creditor lending startup capital is immune.

69. Cf. the example of Ummidia Quadratilla's pantomime artiste in the section below.

70. Interpretations of this skewing have varied. See Garnsey 1980: 44. Jongman 1988: 177. Aspects of work will be explored in the following chapter. Here, the stress is on the shops as businesses.

71. Dixon 1992c, Meiggs 1973: 224. See Plate 13 for Ostian shops.

72. This conclusion is strengthened by the elaboration of others in the network within the nine-line inscription. Two are freed slaves of both Bromius and Curiatia, one a *deliciae* (child-slave) of them both, one a freed slave of Publius and one a freed slave of Curiatia. Only Bromius has an occupational title.

73. The inscription, *CIL* 14. supp. 4698, probably belongs with the relief in Plate 7 and is datable to c. 175-180 (Calza 1978: 37 and 38; Kampen 1981: 64-9). On (*bene*) *meritum* for a financial favour, such as a gift or loan, see Forbis 1990: 500-1, Saller 1982: 20-1.

74. Aurelia and her husband Hermia(s) were fellow-slaves freed by the same owner (*colliberti*). These monuments are limited, but not absolutely fixed by their format and that makes them open to differing interpretations. *CIL* 6.9499 contains a long dual text, flanking the relief shown in Fantham et al. 1994: fig. 11.11. The facing plate, 11.12, depicts Claudia Prepontis, who erected the monument to her 'deserving patron' (*patrono benemerenti*) and herself, *CIL* 6.15002, 15003. The relief shows her and her patron holding right hands, usually a symbol of marriage (taken as such in the text, pp. 320-1), but she does not actually state in the text that she is married to Dionysius.

75. Champlin 1991: 82-102 argues persuasively that most Roman wills actually favoured family. He has collected literary references to *captatio*, pp. 201-2.

76. Calza 1939; *AE* 94 (1940), Dixon 1992b, de Visscher 1963: 239-51.

77. Included in *Digest* 33.1, 34.1.

78. Garnsey & Saller 1987: 33-4, 101-2. Food distributions were sometimes directed to the office-holding élite, sometimes to a wider public.

79. Duncan-Jones 1974: 147-55. The tradition became strained in the later Empire and the top class, the decurionate, was virtually forced to make such endowments. See e.g. Hands 1968, Veyne 1990 (1976). Cf. Garnsey 1974.

80. *CIL* 10.810, 813. But see Moeller 1972 and Jongman 1988: 179-84 on the purpose of the building.

81. See Moeller 1976, Jongman 1988, for opposed views both on cloth in the Pompeian economy and on the importance of the fullers' guilds. *Collegia* were formed for various purposes, including burial clubs.

82. If Eumachia owned a fulling business or had any other specific links with the trade, we do not know of them. Julia Domna was celebrated on one coin as 'mother of the [military] camp', MATER CASTRORVM, Mattingly *CRE* 5.1: 164, no. 56 plate 28.8 rev. and on another as 'mother of the Augusti [princes], mother of the senate, mother of the fatherland' (MAT AVGG MAT SEN M PATRI), 5.1:432, no. 11 pl. 67.12 rev. On the monument of the Volusii at Rome, Gravia is described as PATRONA DECVRIONV(M) – *CIL* 6.10346; *CIL* 9.2687 celebrates the MATER COLLEG[I] CENTONARIOR (guild of patch-workers or rag-merchants) – Waltzing IV, pp. 379, 393.

83. *CIL* 10.6328 = *ILS* 6278.

84. *CIL* 14.2827= *ILS* 6294 (Duncan-Jones 1974: 231). Other examples include *CIL* 10.5918 (Anagnia), 10.7352 (Sicily), 10.109 (Croton), 9.22 (Lupiae).

85. Apuleius *Apologia* 87.

86. Koortbojian (1996: 223-5) reads the whole monument as a biographical tribute to Naevoleia's husband and therefore takes the distribution scene on the funeral monument to refer to beneficence performed by Faustus alone during his lifetime.

87. On the contrast between the capitalist stress on material accumulation versus the gift-economy accumulation of obligation, see Gregory 1982: 51; Dixon 1993b: 457-60.

88. There is now a substantial body of scholarship on alimentary schemes for children, Duncan-Jones 1974: 144-7; Dixon 1988: 86-8 for brief summaries. And see Rawson (forthcoming).

89. Pliny's alimentary foundation, established in his lifetime for poor children of Comum, is attested in *ILS* 2927 and Pliny *Letters* 7.18. 2, 1.8.10-11. Sherwin-White *ad loc.* pp. 422-3 has a good discussion of his scheme and others. See also Veyne 1957, 1958. Pliny also established in his will a foundation for 100 of his former slaves. On the range of his generosity, especially to Comum, see *Letters* 5.7.3, Duncan-Jones 1974: 27-31.

90. *RIC* Trajan, 759 rev., with the legend PIETAS AVGVST[A], showing a women with two girls, may celebrate the imperial alimentary programmes.

91. SHA *Pius* 8.1, *RIC* Pius 398-9; SHA *Marcus* 26.6. And see Dixon 1988: 87, Currie 1996, Rawson (forthcoming).

92. In spite of uncertainty about the authenticity of part of the aunt's will – Fronto *Ad amicos* 1.14 (Naber p. 183).

93. The *puellae faustinianae*, which had been founded by Antoninus Pius (SHA *Pius* 8.1; *RIC* Pius, 398-9) – SHA *Marcus* 26.6.

94. *ILS* 6675 = Bruns 145b.

95. *CIL* 10.6328 = *ILS* 6278. The boys received 20 sestertii a month until they turned sixteen, the girls 16 sestertii per month until they turned fourteen. These are typical differentials between the sexes.

96. *CIL* 14.4 450.

97. Duncan-Jones 1974: 229. See also pp. 144-5 on the donation of Fabia Agrippina and the Tarracina scheme of C(G)aelia Macrina; Mrozek 1988: 158 ff.

98. Duncan-Jones 1974: 228. His argument is that the children referred to as *alumni variani* were beneficiaries of a scheme established by a local dignitary of Capua. He suggests that Matidia's Campanian connections make it likely.

99. *Sportulae* again – Mrozek 1988: esp. 162-6.

100. McDonalds' practice of donating computers to schools and establishing children's hospitals has been challenged by some brave souls. When their practice (well-established in the USA) of giving free food to police was noted by Australian authorities, it was forbidden, an interesting reminder of how the line between patronage and corruption is arbitrarily determined by different cultures.

101. The role of food in such re-distributions and in establishing or maintaining the status of the donors has been extensively discussed by anthropologists, ranging from Mauss to Lévi-Strauss. Pot-latch and the Melanesian 'big-man' phenomenon have attracted particular attention (e.g. Mauss 1954: 100; Sahlins 1966: 166-7).

102. Modern corporations gain tax benefits and *kudos* from gifts to the arts, sports and the community, as well as extremely cheap advertising. International aid reflects foreign policy and sometimes economic interest, as in the donation in 1975 by the Australian government of surplus wheat (difficult to sell on world markets in a time of glut) to Senegal, Mali and Mauretania, as relief for the Sahel drought – 'Le Soleil' (Dakar newspaper), Senegal, 9 April 1975.

103. See Duncan-Jones 1974: 171-84 for estimates.

104. Women were commonly excluded from many *sportulae* – Duncan-Jones 1974: 143.

105. Cf. the Greek husband (Euphrosynus) and wife (Epigone) celebrated at the end of the first century CE by the people of Mantinea for competing with each other in their civic donations, including public banquets and sacrifices – *IG* 5.2.268, esp. lines 32 ff.

106. *AE* 1964, 106; Duncan-Jones 1974: 227.

107. See Corbier 1990 for north African examples of titles for the patrons of towns, Waltzing 1900 on corporations (*collegia*).

108. *Letters* 7.24. Cf. 8.18 on Domitius Tullus.

109. On the amphitheatre and temple she built for Casinum, see *CIL* 10.5813 (*ILS* 5628). *AE* 1946, 174 seems to indicate that she restored a theatre which her father had built, but see now Fora 1992.

110. *ILS* 5183. Cf. *Ep.* 7.14.7.

111. Like many others, Sassia set her trained slave (in this case, a doctor) up in a shop – Cicero *Pro Cluentio* 178.

112. Tacitus *Annals* 3.24 on governors' wives; *Annals* 2.34 on Urgulania, *Annals* 13.18-19 on Agrippina minor (cf. Suetonius *Nero* 34).

113. Woodcock 1998. Cf. Purcell 1986, Flory 1993, Bartman 1999: 123. But Flory 1997 points out that for a long time Livia was not marked out by special honours. Her position changed when it became evident that her line might have to provide Augustus' heir.

114. During Augustus' rule, Livia acquired tribunician sacrosanctity, freedom from *tutela* and the right of children – Dio 49.38.1, 55.2.5. And see Dixon 1988: 89-90, Woodcock 1998. On honours granted in his will: Suetonius *Augustus* 101, Tacitus *Annals* 1.8.2.

115. Dio 56.46.1 on her priesthood. She was apparently official organiser of Augustus' funeral and of the annual games in his memory – Tacitus *Annals* 1.73, Dio 56.46.5. Her provincial accolades include *CIL* 2.2038, and a bronze coin, both from Baetica (*genetrix orbis*) – Ehrenberg & Jones 1955: 94 (no.124), and see Bartman 1999: 199-211 for titles, especially on statue and altar bases.

116. Dio 57.12 on her receptions. She advanced senatorial careers (including that of Galba, who was also named in her will – Suetonius *Galba* 5) and contributed to the dowries of senators' daughters – Dio 58.2. Otho's grandfather was brought up in Livia's home and owed his place in the senate to her – Suetonius *Otho* 1. Her aid to fire victims was recorded officially – Dio 57.16. See Bartman 1999: 107 for the plausible association of her honours in Asia Minor with the earthquakes of 18 CE and pp. 92-3 on her religious benefactions at Rome.

117. Bartman 1999: 114 on the statues; Kokkinos 1992: 70-1 on the land-holdings.

118. Dio 58.2.3 and Tacitus *Annals* 1.14 confirm attempts to confer on Livia the title of *parens* or *mater patriae* 'mother of her country' during her lifetime and on her death. For games and a temple dedicated in honour of her recovery, Tacitus *Annals* 3.64, 3.71.

119. *Annals* 14.11 ff. It also bears an interesting resemblance to creative accounts in modern tabloids of domestic scenes in palaces and Hollywood mansions.

120. Stripped of its clever editorialising, Tacitus' own account supports this reading, e.g. *Annals* 4.8; 4.15. Cf. Suetonius *Tiberius* 26 and see Bauman 1998: 132.

121. Historians today differ on Livia's role – cf. Bauman 1992: 133-8 with Bartman 1999: 92-3, 108-12. The stylised and moralising character of ancient accounts makes it difficult to assess them. Cf. Fischler 1994 and Chapter 9 below.

122. Saller 1982: 195-9 includes examples of centurions' and governors' wives honoured for their part in such promotions. Cf. Pliny *Letters* 9.28 on the empress Plotina's patronage, at Pliny's request, of Voconius Romanus. Nero's mother Agrippina minor promoted Seneca's career – Tacitus *Annals* 12.8.

123. e.g. the legendary Volumnia, who stopped her son Coriolanus from capturing Rome (Plutarch *Coriolanus* 37), or the successful appeal by the mother of Marcus Antonius for her brother's life in the civil war – Appian *Bella civilia* 4.37, Dio 47.8.5. These accounts mention the sons' bitterness.

124. For the inscriptions of the Monumentum Liviae, see *CIL* 6.3926-4326. Literary sources claim Tiberius did not carry out the provisions of her will – Suetonius *Tiberius* 51, *Galba* 5; Dio/Zon. 58.2.3a.

125. Bartman 1999: 108-14 infers an orchestrated 'feminine' public image from the material evidence, in opposition to the literary insistence on mother-son conflict. Cf. Grant's argument (1954: 138-9) that Tiberius stressed the religious aspects of Livia's position.

126. Dio 57.12.5. Cf. the feast at Veii, mentioned above, donated by a husband and wife – *ILS* 6583.

127. As evidenced by sycophantic literary references – Velleius Paterculus 2.130.5, Ovid *Tristia* 4.2.

8. Women's work: perceptions of public and private

1. And see the quotation in Chapter 7 from *De officiis* 1.150 for the part of the passage which concerns commerce.

2. e.g. Cicero *De officiis* 1.150, 2.87-90; Aristotle *Politics* 1256-1328.

3. Cf. Pliny *Letters* 1.9 (a day in Rome) and the 'agricultural' works by Columella (esp. the prefaces to books 9 and 10) or Varro on running an estate.

4. e.g. Gummerus 1913 (iconographic); Loane 1938 (esp. inscriptions); Maxey 1938 (law), von Petrikovits 1981. Theoretical analyses of concepts such as *otium* (loosely translatable as 'leisure') are based on literary discussions, e.g. André 1966.

5. Cf. the observation of Scott and Tilly 1975, that nineteenth-century women continued to define themselves primarily in family terms in spite of changes in their involvement in paid work under industrialisation. Cf. Pleck 1976: esp. 184-6.

6. e.g. *CIL* 6.9683 to Abudia Megiste, a vegetable seller (*negotiatrix frumentaria*).

7. A slave nurse from Rome was commemorated by her partner as both *contubernalis* and nurse of the owner-family – *CIL* 6.12023. Slaves had no right to marry under Roman law, but they did form unions (*contubernia*) and maintained family ties even when they were separated by sale – Rawson 1966. They sometimes refer in inscriptions to their *de facto* spouses as *contubernales* even after manumission has conferred on them the right to use the term *coniuges* (spouses) – Dixon 1992a: 53-5.

8. *CIL* 6.21151, 16592, to wetnurses by their husbands; and see Treggiari 1976 for nurses and midwives generally, Parker 1997 on women doctors, Kampen 1981: 116-17 on midwives.

9. See the list at Evans 1991: 218, app. vii. Status is not indicated in most cases but, where it is, it is servile.

10. Livy 1.57.9. Cloth woven by Tanaquil for the king Servius Tullius still occupied an honoured place in the shrine of Fortuna in the later part of the first century CE – Pliny *Natural History* 8.19.

11. *CIL* 6.15 346.

12. See Treggiari 1991: 375, Larsson Lovén 1998a and cf. *CIL* 6.10230, 11602.

13. Williams 1958: 21 n. 20; on the issue of 'likeness' in portraits generally, consider the comments of (F.S.) Kleiner in his 1996 review of two books on representations of women of the imperial family.

14. Columella *De re rustica* 12 *pr*. 9. Cf . Juvenal 6.287-91.

15. Asconius on *Pro Milone* 43C. See Balsdon 1962: 270.

16. e.g. Williams 1958: 21; Treggiari 1976: 83, Larsson Lovén 1998a: 89-91 – all referring to Suetonius *Divus Augustus* 64.2.

17. Pomponius at *Digest* 24.1.31 *pr*. and 1.

18. Private communications with Prof. Wallace-Hadrill, Dr J. Berry. The 1980 report accompanying the exhibition of finds from the 1975-1980 Italo-Scandinavian dig of Ficana (modern Acilia), a town near Rome, suggests, on the basis of the size (rather than the quantities) of decorated loom-weights found that their purpose went beyond that of everyday domestic provision (Brandt 1980: 118). One problem is that the loom-weights, though included routinely in modern site reports, are not systematically compared with finds from other sites and scholars seldom spell out their reasons for conclusions about the scale of production.

19. Discussions of task specialisation include Frayn 1984: 148-53, Moeller 1976: 74-82.

20. e.g. Larsson Lovén 1998a: 87-8, 1998b. But see Treggiari's list (1976: 81-5) of women named in *CIL* 6 inscriptions for jobs connected with cloth production.

21. Ulpian at *Digest* 33.7.12.5, citing Trebatius; Paul *Sententiae* 3.6.37.

22. Maxey 1938: 32 translates *lanificae* as 'spinners', but the contexts do not justify such a firm and restricted equation – cf. Treggiari 1976: 82, 1979: 68-9. The precise work divisions were of no interest to the jurists, whose concern was with legal issues: the ownership of the slave-women involved, of the materials they used and of the product.

23. See Jones 1974 (1960): 356-7 for the assumption and Moeller 1969: 562 for the suggestion that *lanarii/lanarioi* (without defining adjectives) organised in guilds were weavers. Cf. Waltzing 1895-1900, vol. 2, 153. *Contra*, Dixon 2001.

24. On the moral connotations of *lanifica*, see Williams 1958: 21 n. 20, Lattimore 1942: 23 n. 29. On legal uses, see *Digest* 33.7.12.5, discussed above.

25. Cultural preconceptions can dominate even those lucky enough to observe their subjects in the field. Rogers 1980: 14-15 has some interesting comments on ethnographers (notably Malinowski) either categorising women's work as 'light work' or, when they noticed this was heavy, acting as if that was an oddity rather than the norm although the evidence of their own notes contradicted such judgements. Discourse and ideology can affect observation and even practice.

26. *CIL* 6.7023. Yet on the same page, LeGall treats comparable terms (e.g. *halicaria*) as problematic. Cf. Treggiari 1979: 67, Joshel 1992a: 212 (n. 26) on similar variations in determining the division of labour between gold leaf beaters/sellers; the *brattiaria* Fulvia Melema *sold* gold leaf which her *brattiaria* husband C. Fulcinius C.l. Hermeros (*CIL* 6.9211) had worked. On the general problem of interpreting *-aria/arius* occupational titles, see von Petrikovits 1981: 69-70, Kampen 1981: 126, Larsson Lovén 1998b.

27. The work was targeted by reformers in the late nineteenth century, when it came to be seen as 'such unwomanly toil' – Moore 1999.

28. e.g. Maxey 1938: 33 on *CIL* 6.9290. Moeller's suggestion (1969: 562) that Italian guilds of *lanarii* were for weavers goes against conventional wisdom about the low status of weavers and their lack of occupational guilds. Jones 1974 (1960): 356-7 assumed that *lanarii/lanarioi* outside Italy were weavers. Cf. Waltzing 1895-1900, vol. 2, 153. Waltzing elsewhere (vol. 4, 94) describes *lanarii* as 'woolworkers'.

29. Legal rulings confirmed that masculine forms – both singular and plural – included women, e.g. *Digest* 50.16.40.1 (Ulpian) on *servi* (slaves) and Gardner 1995: 378-9. But see Larsson Lovén 1998b.

30. Jørgensen 1982: 60. Roman historians regularly use 'freedmen' for freed slaves of both sexes and speak of slave-owners and former owners exclusively in the masculine.

31. See e.g. Finley 1973 for the reaction to Rostovtzeff 1926. For overviews of the subsequent debate about how 'industrial' the ancient economy was, see Greene 1986: 9-16, Potter 1987: 152-71, Jongman 1988: 28-35. Harris 1993: 14-18 has introduced a new perspective on this continuing debate, which he summarises.

32. This general tendency is evident in the modern developing world. Colonisers typically cast the colonised men as less enlightened than themselves in their 'treatment' of women, but feminist development economists have argued that the trend is primarily driven by the gendered nature of western aid, which favours male recipients with technology, leaving women in the underdeveloped, traditional subsistence sector. In Ghana, where women are the traditional traders, English firms put men in charge of modern retail shops, which were regularly stripped of their goods by cartels of market women, who could then control the price. Not a desirable result, but an interesting illustration of cultural clashes and non-political subversion of the categories.

33. Dickinson 1994: 97. Only one woman is named as a potter in a Linear B text. Written records of textile production from Roman Egypt and other late imperial sources mention males more than females in census returns and apprenticeship contracts naming weavers, but fourth-century contracts made by the Roman army with villages or male heads-of-household imply that the actual work was carried out by several family members – Jones 1974: 356-7. The fragmentary *P.Oxy.* 1414 explaining non-compliance of such a contract cites the difficulties of filling a goverment order on the ground that 'those who undertook this work *and their wives* are unable to spin the linen yarn' – Jones 1974: 360.

34. Dickinson 1994: 102-3.

35. Compare Friedl's (1959) observation that Peloponnesian men complained of the burden of their daughters' dowries as a form of coffee-house boasting to other men. They resented as insulting the suggestion that such dowries were accumulated by family labour, notably that of the daughter in question.

36. Earle 1989: 337 and Hunt 1992: 12-13 for early modern England; Kitto 1957 (/1951): 219-35, Cohen 1991: 146-67 on classical Athens. Cohen also has material on modern cultures of the eastern Mediterranean.

37. Eight spinsters, *CIL* 6.6339-6346 (*quasillariae*), three weavers, two male, *CIL* 6.6360-1 (*textores*) and one female, *CIL* 6.6362 (*textrix*), a foreman, *CIL* 6.6300 (*lanipend[us]*), the only example outside the imperial establishments of a male in this position; *CIL* 6.6349-6351 *sarcinatrices* – menders or seamstresses, and a male *sarcinator CIL* 6.6348. See Treggiari 1976: 82-6. Other male specialists include dyers/fullers (*fullones*) *CIL* 6.6287-6290.

38. The *monumentum Liviae*, *CIL* 6.3926-4326, covers a range of job titles other than textile-related titles.

39. e.g. servants associated with the bed-chamber (*cubicularii*), *CIL* 6.6254-6265; housekeeper/bailiff (*vilicus*) *CIL* 6.3929; male supervisors/wool-weighers (*lanipendi*) *CIL* 6.3976, 3977 (cf. above on other examples in the household of the Statilii Tauri). Cf. Kampen 1981: 125 on this general tendency.

40. *Pace* Loane 1938: 70. Treggiari 1976: 82 comments on the work-based style of the *Mon. Statiliorum* epitaphs and Joshel 1992a: 136-8 elaborates on the particular characteristics of work-based epitaphs, whether the shared workplace was a manufactory or large-scale *familia*. Frayn 1984: 162 and Jongman 1988: 178-9 consider the possible involvement of wealthy landowners, including senatorials, in the cloth industry of Roman Italy. See the preceding chapter on the social and legal sanctions against (direct) senatorial involvement in commerce.

41. Pompeian residential houses apparently accommodating (or converted to) spinning, weaving and fulling include VI.viii, 20-1 (Jashemski 1993: 134) and VI.xiv.22 (fullery of Stephanus). Cf. Brion 1960: 132-3, Moeller 1976: 40, 56; Jashemski 1993: 35 for rooms off a peristyle transformed to a shop(s?) – I.vi.8-9; 1993: 150 for a Pompeian residential house (VI.xiv.22) converted to a fullery.

42. VI.13.6, Jashemski 1993 Appendix (vol. 2), p. 147, which includes a plan; cf. Moeller 1976: 40 no. 21. Typically, Jongman 1988: 163-5 challenges the identification.

43. *CIL* 4.1493, 1495-8. The single name without the gentile form of the freed slave or the filiation of the free-born, does not always and necessarily signify slave status, but in this context it is a reasonable deduction.

44. He is characterised as *'fututor'* (fucker) – *CIL* 4.1503. See the brief discussion below of this and of 1510 to *'Amarallis fellatri'*.

45. I.x.8. See Della Corte 1954: 301, Moeller 1976: 39 and Jongman 1988: 163, with an illustration plate xv. The loom-weights are noted by Elia 1934 *NS* 10: 317 = inv. 5165.

46. *CIL* 4.8258-9, 8380-4.

47. e.g. d'Avino 1967, Moeller 1976. Cf. Della Corte 1967: 301 (Ref. 8258-9 = his numbers 586-7, 614-15). The *caupona* is at I.x.3. Cf. Jongman 1988: 163.

48. Skydsgaard 1976, Hopkins 1978, 125-6. Cf. Cicero *Pro Cluentio* 178. The over-representation is relative. See Treggiari 1976: 78 on the low numbers.

49. On the protocols, cf. Treggiari 1976: 78-9.

50. *NS* 1922, 144: D VETVRIVS D L ATTICVS/ PVRPVRAR DE VICO IVGAR/VETVRIA D L TRYPHERA/ARBITRATV.

51. *CIL* 6.37826: *camer*IA L L IARINE FECIT/ *l.cam*ERIO L L THRASONI PATRONO/ *et* L CAMERIO L L ALEXANDRO/ PATRONO EIUS ET / L. CAMERIO ONESIMO LIB ET/ *v*IRO SUO POSTERISQVE OMNIBVS/ *vest*IARIIS TENUARIIS DE VICO TVSC. This could equally mean 'and their descendants, all fine tailors'.

52. A Travertine tablet (*CIL* 6.37820) commemorating a number of Veturii who dyed or sold purple cloth at the Marian monument in Rome specifies beside each name (V = living; Θ = dead) whether the person is alive or dead. There is some difference among scholars about whether the occupational term refers only to the woman, Veturia Fedra, or to all those named. See Barbieri (*ILLRP* 809) and compare Joshel 1992a: 211 n. 16; Treggiari 1979: 71.

53. Classic studies include Gummerus 1913, Zimmer 1983. Histories of ancient seacraft have necessarily leaned heavily on visual evidence and incidentally included scenes with boat-builders, seamen and stevedores, e.g. Casson 1971, Carro 1992-7.

54. See Kampen 1981: 69, 117 on the discrepancy between visual and written representations; Evans 1991: 210-12 and Kampen 1981, LeGall 1970, Treggiari 1976, 1979 on jobs attested in inscriptions.

55. Compare Pliny *Letters* 1.9 for a description of a typical day in his calendar at Rome; Quintilian *Institutio oratoria* 6 *pr.*, Aulus Gellius *Noctes Atticae* preface 23 for the responsibility of running an estate.

56. See *De officiis* 150-1, quoted above and discussed in Chapter 7.

57. Kampen 1981, fig. 90. A small figure displays cloth to a seated woman. Intriguingly, there is a seated female in the dyeing scene of the House of the Vettii mural. She is occupied with a cauldron. Terms such as the feminine *purpuraria* (dyer/seller of purple cloth); *sarcinatrix* (seamstress, mender), etc. attested in inscriptions suggest women's involvement in the processes – e.g. Treggiari 1976.

58. Paul *Sententiae* 2.26.11; *Codex Iustinianus* 9.29.

59. On the presumptive sexuality of Australian barmaids, see Kirkby 1997: 43-4, 55-6, 203-6. Domestic servants today *are* often viewed sexually. The typing is often associated with the particular ethnic groups employed in a culture, so that the sexualisation of, e.g. Filipina maids in Singapore or Hispanic nannies in the USA compounds class and racial stereotypes.

60. Kampen 1982 on the iconography of Roman saleswoman. Cf. Edwards 1997 on the display of the actress and Kirkby 1997: 55 on the particular difficulties of actresses and barmaids in the nineteenth century.

61. Keuls 1985: 229-66 analyses 'the sexual allure of female work' on Greek vase paintings. The Lucretia story reinforces the notion that seeing a beautiful woman at work is a turn-on for a tyrant. Sasson 1992 describes the behaviour of men on a Baghdad street when it seems that a woman's veil might slip and reveal part of her face.

62. Treggiari 1991: 299-300.

63. *CIL* 4.1503, 1510. Cf. *CIL* 4.8380 on Onesimus, in the House of the Minucii (Pompeii I-10-8), Della Corte (1954): 301 (no. 606) and the addition (5365) of CVNNILIN to *CIL* 4.5364.

64. Of course, it might be no joke for its object. It is impossible to tell without a context whether it constitutes aggressive sexual harassment or playful teasing. Della Corte 1954: 121 regards such exchanges as 'inevitabile in un simile agglomeramento di operai dei due sessi'.

65. Juvenal 8.43; Terence *Andria* 74-9. From this, Terence draws moral conclusions about the woman, but none about the men who were prepared to pay more for sex than cloth.

66. The word 'tavern' comes from *taberna*, a general word for shop and the class of shopkeeper/artisans who spilled on to Roman streets from their small, rented premises which doubled as home, workshop and point of sale, were collectively called *tabernarii*, in a masculine plural which embraced the men and women of these small family businesses. But the female singular *tabernaria* had a specific meaning, a woman who kept a bar.

67. For similar examples, see Kampen 1981: 110-11, with intelligent discussion.

68. Paul *Sententiae* 2.26.11; *Codex Iustinianus* 9.29; 9.7.1.

69. In Plate 16, the seated mistress does wear the full matronly costume of *stola* with *palla* over it and is depicted as much older than the maids attending her, in their simple long dresses.

70. For the sarcophagus depicting the fates spinning behind a new-born child, see Dixon 1998, plate 7; for the Forum Transitorium frieze, see d'Ambra 1993: 47-60.

71. Cf. (F.S.) Kleiner 1996: 797.

72. Perhaps the most striking bar scene is on a third-century CE sarcophagus relief from grave 90, Isola Sacra of Ostia, the climax of a harbour narrative, depicting a seaman relaxing after his safe return to the port of Ostia. The barmaid brings a cup to customers at a table, while a dog tries to reach the table-top – see Plate 10.

73. Nepos *Atticus* 13.3. The nineteenth-century category 'servant', employed even in census statistics, covered a range of tasks elsewhere discerned as distinct categories – from specialist saddlers and chefs or barmaids, to more varied agricultural and domestic work – Kirkby 1997: 47.

74. Cf. Columella 12.3.6 on spinning in bad weather which precluded outdoor work and Treggiari 1979: 69 on the possibility that women slaves trained for some other specialist task would spin 'part-time'.

75. LeGall 1970, Treggiari 1976, 1979, Herzig 1983. Treggiari's studies of the Latin inscriptions of the western Roman Empire yielded more than 225 job titles

(1979: 66) for male urban *opifices, tabernarii, mercennarii* and *c.* 35 (p. 78) for their female equivalents – her category does not include rural work, urban domestic specialities or 'professionals' such as midwives, nurses, doctors or teachers (whom she treats in other studies).

9. The allure of 'la dolce vita' in ancient Rome

1. I presented a version of this chapter in September 1999 to the 'Roman Crossings' conference organised in Sydney by Kathryn Welch and Tom Hillard. I benefited enormously from the responses of many participants. I particularly wish to acknowledge Maria Wyke, Tom Hillard and Peter Wiseman – not because they agree with me, but because their critical comments helped me to sharpen my focus, as did Ada Cheung's paper on Renaissance transformations of classical originals. Tom Hillard and Lea Beness were also very generous with bibliographic help.

2. Cf. Chomsky 1995 on the time it takes to absorb new ideas; Richlin 1983: 75 for theories about the conservative roles of humour.

3. The current debate about recovered memory revolves around such possibilities. Family history researches notoriously begin with the debunking of entrenched ideas about individuals and origins rooted in romantic topoi – perhaps trivial to outsiders, but sometimes traumatic and a potential source of friction within families, a theme neatly explored in Sinclair Lewis' *Kingsblood Royal* in which the main character sets out to document the family belief in royal origins only to find an African American in the family tree.

4. The construction of the poisoning Livia in Robert Graves' *Claudius* novels elaborates a possibility thrown up by Tacitus in his characteristically disingenuous 'no prejudice' style as one of a series of options (*Annals* 1.3 and 5). Sian Phillips' unforgettable performance in the television production gave it life and took it to a new audience. The process continues: there is now an 'I, Claudius' website for devotees. Considering the age of the film *Quo Vadis*, it is extraordinary that so many students still *know* that Nero set fire to Rome because they saw Charles Laughton do it (before picking up his seventeenth-century violin). These students in turn often become the teachers and community supporters of classics and ancient history.

5. Films as disparate as Griffith's *Intolerance* and Mel Brooks' *Crazy History of the World* exploit this inherited tradition. Maria Wyke has pointed out to me that the face upturned to nibble at the bunch of grapes has become an enduring icon of Roman decadence. Where the notion of the Roman 'orgy' comes from remains a mystery.

6. The judgement encompassed not only depictions of sexual acts, but the ubiquitous religious and apotropaic representations of the phallus, which many publishers continue to include in coffee-table compilations of Roman/Pompeian 'erotica', presumably on the grounds that they find all genital representations erotic. See Johns 1982, esp. pp. 34-5. Many of these artefacts are only now emerging from the 'secret cabinet' of the National Museum at Naples.

7. The lament for the loss of earlier virtue had many manifestations in Latin literature. The nineteenth/twentieth century emphasis on sex is very telling. Cf. Johns 1982: 34.

8. An expression I take from the titles of Kuhn's *The Power of the Image* and of Zanker's seminal 1988 study of Augustan propaganda and its impact.

9. Cf. Evans Grubbs 1995: 55-6. The older style of scholarly discussion, posited on moral decline (Rawson 1974: 279-80; 1986b: 1-2), is typified by Meyer 1895 and

Plassard 1921, although their factual claims have been controverted by empirical studies, notably Rawson 1974, Treggiari 1981. Evans Grubbs 1995 has debunked any notion of simplistic difference between 'pagan' and 'Christian' approaches to marriage as such.

10. The inverted commas represent the literary construct of the character in each case. Clodia Metelli was certainly the object of Cicero's attack in the *Pro Caelio*.

11. Notably, Skinner 1983, Wiseman 1985: 15-53, Hillard 1981, 1989: 173; Bauman 1992: 69-73. For a bibliography on 'Clodia', see Skinner 1983: 273-4, Bauman 1992: 236-7.

12. This is a summary. Cicero's letters include *Ad familiares* 5.1, 5.2 (62 BCE), *Ad Atticum* 2.1.4, 2.1.5 (mid-60s BCE), *Ad Atticum* 2.9.1, 2.12.2, 2.14.1, 2.22.5 (59 BCE), after the death of Clodia's consular husband Metellus Celer. It is possible that the Clodia who owned the gardens across the Tiber (*Att.* 12.42.2; 13.29.2), convincingly identified by Shackleton Bailey 1966: 412-13 as Clodia Metelli, was a sister – Hillard 1973. Cf. Wiseman 1974: 111-12 on the Clodia of *Ad Atticum* 9.6.3, 9.9.2 (49 BCE) as the former wife of Lucullus.

13. The man I shall refer to throughout as Clodius (although he apparently took that name in 59 BCE) was accused of having attended the all-female religious rite of Bona Dea in drag in order to meet his lover Pompeia, wife of the absent Julius Caesar. Suetonius *Divus Julius* 6, Plutarch *Caesar* 14, Cicero *Ad Atticum* 1.12.3. Cicero's portrait of Clodius has also been influential – Rundell 1979.

14. Apuleius *Apologia* 10, 158 CE. Apuleius presents the key to several poets' devices, to defend his own use of pseudonyms for real boys in his poetry, 9-10. Cf. Ovid *Tristia* 2.427.

15. See esp. Wiseman 1969: 50-60; Hillard 1973.

16. From the 'Bona Dea' incident of December 62 BCE to Clodius' murder in January 52. The consequences of the feud were very serious for Cicero. Clodius secured his exile in 58 BCE and led a mob which demolished his expensive new house. See also Cicero's speech *De domo sua*.

17. Austin's appendix 'Caelius and Catullus' was re-written for the third edition in 1960, but the characterisations remained much the same. His book has been reprinted in paperback since 1988 and is cited in the latest *OCD* entry (1996) for Caelius Rufus.

18. By R.J. Seager and one G.E.F.C. See also the entries for Caelius Rufus (p. 271, by E. Badian) and Catullus (pp. 303-4, by H-P. Syndikos).

19. A free translation might be: 'This ogress, who was more Catullus' leach than his lover.'

20. Wiseman 1985: 53, harking back to his quote from Pope's *Epistle to a Lady: Of the Characters of Women* 207-10 and his own conception of her as instancing the Claudian arrogance noted in hostile traditions. Cf. 1985: 157, with its token reservations and confident assertion: 'What have we learned about "Lesbia" by the end of the first book of Catullus' collected poems? His subject is not so much the woman herself as his own reactions to her; nevertheless, we can recognise in that distorting mirror a will stronger than his, appetites more earthy than his, a beauty, an elegance and a capacity for laughter that captivated him against his better judgement, and perhaps also a certain presence, a *hauteur* that made her intimacy all the more electrifying.' This is a subtle modern development, in which the overt disapproval is not for 'Clodia's' sexual behaviour but for her aristocratic high-handedness.

21. Wiseman (1969), Quinn (1973: 386-8) and Syndikus (1984, vol. 1; 1996:

304) see the metrically grouped arrangement of the only manuscript as intended by Catullus himself. *Contra*, Wheeler 1934. Syndikus (1996) divides the Lesbia poems into two cycles, one involving poems 2, 3, 5, 7, 8, 11 'telling the story of Catullus' love affair from their first courtship through the height of passion to estrangement and the final break up of the affair' and a second, epigrammatic Lesbia cycle (70-87), 'more loosely constructed and not completely chronological'.

22. The poems include (in the order given) 51, 2, 3, 5, 7, 86, 87 (Happiness, ch. 2), 92, 109, 70, 72, 75, 85, 73, 8 (Doubt, ch. 4), 76, 11, 38 (Disillusionment, ch. 6).

23. Williams 1968: esp. 549-57; Quinn 1970: xiv-xv. Wiseman does *not* agree about Caelius (1985: 173) and remains sceptical about the identification of the Catullan Lesbia with Clodia Metelli (1969: 50-60). See Quinn 1973 for a review of Catullan scholarship, esp. pp. 383-5 on changing approaches to the Lesbia poems.

24. They are 5, 7, 43, 51, 58, 72, 75, 79, 83, 86, 87, 92, 107.

25. 91 refers to Gellius' betrayal of their friendship. Cf. Lee 1990: 179. Quinn's list (xvi) is: 2, 5*, 7*, 8, 11, 13, 36, 37, 43*, 51*, 58*, 68, 70, 72*, 75*, 76, 79*, 83*, 85, 86*, 87*, 92*, 104, 107*, 109. The asterisk indicates those poems that actually name 'Lesbia'.

26. Fordyce (1961: xvii) states that 25 of Catullus' poems, *c.* 250 lines out of 2,000, are about Lesbia. At 89, he glosses *meae puellae*, Catullus 2.1 'Lesbia, as in 11.15, 13.11, 36.2'. Cf. 124, Lee 1990: 161, Wiseman 1985: 130.

27. Cf. Fordyce's comments on 11 and 36, 82. The beautiful 8, in which the poet addresses himself (*Miser Catulle, desine ineptire*) is always taken to refer to *his* genuine unhappiness and attempt to recover from the affair with Lesbia, as is 76 (*Siqua recordanti*).

28. The commonplace denunciation of womanly insincerity in love in 70 ('My wife/woman – *mea mulier* – tells me she would not have anyone as a husband rather than me, even if Jupiter himself were to ask for her hand') is commonly linked with 72, addressed to Lesbia ('You once used to say, Lesbia, that you knew only Catullus and would not prefer Jove to me'). See note 36 below. The kissing theme, so famously explored in 5 ('Let us live, my Lesbia, and let us love ... Give me a thousand kisses, then a hundred, ...') and 7 ('You ask, Lesbia, how many of your kisses would be enough and more than enough') re-surfaces in 48, an appeal to Iuventius, to be allowed to kiss his honey-sweet eyes ('as many as three hundred thousand times, nor shall I ever feel I have had enough ...').

29. On Iuventius, see 24, 48, 81, 99. Compare 55 and 58b on Camerius. And see Williams 1968: 549-57.

30. See above for Syndikus' classification of 70-87 as the secondary, epigrammatic cycle. The general division, possibly modelled on the Garland of Meleager, is into the short poems, 1-60, followed by longer poems in more elevated style, then 65-116 in elegiac couplets, with 65-8 distinguished from the epigrams. Not all epigrams are invective.

31. 'It's your fault, Lesbia, that my mind is so pulled apart and so destroyed by its own decency that it can no longer like you, however good you might be, or stop loving you, no matter what you do.'

32. 58 is addressed to Caelius. The unspeakable acts are not quite clear. The word Catullus uses – *glubit* – seems to mean that Lesbia 'peels' the descendants of Remus. But the general sense is plain enough. This more closely resembles the deliberately sordid images of Juvenal 6, e.g. 327-34, or Martial (e.g. 10.81), but in those cases, the object of vilification is not a love object. To my knowledge, the collapsing of genres – unlike other innovations of Catullus – was not taken up by subsequent poets. Catullus 72 (*Dicebas quondam* ...) is a more tasteful (and conventional) elaboration of the stock theme of faithlessness.

33. 56, on the rape of 'my girl's little boy' – not her son, but her pet slave-boy, is ironically addressed to the stern moralist Cato (see Richlin 1983: 11-12 on this device); 57 is one of several poems on Mamurra, some of which include Caesar.

34. 11.17-20. The message is relayed through his friends Furius and Aurelius.

35. Catullus 11.21-4: 'Let her not look again for my love, as it used to be. It is her fault that it has died (or 'fallen' – *cecidit*), like a flower at the edge of the meadow, after it has been touched a glancing blow by the plough as it passes by.' Cf. Sappho 148.ii, Catullus 62, 39-46.

36. It consciously recalls Callimachus Epigram 25, but Kroll and Fordyce agree that Catullus 70 and 72 (which names Lesbia) obviously express genuine feeling, not just art. Cf. Quinn 1970: 244 on Catullus 51, an imitation of Sappho. Similar rationales are behind the inclusion in the Lesbia narrative of poems about friendship betrayed or regrets for the past, such as 8 and 76.

37. On Catullus' criticism of the governor he accompanied to Bithynia – Catullus 10. Cf. Austin 1933: 52. Catullus' poems attacking Caesar include 29, 54, 57 – Suetonius *Divus Julius* 73. Williams 1968: 524-77 draws a complex distinction between the (broadly sincere) personal feelings of Roman elegiac poets and the 'unreal' issues of politics.

38. Quinn 1973: 383-5 for a summary of these self-inflicted problems.

39. Catullus is unusual in attempting to describe a different kind of feeling for Lesbia – characteristically, in a nostalgic reproach: 'I loved you then not only as the crowd loves a mistress but as a father loves his children and sons-in-law' (72.3-4).

40. Or she could die. But (as we saw in Chapter 4) that belongs to a different style of narrative.

41. *Pro Caelio* §§23-5, 51-5. And see Austin 1933: 152-4, Wiseman 1985: 54-74.

42. He plays with the word *meretrix*, which he introduces in his opening lines, *Pro Caelio* 1 (*opes meretriciae*). Cf. Wiseman 1985: 84-6 and see the analysis below.

43. Geffcken 1973, esp. 11, 55-6. Salzman 1982 sees the theme as more serious.

44. In §23, he points out that the previous speaker, Crassus, covered three of the five formal charges. In §30 he states that he will deal with two charges, concerning the gold and the poison – all other accusations are not charges but slander (*omnia sunt alia non crimina sed maledicta*).

45. Wiseman 1985: 54-74 represents a rare examination of the likely events. Badian's *OCD* article on Caelius Rufus simply summarises Cicero's assertions about his life. Cf. Austin 1933: viii, 52; Münzer 1897.

46. The puzzling nick-name '*quadrantaria*', clearly meant to be insulting, was explained by Plutarch *Cicero* 29.2. Cf. Quintilian *Institutio oratorio* 8.65.3. While not wishing to detract from Cicero's artistry, I can't help wondering if the staying power of this image of Clodia might owe something to ingrained adolescent male fantasies about older women (cf. Mrs Robinson in the film *The Graduate* and the associated song). Salzman 1982: 302-3 points out that the Magna Mater celebrations revolve around a myth about a vengeful older woman (Cybele) and her lover (Attis).

47. *libido muliebris*, an expression repeated in the conclusion, at §78; '[being] besieged by the resources of a prostitute' – *oppugnari ... opibus meretriciis* (§1). On Atratinus and his father: Münzer 1897: 1268; Dorey 1958; Wiseman 1985: 67-8.

48. All this within a pseudo-hypothetical setting about *a certain noblewoman*: 'she would seem not only a prostitute, but in fact a forward and provocative prostitute' (*non solum meretrix sed etiam proterua meretrix procaxque uideatur*)

§49. Wiseman's emphasis (1985: 85) on the legal implications of this characterisation is misplaced: as in modern legal systems, the testimony of a prostitute is formally open to challenge in court, but we are dealing here with prejudice and a more general attack on the character and credit of a formidable witness in support of an alternative reading of the events by the defence. It is no more literal than assertions that Piso's grandfather was an auctioneer (Cicero *In Pisonem* frag. ix; cf. §20, §53) or that the boy Cicero wore customers' clothes from his father's laundry – Dio 46.4.4-5. Cf. *De oratore* 2.240-1. Cf. Nisbet 1961: 194-6.

49. e.g. §52, which recalls (perhaps intentionally) the elegiac conceits of love as warfare (*militia amoris*) and slavery (*seruitium amoris*). On the *dux femina* motif generally in the speech, see Geffcken 1973: 37-40.

50. Cf. the many hilarious and outrageously inappropriate female behaviours in Juvenal's sixth satire, e.g. rich women who dominate their husbands (136-41); the athletic wife (246-67) or the wife who corrects her husband's grammar in public (451-6) – all clearly offences against nature.

51. Münzer 1897, Austin 1933 *passim*, esp. the introduction and Appendices. Cf. Wiseman 1985: 54-74, who is more critical.

52. Gruen 1966 shook some longstanding views on Clodius but not the fundamental characterisation. Most of the common claims originate in Cicero *De haruspicum responso* (Rundell 1979: 302). Cicero was particularly affronted by the guarantee of an affordable price for grain, the staple food of the poor (*Pro Sestio* 55) – another emblem of Roman moral decline taken up by modern scholars. Caelius' politics and methods were quite as suspect in Cicero's terms, but the friendship endured and his scholarly 'typing' has taken its cue from Cicero's indulgent tone.

53. Plutarch *Cato maior* 15.3. Such prosecutions were often the first public step in a political career at Rome – Taylor 1949: 2 n. 12.

54. Wiseman 1985: 54-62 (the background to the prosecution), 136 (the identification of Lesbia), 53 ('love of sway'). See also Geffcken 1973: 37-40, Skinner 1983: 286 on the representation of her unfeminine power.

55. Austin 1933: 44-6. Cf. Münzer 1897, Wiseman 1985: 62-9.

56. Cicero *Ad Atticum* 1.3.3 on Tullia's first engagement, 67 BCE. See Shaw 1987 on the likely age at first marriage of upper-class Roman girls.

57. *Ad Atticum* 12.42.2, 13.29.2, *Pro Milone* 75 and possibly *Ad Atticum* 9.6.3, 9.9.2 (mother-in-law of the tribune L. Metellus). Cf. Skinner 1983: 281-3, Wiseman 1985: 52-3. Yet Austin draws on Cicero's correspondence for Caelius' character.

58. Consider once more Asconius, writing *c.* 54-57 CE on Cicero *In Pisonem* 10 (Clark): 'I have not been able to discover who Piso's mother-in-law was, since it appears the authors have not, in the case of the houses and families, passed on the names of the women as they have those of the men, except in the case of distinguished women.'

59. That does not mean that Roman politicians enjoyed being abused. Plutarch tells us (*Cicero* 25-6) that Cicero offended many leading men by his witty (and immensely repeatable) insults. Mark Antony and his wife Fulvia marked him out for special treatment because of his attacks (*Cicero* 48). Caesar was formally reconciled to Catullus (Suetonius *Divus Iulius* 73). But such insults were part and parcel of Roman political life in the Republic, institutionalised in the ritual abuse of the triumphing general and the Saturnalia (49). See Syme 1939: 149-51.

60. Although we hear little of him, there is no argument that *he* 'vanished'. Cicero attributed the attack on Caelius in February 54 to the *gens Claudia*, presumably Publius, Appius and Clodia Metelli. It seems to have come to nothing (*Ad Quintum fratrem* 2.12.2; 2.13.2).

61. Dorey 1958 seems to have led this change, not followed by Syme 1964: 25, but echoed by Balsdon 1962, Hillard 1989, Wiseman 1985. Cf. Gruen 1974: 308.

62. e.g. Cicero *De oratore* 2.217-332 on wit is mostly about entertaining attacks on character; Quintilian *Institutio oratoria* 12.8. Nisbet 1961: 192-197 has a good summary of the usual headings. Cf. Lenaghan 1969: 77.

63. Cicero *In Pisonem* 13,22,42, 66-67 (Piso at dinner); *CIL* 11.672: 9-11, Suetonius *Divus Augustus* 68 (sexual accusations against Octavian); pseudo-Sallust *Inv. in Cic.* 2.2, Fufius Calenus at Dio 46.18.6 (Cicero and his daughter Tullia); Catullus 29,57 (Caesar and Mamurra having oral sex with each other).

64. There were, to be sure, some successful propaganda campaigns, e.g. Marius' supplanting of the general Metellus in his command in Numidia (Sallust *Bellum Iugurthinum* 84 ff.) and Octavian's brilliant orchestration of images to discredit Antonius (Mark Antony) – Zanker 1988: 33-77.

65. Martial 11.20.3-8 (Octavian's poem purportedly to Fulvia). See Hallett 1977: 16-163 for a discussion of its genuineness.

66. Mark Antony's wife and brother, who represented him in his absence in armed conflict with Octavian 41/40 BCE – Livy *Periochae* 125-6, Velleius Paterculus 2.74. For the insults: *CIL* 11.6721.13-14 (against Lucius); 5 (against Fulvia). See Hallett 1977.

67. This point holds even if it was another sister he dealt with in 49 and 45 BCE, since Cicero had publicly accused her brother and either her or her sister of pretty awful things, including promiscuity, incest and murder. Clodius Pulcher's death would not necessarily have opened the way to reconciliation, since Cicero had been prepared to defend his murderer.

68. It was a commonplace for lyric poets to lament that they were rejected by a mercenary beloved in favour of wealthier suitors (Horace *Odes* 3.7; cf. the epigrams *AP* 5.46,101, Martial 12.65). On the desiring older woman, see again Richlin 1983: 109-16. Examples from Martial include 3.93, 10.67, 10.90. In 2.34, 4.28 he criticises women who fritter their wealth away on young lovers. Cf. Horace *Epodes* 8,12. On Clodia's loan, see *Pro Caelio* 31, 36.

69. The empress Messalina was depicted as using her position to force men to have sex with her, e.g. Dio 60.27.4 (Vinicius) and Tacitus *Annals* 11.36 (Mnester). Cf. Martial 11.20 and for the stereotype generally, see Skinner 1983: 286 n., Dixon 1992b.

70. Not all Catullus' epigrams are insulting, but only the epigrams can house abuse and the things that go with it, like bodily description. Within the elegiac couplets (65-116), the nearest to a physical description is in the criticism of a local beauty in 43 whose nose is not small, her foot not beautiful, her eyes not black, her mouth not dry, her language insufficiently elegant – the opposite of Lesbia.

71. Cf. the rumour about Sempronia poisoning her husband Aemilianus in the second century BCE – Appian *Bella civilia* 1.20, Livy 59. The many accusations against senatorial women targeted for their worship of Bacchus in 186 BCE included conspiracy to poison their husbands – Liv. 39.7-19. Balsdon 1962: 30-1 summarises notable scandals and points out that in past ages deliberate poisoning was often rumoured in cases which could now be diagnosed as natural. Poisoning can cause symptoms similar to food poisoning. But deep-seated cultural fears also play a part.

72. Wiseman 1985: 40-3 likens Clodia to twentieth-century political hostesses who 'provide an opportunity for political gossip to be disseminated, but they are not themselves political figures of any importance'. Hillard has argued in several works that women of the Republican political élite were without political power and has used Clodia Metelli as a prime example of his view, e.g. 1981, 1983, 1989, 1992, esp. 48-53. Several of us continue to debate the issue, in print and in correspondence. See Skinner 1983: 273 n. for earlier references.

73. 'By augmenting masculine suspicion of a woman who has achieved prominence outside the home, the *Pro Caelio* slyly reinforces patriarchal values. It argues that females cannot be trusted with power; given the freedom to exercise it, they will automatically employ it for corrupt ends' (Skinner 1983: 286). For the argument that incest decodes as political alignment, see Hillard 1973, Skinner 1982.

74. Wiseman 1985: 52. Although some of these supposed events are referenced from other sources (Plutarch *Cicero* 29.4, based on *Pro Caelio* 62; Quintilian 8.6.52; 6.3.25), all but one originate in *Pro Caelio* allusions to contemporary gossip, in the usual fashion of ancient forensic speeches. See Cohen 1991, esp. 240, Hunter 1994: 118-19 for discussions of this technique in Attic speeches. The reference to chants in the theatre comes from a letter from Cicero to his brother Quintus in 56 BCE, *Ad Quintum fratrem* 2.3.2. Clodius led anti-Pompeian chants and the other side ran counter-chants, which included 'every kind of foul accusation, finally verses of the most obscene kind against Clodius and Clodia'. Most of the letter is given over to Clodius' chants, which are the ones Plutarch chose to reproduce in his life of Pompey.

75. See esp. E. Rawson 1976, Dixon 1986, Gardner 1986, Setälä 1998 and Chapters 6-8 above on the legal and financial activies of Roman women in the late Republic. The arguments of Skinner and Wiseman and my own impression are both based on the possibility that Cicero's approaches in 49 BCE were to Clodia Metelli rather than her sisters (Shackleton Bailey 1960: 95-7; Wiseman 1974: 111-12). See below.

76. See e.g. *Pro Roscio Amerino* §27, Dixon 1983: 94-5.

77. Cf. Delia 1991: 199: 'One of Cicero's rhetorical techniques was to slander the female relations of an enemy so as to make him appear utterly vile.' She uses this argument to play down the political role of Fulvia. Cf. Hillard 1989: 176. The idea that women did not exercise the restraint expected from men of their station and therefore needed external control was enapsulated in *impotentia muliebris*, a concept invoked to describe womanly jealousy and anger as well as lust. Cf. Livy 34.2 (Cato the Elder); Tacitus *Annals* 3.33.3 (Caecina Severus).

78. There was certainly nothing remarkable about a Roman woman lending out money at interest or manumitting her slaves. Cf. Cohen 1991: 240 on Attic law-court speeches: 'For the historian, the question is not that of determining the social reality "behind" the lies: it is forever lost to us whether or not a particular marriage, or adoption, or making of a will in Isaeus actually took place.'

79. The suggestion of an anonymous referee – Skinner 1983: 286 n.

80. Its published version, which appeared soon afterwards (Salzman 1982) was clearly well known to Quintilian, whose rhetorical school flourished in Rome from the mid-sixties CE.

81. Schol. Bob. on Cicero *Pro Sestio* 116, in which Cicero made a passing reference to Clodius' familiarity with his sister's 'ballets' (*embolia*), presumably a *double entendre* which should amuse fans of *Lucky Jim*.

82. After all, men were subjected to fairly standard accusations of gluttony, incest and dancing (Austin 1933: xiv). The *Pro Sestio* passage which inspired the quoted gloss is sarcastic about Clodius' familiarity with games, pantomime and dancing. Cf. Macrobius *Saturnalia* 3.14.

83. Lines 19-25, *CIL* 6.10230 = *ILS* 8394. This awkwardly phrased inscription is almost certainly taken from the *laudatio* which the commissioning author delivered at his mother's funeral.

84. Lines 26-8. Further elaborations are cut short by damage to the inscription after line 29. The damage also reverses the usual situation – in this case, we know the mother's name but not the son's.

85. For the changes and the constants, see Rose 1997, Wood 1999. Cf. Pliny *Panegyricus* 83-4 on Trajan's wife and sister. The coin imagery is well illustrated in Giacosa 1977.

86. Velleius Paterculus 2.100, Seneca *De beneficiis* 6.32, Pliny *Natural History* 21.9 on Julia (the Elder) and cf. Richlin 1992. On Messalina, see Pliny *Natural History* 10.72, Juvenal 6.114-32. Right-wing newspapers in Greece waged political war for some time on Mrs Papandreou (whom they called MIMI in their headlines). She was much younger than her husband and they characterised her, even in her widowhood, as a jumped-up air hostess, in an attempt to undermine her political credibility – a classic instance of the 'scheming concubine' syndrome (Dixon 1992b).

87. Tacitus *Annals* 13.45.2; Dio *Epit.* 61.(60).29.5-6 (Xiph.), 6a (Zon.).

88. See references above, and Dio *Epit.*, 61 (60) 31. 1-5 (Exc. Val.) In my own Classics Department, the student association held a popular debate in 1999 on whether Monica Lewinsky was more sexually adventurous than Messalina. A living woman can become discourse.

89. Consider the reverse coin issue depicted by Wood 1999, fig. 20. It features her bust between those of her two sons, Gaius and Lucius, *RIC* 1 (2nd ed.) 404, 405. See Bartman 1999: 215-16 on other public portrayals.

90. See Giacosa 1977 and Wood 1999 for a selection of imagery.

91. Cf. Boatwright 1991 on the relative 'subservience and impotence' of the imperial women of the early second century CE.

92. Censors claimed to be acting in the public interest but (as in modern political scandals) always targeted their enemies, never their political allies. For examples, see Valerius Maximus 2.9; Cicero *De oratore* 2.268, 272.

93. Plutarch *Numa* 10.4-7; Dionysius of Halicarnassus 2.6.7.3-4; 9.40.3 for the traditional punishment, very slightly modified over time. Scandals erupted from time to time, e.g. 114-113 CE (Aemilia, Licinia, Marcia) – Dio 26.87 (Exc. Val.). Cf. Bauman 1992: 52-8. The last execution of a Vestal was *c.* 83-86 CE, under Domitian – Pliny *Letters* 4.11.6.

94. A Vestal's intercession was difficult to resist – e.g. Suetonius *Tiberius* 5.4.6. Cf. the role of Cicero's sister-in-law, the Vestal Fabia, in his consulship – Plutarch *Cicero* 20.

95. Cf. Kampen 1981: 110 on representations of women shopkeepers, barmaids and bar-managers.

96. Amaryllis (spelt with a 'y') is listed as a spinner on a list on the wall of the weaving workshop in the peristyle of M. Terentius Eudoxus' house in Pompeii – line 3, *CIL* 4.1507. In the entry of the house, some wit has written AMARILLIS FELLATRI ('cock-sucker') – *CIL* 4.1509.

97. On ancient conceptions of history, Cicero *De legibus* 1.2.5, Pliny *Letters* 5.8.9, Livy, preface, Aulus Gellius *Noctes Atticae* 5.18.6-9. Biography, a somewhat less dignified medium, could admit more personal – and therefore, more sensational – detail, but Tacitus also insisted on an exemplary role for his *Agricola*, 1.1.

98. Livy 39.7-19; *CIL* 1.581 on the Bacchanalian persecutions; Suetonius *Tiberius* 2 on the trial of Claudia for treason in the third century BCE. after her arrogant public joke about a disastrous Roman naval defeat involving her brother.

99. On Antonius – Plutarch *Antonius* 10.3. Cf. Velleius Paterculus 2.74 on Fulvia's 'manliness'. On Claudius, see Suetonius' *Life*, esp. 29. On Cato the Elder, Livy 34.2-4.

100. Dio 55.10.14 (Julia); Tacitus *Annals* 11.37-38, Dio *Epit.* 61 (60).31 (Messalina). We do not know why others were executed, when some of her alleged lovers were relegated to island-exile. Cf. Bauman 1992: 108-24.

101. *Annals* 14.63. See Gallivan 1974 on Tacitus' distortion of her age to make her fate even more pitiful.

102. Treason and adultery accusations are difficult to disentangle – Bauman 1974: 131-2 and see above on the implications of Julia's trial. Cf. Tacitus *Annals* 6.47.2 on Albucilla and Schol ad Juv. 6.158 on the wife of Aemilius Paullus. In the aftermath of the plot against the emperor Gaius in 39 CE, his sisters Livilla and Agrippina and their alleged lover Tigellinus were all banished. On the Stoic dissidents and others represented as victims, see Pliny *Letters* 3.11 (Gratilla), 7.19, 9.13. The 1999 trial of the Malaysian politician Anwhar Ibrahim for sodomy was generally interpreted as a punishment for his political opposition.

103. Qualities praised in the wives of the dissident martyrs – Tacitus *Histories* 1.3.1.

104. Delia 1991, Virlouvet 1994 (Fulvia), Hillard 1989, 1992 (Clodia and Servilia) belong to the minimising school; Dixon 1983, Skinner 1983 favour political interpretations.

105. Finley's views are as likely to have been shaped by a reading of ancient literature as by Balsdon. I regard Syme's discussions of political women as more nuanced and informed, *pace* Skinner 1983: 274. But it is clearly a matter of personal judgement.

106. e.g. in Colleen McCullough's *Caesar's Women*; Stephen Saylor's *The Venus Throw* (Clodia also appears in *A Murder on the Appian Way*). Wiseman 1975 and 1985: 230-41 lists examples of Lesbia in fiction.

107. Cf. the pious care of Lee 1990: xx with p. 177, on Catullus 79. On 107 he quotes Fordyce without comment. In their 1996 *OCD* articles, Badian ('Caelius Rufus'), Seager ('Clodia') and Syndikus ('Catullus') unhesitatingly make the identification.

108. Cf. again Cohen 1991: 240 on the difficulties of abstracting from Attic law-court speeches 'the cultural meaning of many of the exaggerations, lies distortions, and fabrications with which the orators are replete.'

109. I am not suggesting that I have done that in this chapter, where my main concern has been to discuss the basis of enduring stereotypes.

110. Pliny *Letters* 9.13 on Helvidia, 6.33 on the lawsuit.

111. Tacitus *Agricola* 4.2-3; cf. 6.1. The canon of good mothers includes Volumnia (Plutarch *Coriolanus* 33-36), Cornelia (Plutarch *Tiberius Gracchus* 1, *Gaius Gracchus* 19), Aurelia (Tacitus *Dialogus* 28) – Dixon 1993: 129-35. See chapters 10 and 11 of Wyke's forthcoming book on modern representations of Messalina.

Bibliography

Note on abbreviations

Journal abbreviations are listed in *L'Année philologique* and online at
http://www.chass.utoronto.ca/amphoras/revues.txt
I have given in full references to most foreign and non-classical journals or journals
cited only once. The following abbreviations are used in the text and notes:

AE L'Année épigraphique (1888-).
ANRW Aufstieg und Niedergang der römischen Welt (1972-) ed. H. Temporini & W.
   Haase. Berlin.
CRE Coins of the Roman Empire in the British Museum (1965-) ed. Harold
   Mattingly. London: The Trustees of the British Museum
CIL Corpus Inscriptionum Latinarum (1863-).
EMC / CV Échos du monde classique / Classical Views.
FIRA Fontes Iuris Romani Antejustiniani in Usum Scholarum, 3 vols (1940) eds.
   S. Riccobono, J. Baviera, C. Ferrini, J. Furlani & V. Arangio-Ruiz.
IG Inscriptiones Graecae.
ILLRP Inscriptiones Latinae Liberae Rei Publicae (1963-) ed. A. Degrassi
ILS Inscriptiones Latinae Selectae (1962) ed. H. Dessau. Berlin.
NS Nuove scavi. Series.
OCD Oxford Classical Dictionary, 3rd edition (1996) ed. S. Hornblower & A.
   Spawforth. Oxford: Oxford University Press.
RE Realencyclopädie der klassischen Altertumswissenschaft (1894-).
RIC The Roman Imperial Coinage (1923-1994) ed. H. Mattingly & E.A. Sydenham.
   London: Spink.
SHA Scriptores Historiae Augustae

*

Adams, J. 1982 *The Latin Sexual Vocabulary*. London: Duckworth.
Africa, T. 1978 'The Mask of an Assassin', *Journal of Interdisciplinary History* 8:
   599-626.
d'Ambra, E. 1993 *Private Lives, Imperial Virtues: The Frieze of the Forum Transitorium in Rome*. Princeton: Princeton University Press.
———— 1996 'The Calculus of Venus' in N. Kampen ed. *Sexuality in Ancient Art*.
   Cambridge: Cambridge University Press: 219-32.
Anderson, W.S. 1956 'Juvenal VI. A problem of structure', *Classical Philology* 51:
   73-94.
André, J. 1966 *L'Otium dans la vie morale et intellectuelle romaine des origines à*

l'époque augustéene. Paris: Faculté des lettres et sciences humaines ('Recherches' XXX).

Andreau, J. 1977 'Fondations privées et rapports sociaux en Italie romaine (Ier-IIIème siècle ap. J.-C.)', *Ktema*: 157-209.

Andreau, J. & H. Bruhns eds 1990 *Parenté et stratégies familiales dans l'Antiquité romaine*. Rome: École française de Rome.

Arangio-Ruiz, V. 1954 *Le Persone sui iuris e la capacità di agire. Tutela e cura*. Naples: Loffredo.

Archer, L.J., S. Fischler & M. Wyke eds 1994 *Women in Ancient Societies: An Illusion of the Night*. London: Macmillan.

d'Arms, J.H. 1970 *Romans on the Bay of Naples: A Social and Cultural Study of Villas and their Owners from 150 B.C. to A.D. 400*. Cambridge, Massachusetts: Harvard University Press.

——— 1977 'M.I. Rostovtzeff and M.I. Finley: the status of traders in the Roman world' in d'Arms & Eadie 1977: 159-80.

——— 1980 'Republican senators' involvement in commerce in the late Republic: some Ciceronian evidence', pp. 77-90 in J.H. d'Arms & Kopf eds *The Seaborne Commerce of Ancient Rome: Studies in Archaeology and History. Studies in Archaeology and History*. Rome: MAAR 36.

——— 1981 *Commerce and Social Standing in Ancient Rome*. Cambridge, Massachusetts: Harvard University Press.

d'Arms, J.H. & J.W. Eadie eds 1977 *Ancient and Modern: Essays in Honor of G.F. Else*. Ann Arbor: Michigan University Press.

Asser, W.D.H. 1971 *The Procurator in the Development of Agency in Roman Law and Later Civil Law*. Dissertation, Trinity College, Cambridge.

Austin, R.G.A. 1933 *M. Tulli Ciceronis pro M. Caelio oratio*. Oxford: Clarendon (revised 3rd edition 1960).

d'Avino, M. 1967 *The Women of Pompeii* (trans. M. Hope Jones & L. Nusco). Naples: Loffredo.

Badian, E. 1996 'M. Caelius Rufus', article in *OCD*: 271.

Balsdon, J.P.V.D. 1962 *Roman Women: Their History and their Habits*. London: Bodley Head.

Barrett, D.S. 1984 'Martial, Jews and circumcision', *LCM* 9.3: 42-6.

Bartman, E. 1999 *Portraits of Livia: Imaging the Imperial Woman in Augustan Rome*. Cambridge: Cambridge University Press.

Bashar, N. 1984 'Women and the concept of change in history' in Dixon & Munford 1984: 43-6.

Bauman, R. 1992 *Women and Politics in Ancient Rome*. London: Routledge.

Beard, M. 1999 'The erotics of rape. Livy, Ovid and the Sabine women' in Setälä & Savunen 1999: 1-10.

Beaucamp, J. 1976 'Le vocabulaire de la faiblesse féminine dans les textes juridiques romains du IIIe ou VIe siècle', *Revue historique du droit français et étranger* 54: 485-509.

Blanshard, A. 2000 'Hellenic fantasies: aesthetics and desire in John Addington Symonds' "A problem in Greek Ethick" ', *Dialogos* (in press).

Bloch, H. 1947-8 *Supplement to Volume 15,1 of the Corpus Inscriptionum Latinarum. Including complete indices to the Roman brickstamps*. Cambridge, Massachusetts: Harvard Studies in Classical Philology: 46-9 (reprinted 1967 by 'l'Erma' di Bretschneider, Rome).

Blok, J. 1987 'Sexual asymmetry: a historiographical essay' in Blok & Mason 1987: 1-57.

Bibliography

Blok, J. & P. Mason eds 1987 *Sexual Asymmetry: Studies in Ancient Society*. Amsterdam: Gieben.

Boatwright, M. 1991 'The imperial women of the early second century A.C.', *AJP* 112: 513-40.

―――― 1992 'Matidia the Younger', *EMC/CV* 36 (N.S.11): 19-32.

Boissier, G. 1873 'Les Femmes à Rome, leur éducation et leur rôle dans la société romaine', *Revue des deux mondes* (seconde période) 108: 525-53.

Bradley, K.R. 1978 *Suetonius's Life of Nero: An Historical Commentary*. Brussels: Latomus (Coll. Latomus 157).

―――― 1985 'Ideals of marriage in Suetonius' *Caesares*', *Rivista storica dell' antichità* 15: 77-95.

―――― 1986 'Wet-nursing at Rome: a study in social relations' in Rawson ed. 1986: 201-29.

Brandt, R. 1980 'La vita quotidiana à Ficana', *Ficana: una pietra miliare sulla strada per Roma* (travelling exhibition of finds from the 1975-1980 Italian-Scandinavian dig at Ficana, modern Acilia). Copenhagen: Museum Tusculanum: 111-22.

Braund, S. ed. 1989a *Satire and Society in Ancient Rome*. Exeter: University of Exeter Press (Exeter Studies in History no. 23).

―――― 1989b 'Introduction', in Braund 1989a: 1-3.

―――― 1989c 'City and country in Roman satire' in Braund 1989a: 23-47.

―――― 1992 'Juvenal – misogynist or misogamist?' *Journal of Roman Studies* 82: 71-86.

―――― (forthcoming 2001) 'Genre', introduction to the section on *genre* in S. Harrison ed., *Ideas and the Classics: Scholarship, Theory and Classical Literature*, Oxford: Oxford University Press.

Braund, S. & B. Gold eds 1998 *Vile Bodies*, special issue of *Arethusa* 31.3.

Brion, M. 1960 *Pompeii and Herculaneum, the Glory and the Grief*. London: Elek (trans. J. Rosenberg – reprinted 1973 Cardinal).

Brown, S. 1997 ' "Ways of seeing" women in antiquity: an introduction to feminism in classical archaeology and ancient art history' in Koloski-Ostrow & Lyons 1997: 12-42.

Browner, C. 1986 'The politics of reproduction in a Mexican village', *Signs* 11.4: 710-24.

Brownmiller, S. 1976 *Against Our Will: Men, Women and Rape*. New York: Bantam.

Bulwer-Lytton, E. 1834 *The Last Days of Pompeii* (reprinted 1839, Paris: Baudry's European Library).

Calza, G. 1939 'Epigrafe sepolcrale contenente disposizioni testamentarii', *Epigraphica* 1: 160-2.

―――― 1978 'Ritratti romani dal 160 circa alla metà del III sec.d.C.', *Scavi di Ostia* 9.

Cameron, A. ed. 1989a *History as Text. The Writing of Ancient History*. London: Duckworth.

―――― 1989b 'Introduction: the writing of history' in Cameron 1989a: 1-10.

Cameron, A. & A. Kuhrt eds 1983 *Images of Women in Antiquity*. Beckenham: Croom Helm.

Carcopino, J. 1940 *Daily Life in Ancient Rome: The People and the City at the Height of the Empire* (trans. from the French by E.O. Lorimer). New Haven: Harvard University Press (1941, London: Routledge).

Carro, D. 1992-7 *Classica. Storia della Marina di Roma. Testimonianze dall' Antichità*. Rome: Rivista Marittima.

207

Bibliography

Casson, L. 1971 *Ships and Seamanship in the Ancient World*. Princeton University Press (reprinted 1995, Johns Hopkins University Press).

Champlin, E. 1991 *Final Judgements: Duty and Emotion in Roman Wills, 200 B.C. – A.D. 250*. Berkeley: University of California Press.

Chastagnol, A. 1979 'Les Femmes dans l'ordre sénatorial: titulature et rang social à Rome', *Revue historique* 103: 3-28.

Chomsky, N. 1995 'Visions of freedom', audio-tape of talk delivered at Sydney Town Hall, 21 January 1995.

Clark, A. 1919 (/1968) *Working Life of Women in the Seventeenth Century*. London: Cass.

Clark, G. 1989 'Women in the ancient world', *Greece & Rome. New Surveys in the Classics* 21.

Clark, G. & H. King 1994 'Contraceptives of old', *Chemistry and Industry* 18: 722.

Clarke J. 1996 'Hypersexual black men in Augustan baths: ideal somatypes and apotropaic magic' in Kampen 1996: 184-98.

―――― 1998 *Looking at Lovemaking: Constructions of Sexuality in Roman Art, 100 BC – AD 250*. Berkeley: University of California Press.

Cohen, D. 1991 *Law, Sexuality and Society: The Enforcement of Morals in Classical Athens*. Cambridge: Cambridge University Press.

Cohen, D. & R.P. Saller 1994 'Foucault on sexuality in Greco-Roman antiquity' in Goldstein 1994: 35-59.

Cole, S.G. ed. 1984 *Male and Female in Greek Cult* (special issue, *ZPE* 55).

Corbett, P.E. 1930 *The Roman Law of Marriage*. London: Clarendon.

Corbier, M. 1990 'Usages publics du vocabulaire de la parenté', *L'Africa romana: Atti del VII Convegno di studio Sassari 15-17 dec. 1989*. ed. A. Mastino. Sassari Gallizi: Dip. Di storia dell'università degli studi di Sassari no. 16: 815-54.

Cornish, F.W. 1926 *Catullus, Tibullus and Pervigilium Veneris*. Cambridge, Massachusetts: Loeb Classical Library.

Cornwall, A. & N. Lindisfarne eds 1994 *Dislocating Masculinity: Comparative Ethnographies*. London: Routledge.

Cotton, H. 1981 *Documentary Letters of Recommendation in Latin from the Roman Empire*. Königstein: Anton Hain (Beiträge zur klassischen Philologie 132).

Courtney, E.E. 1980 *A Commentary on the Satires of Juvenal*. London: Athlone.

Coyne, P. n.d. 'From Tacitus to television. The empress Livia and the novels of Graves, Howatch and Massie' (unpublished paper).

Crawford, D.J. 1976 'Imperial estates' in Finley 1976: 35-70.

Crook, J.A. 1967 *Law and Life of Rome, 90 B.C. – A.D. 212*. London: Thames & Hudson.

―――― 1986a 'Women and succession in Roman law' in Rawson 1986a: 58-82.

―――― 1986b 'Feminine inadequacy and the *senatusconsultum velleianum*' in Rawson 1986a: 83-92.

Csillag, P. 1976 *The Augustan Laws on Family Relations*. Budapest: Akademiai Kiado.

Culham, P. 1987 'Ten years after Pomeroy: studies of the image and reality of women in antiquity' in Skinner ed.

―――― 1990 'Decentering the text: the case of Ovid' *Helios* 17.2: 161-70.

Currie, S. 1996 'The empire of adults: the representation of children on Trajan's arch at Beneventum' in Elsner 1996: 153-81.

Daube, D. 1965 'Licinnia's dowry' *Studi in Onore di Biondo Biondi* vol. 1. Milan: 199-212.

Davis, N.Z. 1983 *The Return of Martin Guerre*. London & Cambridge, Massachusetts: Harvard University Press.

Deacy, S. & K.F. Pierce eds 1997 *Rape in Antiquity: Sexual Violence in the Greek and Roman Worlds*. London: Duckworth.

Dean-Jones, L. 1992 'The politics of pleasure' *Helios* 19.1-2: 72-91.

――――― 1994 *Women's Bodies in Classical Greek Science*. Oxford: Clarendon.

Delia, D. 1991 'Fulvia reconsidered' in Pomeroy 1991a: 197-217.

Della Corte 1954 *Case ed Abitanti di Pompeii*. Rome: 'L'Erma' di Bretschneider (2nd ed.).

Dickinson, O.T.P.K. 1994 *The Aegean Bronze Age*. Cambridge: Cambridge University Press.

Diehl, E. 1925-1967 *Inscriptiones Latinae Christianae Veteres* (4 vols) Berlin.

――――― 1930 *Pompeianische Wandinschriften und Verwandtes*. Berlin: de Gruyter.

Dixon, S. 1983 'A family business: women's role in patronage and politics at Rome 80-44 BC', *Classica et Mediaevalia* 34: 91-112.

――――― 1984 '*Infirmitas sexus*: womanly weakness in Roman law', *Tijdschrift voor Rechtsgeschiedenis / Revue d'Histoire du droit* 52: 343-71 (reprinted in this vol. in abbreviated form as Chapter 6).

――――― 1985 'Breaking the law to do the right thing: the gradual erosion of the Voconian law in Ancient Rome', *Adelaide Law Review* 9: 519-34.

――――― 1986 'Family finances. Terentia and Tullia' in Rawson 1986a: 93-120 (reprinted from *Antichthon* 18: 78-101).

――――― 1988 *The Roman Mother*. London: Croom Helm/Routledge.

――――― 1991 'The sentimental ideal of the Roman family', B. Rawson ed. *Marriage, Divorce and Children in Ancient Rome*. Oxford: Oxford University Press: 99-113.

――――― 1992a *The Roman Family*. Baltimore: Johns Hopkins University Press.

――――― 1992b 'Conclusion – the enduring theme: domineering dowagers and scheming concubines' in Garlick, Dixon & Allen 1992: 209-25.

――――― 1992c 'A woman of substance: Iunia Libertas of Ostia', *Helios* 19: 162-74, ed. Konstan.

――――― 1993a ' "A Lousy Ingrate": honour and patronage in the American mafia and ancient Rome', *International Journal of Moral and Social Studies* 8: 61-72.

――――― 1993b 'The meaning of gift and debt in the Roman elite', *EMC / CV* 37 (n.s.12): 451-64.

――――― 1997 'Conflict in the Roman family' in Rawson & Weaver 1997: 149-67.

――――― 2001 'How can you count them when they aren't there? New perspectives on Roman cloth production', forthcoming in *Opuscula Romana* 25.

Dixon, S. & T. Munford eds 1984 *Pre-Industrial Women: Interdisciplinary Perspectives*. Canberra: ANU Women's History Group.

Dorey, T.A. 1958 'Cicero, Clodia and the Pro Caelio', *Greece and Rome* 27: 175-80.

Dougherty, C. 1998 'Sowing the seeds of violence. Rape, women and the land' in M. Wyke ed. *Parchments of Gender: Deciphering the Bodies of Antiquity*. Oxford: Clarendon.: 267-84.

Duncan-Jones, R. 1964 'The Purpose and organisation of the *alimenta*', *Publications of the British School at Rome* 32: 123-46.

――――― 1974 *The Economy of the Roman Empire: Quantitative Studies*. Cambridge: Cambridge University Press.

Dupont, F. 1990 'Peut-on utiliser les textes satiriques comme documents sur la civilisation romaine? Un exemple: la nourriture', *LALIES* IX: 163-71.

Earle, P. 1989 'The female labour market in London in the late seventeenth and early eighteenth centuries', *Economic History Review* 2nd ser. 42.3: 328-53.

Bibliography

Edwards, C. 1993 *The Politics of Immorality*. Cambridge: Cambridge University Press.

—— 1997 'Unspeakable professions: public performance and prostitution in ancient Rome' in Hallett & Skinner 1997: 66-95.

Ehrenberg, V. & A.H.M. Jones 1955 *Documents Illustrating the Reigns of Augustus and Tiberius* (2nd edition). Oxford: Clarendon.

Elsner, J. ed. 1996 *Art and Text in Roman Culture*. Cambridge: Cambridge University Press.

Étienne, R. 1973 'La Conscience médicale antique et la vie des enfants', *Annales de démographie historique* (special issue, *Enfant et société*: 15-61).

Evans, J.K. 1991 *War, Women and Children in Ancient Rome*. London, New York: Routledge.

Evans Grubbs, J. 1989 'Abduction marriage in antiquity: a law of Constantine and its social context', *Journal of Roman Studies* 79: 59-83.

—— 1995 *Law and Family in Late Antiquity: The Emperor Constantine's Marriage Legislation*. Oxford: Clarendon.

Eyben, E. 1980-1981 'Family planning in Graeco-Roman antiquity', *Ancient Society* 11-12: 5-82.

Eyre, E.J. 1845 *Journals of Expeditions of Discovery into Central Australia and Overland*. London: Boone.

Fabré, G. 1981 *Libertus: recherches sur les rapports patron-affranchi à la fin de la République romaine*. Rome: École française de Rome.

Fantham, E. 1986 'Women in antiquity: a selective (and subjective) survey 1979-1984', *Échos du monde classique/Classical Views* (*EMC/CV*) n.s. 5.1: 1-24.

—— 1998 *Ovid Fasti Book IV*. Cambridge: Cambridge University Press.

Fantham, E., H.P. Foley, N.B. Kampen, S.B. Pomeroy, H.A. Shapiro 1994 *Women in the Classical World*. New York, Oxford: Oxford University Press.

Finley, M.I. 1965 'The silent women of ancient Rome', *Horizon* 7: 57-64 (reprinted 1967 in *Aspects of Antiquity: Discoveries and Controversies*: 129-42. New York: Viking).

—— 1973 *The Ancient Economy*. London: Chatto & Windus.

—— 1976 ed. *Studies in Roman Property*. Cambridge: Cambridge University Press.

Fischler, S. 1994 'Social stereotypes and historical analysis: the case of the imperial women at Rome' in Archer, Fischler & Wyke 1994: 115-33.

Fitzgerald, F. Scott 1966 *The Beautiful and the Damned*. Harmondsworth: Penguin (from 1922 original).

Fleming, T. 1986 'Des dames du temps jadis', *CJ* 82.1: 73-80.

Flory, M.B. 1978 'Family in *familia*: kinship and community in slavery', *AJAH* 3: 78-95.

—— 1984 '*Sic exempla parantur*: Livia's shrine to Concordia and the Porticus Liviae', *Historia* 33: 309-30.

—— 1993 'Livia and the history of public honorific statues for women in Rome', *TAPA* 123: 287-308.

—— 1997 'The meaning of *Augusta* in the Julio-Claudian period', *AJAH* 13.2: 113-38.

Foley, H.P. ed. 1981 *Reflections of Women in Antiquity*. New York: Gordon and Breach Science Publishers.

Fora, M. 1992 'Ummidia Quadratilla ed il restauro del teatro di Cassino', *ZPE* 94: 269-73.

Forbis, E. 1990 'Women's public image in Italian inscriptions', *AJP* 111: 493-512.

Bibliography

Fordyce, C.J. 1961 *Catullus: A Commentary*. Oxford: Clarendon.

Foucault, M. 1984/1990 *The Use of Pleasure*, vol. 2 of *The History of Sexuality*. (trans. R. Hurley 1990 New York: Vintage Books from the 1984 original publication, *L'Usage des plaisirs* Paris: Gallimard).

Foxhall, L. & J. Salmon eds 1998 *Thinking Men: Masculinity and its Self-Representation in the Classical Tradition*. London, New York: Routledge.

—— 1999 *When Men were Men: Masculinity, Power and Identity in Classical Antiquity*. London, New York: Routledge.

Förtsch, B. 1935 *Die politische Rolle der Frau in dem Republik*. Würzburg: Würzburger Studien zur Altertumswissenschaft 5.

Fraschetti, A. ed. 1994a *Roma al femminile*. Roma-Bari: Laterza.

—— 1994b 'Livia, la politica' in Fraschetti 1994a: 123-51.

Frayn, J.M. 1984 *Sheep-Rearing and the Wool Trade in Italy during the Roman Period*. Liverpool: Francis Cairns.

Friedl, E. 1959 'Dowry and inheritance in modern Greece', *Transactions of the New York Academy of Sciences* ser. 2: 49-54.

Gagé, J. 1963 *Matronalia: essai sur les dévotions et les organisations cultuelles des femmes dans l'ancienne Rome*. Bruxelles: Latomus.

Gallivan, P.A. 1974 'Confusion concerning the age of Octavia', *Latomus* 33: 116-17.

Gamel, M-K. 1990 'Reading "Reality" ', *Helios* 17: 171-4.

Gardner, J. 1995 'Gender-role assumptions in Roman law', *EMC / CV* 39 (n.s. 14): 377-400.

—— 1986 *Women in Roman Law and Society*. London: Croom Helm.

—— 1999 'Women in business life: some evidence from Puteoli' in Setälä & Savunen 1999: 11-27.

Garlick, B., S. Dixon & P. Allen eds 1992 *Stereotypes of Women in Power. Historical Perspectives and Revisionist Views*. New York, Westport Conn.: Greenwood.

Garnsey, P. 1970 *Social Status and Legal Privilege in the Roman Empire*. Oxford: Clarendon.

—— 1974 'Aspects of the decline of the urban aristocracy in the empire', *ANRW* ii.1: 229-52.

—— 1976 'Urban property investment', in Finley 1976: 123-36.

—— ed. 1980 *Non-Slave Labour in the Roman World*. Cambridge: Cambridge Philological Society (supp. vol. 6).

Garnsey, P. & R.P. Saller 1987 *The Roman Empire: Economy, Society and Culture*. London: Duckworth, and Berkeley: University of California Press.

Geddes, A. 1975 'The philosophic notion of women in antiquity', *Antichthon* 9: 35-40.

Geffcken, K.A. 1973 *Comedy in the Pro Caelio*. Leyden: Brill (Memnosyne Supplement 30).

Giacosa, G. 1977 *Women of the Caesars: Their Lives and Portraits on Coins*. Milan: Arte e Moneta.

Gibbon, E. 1776-1788 *The Decline and Fall of the Roman Empire* (reprinted 1910, London: Dent).

Gide, P. 1885 *Étude sur la condition privée de la Femme dans le droit ancien et moderne et en particulier sur le sénatus-consulte velléien*. Paris.

Gilmore, D. 1987 *Honor and Shame: The Unity of the Mediterranean*. Washington.

Gleason, M. 1995 *Making Men: Sophists and Self-presentation in Ancient Rome*. Princeton: Princeton University Press.

Gold, B.K. ed. 1982 *Literary and Artistic Patronage in Ancient Rome*. Austin: Texas University Press.

Bibliography

——— 1993 ' "But Ariadne was never there in the first place": finding the female in Roman poetry' in Rabinowitz & Richlin 1993: 75-101.

——— 1998 ' "The house I live in is not my own": women's bodies in Juvenal's *Satires'* in Braund & Gold 1998: 369-86.

Golden, M. 1981 'Demography and the exposure of girls at Athens', *Phoenix* 35: 316-51.

Golden, M. 1992 'Continuity, change and the study of ancient childhood', *EMC / CV* 36 n.s. 11: 7-18.

Goldstein, J. ed. 1994 *Foucault and the Writing of History*. Oxford: Blackwell.

Gomme, A.W. 1925 'The position of women in Athens in the fifth and fourth centuries', *CP* 20: 1-26.

Goodwater, L. 1975 *Women in Antiquity: An Annotated Bibliography*. Metuchen, N.J.: Scarecrow Press.

Grant, M. 1954 *Roman Imperial Money*. Edinburgh: Nelson.

deGrassi, A. 1963 *Inscriptiones Italiae*. 13.2. Florence: La nuova Italia.

Green, P. 1967 *Juvenal. The Sixteen Satires*. Translation, with an introduction and notes. Harmondsworth: Penguin.

Greene, K. 1986/1990 *The Archaeology of the Roman Economy*. Berkeley: University of California Press.

Gregory, C.A. 1982 *Gifts and Commodities*. London, New York: Academic Press.

Grubbs – see Evans Grubbs

Gruen, E. 1966 'P. Clodius: instrument or independent agent?' *Phoenix* 20: 120-30.

——— 1974 *The Last Generation of the Roman Republic*. Berkeley: University of California Press.

Guiducci, A. 1989 *Perdute nella storia. Storia delle donne dal I al VII secolo d.C.* Florence: Sansoni.

Gummerus, H. 1913 'Darstellungen aus dem Handwerk auf Römischen Grab- und Votivsteinen in Italien', *Jahrbuch des deutschen archäologischen Instituts* 28: 63-126.

——— 1916 'Industri und Handel (Rom)', *RE* IX: 1449=1534.

Hahn, U. 1994 *Die Frauen der römischen Kaiserhauses und ihre Ehrungen*. Mainz am Rhein: Philipp von Zabern.

Haley, S.P. 1993 'Black feminist thought and classics: re-membering, re-claiming, re-empowering' in Rabinowitz & Richlin 1993: 23-43.

Hallett, J.P. 1973 'The role of women in Roman elegy: counter-cultural feminism', *Arethusa* 6: 103-24 (reprinted in Peradotto & Sullivan 1984: 241-62).

——— 1977 *'Perusinae glandes* and the changing name of Augustus', *AJAH* 2: 151-71.

——— 1984 *Fathers and Daughters in Roman Society: Women and the Elite Family*. Princeton: Princeton University Press.

——— 1989 'Women as "Same" and "Other" in the Classical Roman Elite', *Helios* 16.1: 59-78.

——— 1992 'Heeding our native informants: the use of literary texts in recovering elite Roman attitudes towards age, gender and social status', *EMC / CV* 36 (n.s. 11): 333-55.

——— 1993 'Martial's Sulpicia and Propertius' Cynthia' in M. DeForest, ed. *Woman's Power, Man's Game: Essays in Classical Antiquity in Honor of Joy K. King*. Chicago: Bolchazy-Carducci: 322-53. (originally published 1992 in *Classical World* 86.2: 199-24).

Hallett, J.P. & M.B. Skinner eds 1997 *Roman Sexualities*. Princeton: Princeton University Press.

Bibliography

Halperin, D.M. 1994 'Historicizing the subject of desire: sexual preferences and erotic identities in the pseudo-Lucianic *Erotes*' in Goldstein: 19-34.

Hands, A.R. 1968 *Charities and Social Aid in Greece and Rome*. London: Thames and Hudson.

Hanson, A. 1992 'Conception, gestation and the origin of female nature in the *Corpus Hippocraticum*', *Helios* 19.1-2: 31-71.

Harris, W.V. 1993 'Between archaic and modern: some current problems in the history of the Roman economy', in Harris ed. *The Inscribed Economy: Production and Distribution in the Roman Empire in the Light of the Instrumentum Domesticum*. Ann Arbor: Journal of Roman Archaeology (supp. ser. VI): 11-29.

Haury, A. 1956 'Philotime et la vente des biens de Milon', *Revue des études latines* 34: 179-90.

Hawley, R. & B. Levick eds 1995 *Women in Antiquity: New Assessments*. London: Routledge.

Hecker, E.A. 1910 *A Short History of Women's Rights from the Days of Augustus to the Present Time: With Special Reference to England and the United States*. New York: Putnam's Sons.

Helen, T. 1975(-1977) *Organization of Roman Brick Production in the First and Second Centuries AD: An Interpretion of Roman Brick Stamps*. Helsinki: Finnish Academy (Annales Academiae Scientiarum Fennicae, Diss. Hum. Litt. 5).

Hellegouarc'h, J. 1963 *Le Vocabulaire latin des relations et des partis politiques sous la république*. Paris: Les belles letters (reprinted 1972).

Henderson, J.G.W. 1989a 'Satire writes "Woman": gendersong', *Proceedings of the Cambridge Philological Society* 215 (n.s. 35): 50-80.

───── 1989b 'Not "Women in Roman Satire" but "When Satire Writes Woman"' in Braund 1989a: 89-125.

───── 1989c 'Livy and the invention of history' in Cameron 1989a: 66-85.

Herzig, H.E. 1983 'Frauen in Ostia. Ein Beitrag zur Sozialgeschichte der Hafenstadt Roms', *Historia* 32: 77-92.

Hillard, T.W. 1973 'The Clodii Pulchri 76-48 B.C.: studies in their political cohesion', unpublished doctoral thesis, Macquarie University, Australia.

───── 1981 ' "*In triclinio Coam, in cubiculo Nolam*": Lesbia and the other Clodia', *Liverpool Classical Monthly* 6.6 (June): 149-54.

───── 1983 '*Materna auctoritas*: the political influence of Roman matronae', *Classicum* 22 (ix:1): 10-13.

───── 1989 'Republican politics, women and the evidence', *Helios* 16: 165-82.

───── 1992 'On the stage, behind the curtain: images of politically active women in the Late Roman Republic' in Garlick, Dixon & Allen 1992: 37-64.

Hind, J. 1972 'The death of Agrippina and the finale of the *Oedipus* of Seneca', *Australasian Universities Modern Languages Association* (*AUMLA*) 38: 204-11.

Hobson, D. 1984a 'The role of women in the economic life of Roman Egypt: a case study from first century Tebtunis', *EMC/CV* 28 (n.s. 3): 373-90.

───── 1984b, 'House and household in Roman Egypt', *Yale Classical Studies* 28: 211-29.

Hopkins, (M.) K. 1965a 'The age of Roman girls at marriage', *Population Studies* 18: 309-27.

───── 1965b 'Contraception in the Roman empire', *Comparative Studies in Society and History* 8: 124-51.

───── 1966 'On the probable age structure of the Roman population', *Population Studies* 20: 245-64.

───── 1978 *Conquerors and Slaves*. Cambridge: Cambridge University Press.

Bibliography

—— 1983a *Death and Renewal*. Cambridge: Cambridge University Press.

—— 1983b 'Introduction', pp. ix-xxiv in P. Garnsey, K. Hopkins & C.R. Whittaker eds *Trade in the Ancient Economy*. Berkeley: University of California Press.

Hornblower, S. & A. Spawforth eds 1996 *Oxford Classical Dictionary*, 3rd edition. Oxford, New York: Oxford University Press.

Huchthausen, U. 1974 'Herkunft und ökonomische Stellung weiblicher Adressaten von Reskripten des *Codex Iustinianus* (2. und 3. Jh. u.Z.)', *Klio* 56: 199-228.

—— 1976 'Zu kaiserlichen Reskripten an weiblicher Adressaten aus der Zeit Diokletians (284-305 u.z.)', *Klio* 58: 55-85.

Hudson, N.A. 1989 'Food in Roman satire' in Braund 1989a: 69-87.

Hughes, D.O. 1978 'From brideprice to dowry in Mediterranean Europe', *Journal of Family History* 3: 262-96.

Hunt, L. 1992 'Wife-beating, domesticity and women's independence in eighteenth-century London', *Gender and History* 4.1: 10-33.

Hunter, V. 1994 *Policing Athens: Social Control in the Attic Lawsuits, 420-320 B.C.* Princeton, N.J.: Princeton.

Huttunen, P. 1974 *The Social Strata in the Imperial City of Rome: A Quantitative Study of the Social Representation in the Epitaphs Published in the CIL VI*. Oulu: University of Oulu.

Irigaray, L. 1995 'The question of the other', *Yale French Studies* 87: 7-19.

Jashemski, W.F. 1979 *The Gardens of Pompeii, Herculaneum and the Villas Destroyed by Vesuvius*. New Rochelle, New York: Caratzas.

—— 1993 Appendix (vol. 2).

Johns, C. 1982 *Sex or Symbol? Erotic Images of Greece and Rome*. London: British Museum Press.

Jolowicz, H.F. 1972 (/B. Nicholas) *Historical Introduction to the Study of Roman Law*. Cambridge: Cambridge University Press (3rd edition from 1932/1952 original).

Jones, A.H.M. 1974 'The cloth industry under the Roman empire', pp. 350-64, in *The Roman Economy* ed. P.A. Brunt, Oxford: Blackwell (reprint of 1960 article, *Economic History Review* 13: 183-92).

Jongman, W. 1988 *The Economy and Society of Pompeii*. Amsterdam: Gieben.

Joplin, P.K. 1990 'Ritual work on human flesh: Livy's Lucretia and the rape of the body politic', *Helios* 17: 51-70.

Jørgensen, K. 1982 'The invisible woman – some methodological considerations' in M LeWinter ed. *Theoretical and Methodological Problems in Research on Women in Developing Countries*. Copenhagen: Women's Social Research Centre: 57-65.

Joshel, S. 1992a *Work, Identity and Social Status at Rome: A Study of the Occupational Inscriptions at Rome*. Norman: University of Oklahoma Press.

—— 1992b 'The Body Female and the Body Politic: Livy's Lucretia and Verginia' in Richlin 1992a: 112-30.

—— 1997 'Female desire and the discourse of empire: Tacitus's Messalina' in Hallett & Skinner 1997: 221-54.

Just, R. 1975 'Conceptions of women in classical Athens', *Journal of the Anthropological Society of Oxford* 6: 153-70.

Kampen, N. 1981 *Image and Status: Roman Working Women in Ostia*. Berlin: Mann.

—— 1982 'Social status and gender in Roman art: the case of the saleswoman' in N. Broude & M. Garrard eds *Feminism and Art History: Questioning the Litany*: 62-77.

Bibliography

———— 1991 'Between public and private: women as historical subjects in Roman art' in Pomeroy 1991a: 218-48.

———— ed. 1996 *Sexuality in Ancient Art*. Cambridge: Cambridge University Press.

Kaplan, M. 1979 '*Agrippina semper atrox: A Study in Tacitus' Characterization of Women*', C. Deroux ed. *Studies in Latin Literature and Roman History I*. Brussels: Coll. *Latomus* 164: 410-17.

Kaser, M. 1971-1975 *Das römische Privatrecht*. Munich: Beck.

Keegan, P. 2000 'GAIA: the inverse function of C as an integral calculation of gender', unpublished paper delivered at the third *Feminism and the Classics* Conference ('The New Generation'), University of Southern California, May 2000.

Keuls, E.C. 1985 *The Reign of the Phallus: Sexual Politics in Ancient Athens*. Berkeley: University of California Press.

Kinchin Smith, F. & T.W. Melluish 1942 *Catullus. Selections from the Poems* (rev. 1946, subsequently reprinted, London: Allen & Unwin).

King, H. 1993 'Producing woman: Hippocratic gynaecology' in Archer, Fischler & Wyke 1993: 102-14.

———— 1998 *Hippocrates' Woman: Reading the Female Body in Ancient Greece*. London, New York: Routledge.

Kirkby, D. 1997 *Barmaids*. Cambridge: Cambridge University Press.

Kitto, H.D.F. 1951 *The Greeks*. Harmondsworth: Penguin. 2nd ed. 1957.

Kleiner, D.E. 1992 *Roman Sculpture*. London, New Haven: Yale University Press.

Kleiner, F.S. 1996 Review of T. Micocki *Les Impératrices et princesses romaines assimilées à des déesses: Étude iconologique* and R.Tansini *I Ritratti di Agrippina maggiore*, *American Journal of Archaeology* 100: 797-8.

Knox, P.E. 1995 *Ovid Heroides. Select Epistles*. Cambridge: Cambridge University Press.

Kokkinos, N. 1992 *Antonia Augusta: Portrait of a Great Roman Lady*. London, New York: Routledge.

Koloski-Ostrow, A. & C.L. Lyons eds 1997 *Naked Truths: Women, Sexuality and Gender in Classical Art and Archaeology*. London, New York: Routledge.

Konstan, D. ed. 1992 *Documenting Gender: Women and Men in Non-Literary Classical Texts*. Special issue of *Helios* (19.1 + 2). Lubbock, Texas: Texas Tech University Press.

Konstan, D. & M. Nussbaum eds 1990 *Sexuality in Greek and Roman Society*. Special issue of *differences* (2.1).

Koortbojian, M. 1996 '*In commemorationem mortuorum*: text and image along the "streets of tombs"' in Elsner 1996: 210-33.

Kroll, W. 1923 *C. Valerius Catullus*. Leipzig: Teubner (3rd edition reprinted Stuttgart, 1959).

Kuhn, A. ed. 1985 *The Power of the Image: Essays on Representation and Sexuality*. London: Routledge & Kegan Paul.

Lacey, W.K. 1968 *The Family in Classical Greece*. London: Thames & Hudson.

Lanfranchi, F. 1938 *Il diritto nei retori romani*. Milan: Giuffrè.

Larsson Lovén, L. 1998a 'LANAM FECIT – woolworking and female virtue' in Larsson Lovén & A. Strömberg 1998: 85-95.

———— 1998b 'Male and female professions in the textile production of Roman Italy', pp. 73-8, in L. Bender Jørgensen & C. Rinaldo eds *Textiles in European Archaeology*. Göteborg: GOTARC ser. A, vol. 1.

Larsson Lovén, L. & A. Strömberg eds 1998 *Aspects of Women in Antiquity*. Jonsered, Sweden: Paul Åstrom.

Bibliography

Lattimore, R. 1942 *Themes in Greek and Latin Epitaphs*. Urbana: University of Illinois Press.

Laurence, R. 1994 *Roman Pompeii: Space and Society*. London: Routledge.

Lee, G. 1990 *The Poems of Catullus: A New Translation by Guy Lee*. Oxford: Oxford University Press (reprinted 1991 in paperback World's Classics series).

Lefkowitz, M.R. 1986 *Women in Greek Myth*. London: Duckworth.

Lefkowitz, M.R. & M.B. Fant eds 1975 *Women in Greece and Rome*. London: Duckworth.

—— 1982/1992 *Women's Life in Greece and Rome. A Source Book in Translation*. London: Duckworth.

LeGall, J. 1970 'Les Métiers des femmes au Corpus Inscriptionum Latinarum', pp. 123-30, in *Mélanges M. Durry* (reprinted from *REL* 47 (bis) 1969: 123-30).

Lenaghan, J.O. 1969 *Commentary on Cicero's De Haruspicum Responsis*. The Hague: Mouton.

Levy, E. ed. 1983 *La Femme dans les sociétés antiques*. Strasbourg: *Actes des colloques de Strasbourg* (mai 1980 et mars 1981). Strasbourg: Université des Sciences Humaines de Strasbourg.

LeWinter, M. ed. 1982 *Theoretical and Methodological Problems in Research on Women in Developing Countries*. Arbeijdsnotat nr 5/82, Copenhagen: Women's Social Research Centre.

Lind, L.R. 1979 'Roman moral conservatism', pp. 7-58 in C. Deroux (ed.) *Studies in Latin Literature* vol. I (Collection Latomus vol.164). Brussels.

Lindsay, H. 1994 'Revenge on the tyrant: the assassinations of Philip II and Caligula', *Eranos* 92: 73-84.

Loane, H.J. 1938 *Industry and Commerce of the City of Rome (50 B.C. – 200 A.D.)*. Baltimore: The Johns Hopkins University Press.

Loraux, N. 1981 *Les Enfants d'Athéna: idées athéniennes sur la citoyenneté et la division des sexes*. Paris: Maspero, Textes à l'appui (published 1993 in English as *The Children of Athena: Athenian Ideas about Citizenship and the Division between the Sexes*, trans. C. Levine. Princeton: Princeton University Press).

Lyne, R.A.M. 1980 *The Latin Love Poets from Catullus to Horace*. Oxford: Clarendon.

McDonnell, M. 1987 'The speech of Numidicus at Gellius, *NA* 1.6', *AJP* 108: 81-94.

McGinn, T.A.J. 1998 *Prostitution, Sexuality, and the Law in Ancient Rome*. Oxford: Oxford University Press.

MacMullen, R. 1980 'Woman in public in the Roman empire', *Historia* 29: 208-18.

Manacorda, D. 1975 'The *ager Cosanus* tra tarda repubblica e impero: forme di produzione', in d'Arms & Kopf: 173-84.

—— 1978 'The *ager cosanus* and the production of the amphorae of Sestius: new evidence and a reassessment', *JRS* 68: 122-31.

de Maria, R. 1966 *Clodia*. London: Consul.

Marshall, P.K. 1977 *Cornelii Nepotis Vitae cum Fragmentis*. Leipzig: Teubner.

Mason, H.A. 1963 'Is Juvenal a classic?' in J.P. Sullivan ed. *Critical Essays on Roman Literature: Satire*. London: Athlone: 93-176.

Mauss, M. 1954 *The Gift* trans. I. Cunnison from original 'Essai sur le don'. London: Cohen and West (corrected reprint 1969).

Maxey, M. 1938 *Occupations of the Lower Classes in Roman Society* (orig. published Chicago: University of Chicago Press; reprinted in M. Parke & M. Maxey 1975 *Two Studies in the Roman Lower Classes*. New York: Arno).

Meiggs, R. 1973 *Roman Ostia*. Oxford: Oxford University Press.

216

Bibliography

Meyer, P.M. 1895 *Der römische Konkubinat nach den Rechtsquellen und der Inschriften*. Leipzig: Teubner (reprinted 1966 Aalen: Scientia).

Michel, J.H. 1962 *Gratuité en droit romain*. Brussels: Université libre de Bruxelles.

Millennium: Tribal Wisdom and the Modern World. 1992 Magazine version, linked with the television series produced by M. Grant and featuring D. Maybury-Lewis. Fitzroy, Australia: Bluestone Media.

Mitford, J. 1961 *Hons and Rebels*. London: Victor Gollancz (Readers' Union).

Mitford, N. 1988 *The Pursuit of Love*. Harmondsworth: Penguin (reprint of 1945 original).

Modrzejewski, J. 1974 'À propos de la tutelle dative des Femmes dans l'Égypte romain', *Akten des XIII. Internationales Papyrologenkongresses* (Munich): 265-92.

Moeller, W. 1969 'The male weavers at Pompeii', *Technology and Culture* 10: 561-6.

—— 1972 'The building of Eumachia: a reconsideration', *AJA* 76: 323-7.

—— 1976 *The Wool Trade in Ancient Pompeii*. Leiden: Brill.

Montevecchi, O. 1982 'Contratti di baliatico e vendite fiduciarie a Tebtynis', *Aegyptus* 52: 148-61.

Moore, C. 1999 ' "Unwomanly toil": the women nailmakers of the late 19th century', *Family Tree Magazine*, November 1999: 27-8.

Morris, I. 1992 *Death-Ritual and Social Structure in Classical Antiquity*. Cambridge: Cambridge University Press.

Morton, A. 1999 'Give me a head with hair', paper presented at the *Text, Artifact, Context* conference, Macquarie University, Australia, October 1999.

Mrozek, S. 1988 'Die Privaten alimentarstiftungen in der römischen Kaiserzeit', ed. H. Kloft, *Sozialmassnahmen und Fürsorge. Zur Eigenart antiker Sozialpolitik. Grazer Beiträge Supplementband III*. Horn/Österreich Berger: 155-66.

Münzer, F. 1897 'M.Caelius Rufus,' *RE* 3.1: 1266-72 (Caelius no. 35).

—— 1900 'Clodia' *RE* 4.1: 105-7 (Clodius no. 66, Clodia Metelli), 107 (no. 67, Clodia Luculli), 108 (no. 72, Clodia Tertia, wife of Q. Marcius Rex).

Mustakallio, K. 1999 'Legendary women and female groups in Livy' in Setälä & Savunen 1999: 53-64.

Nardi, E. 1971 *Procurato aborto nel mondo greco romano*. Milan: Giuffrè.

Nimis, S. 1984 'Fussnoten: das Fundament der Wissenschaft', *Arethusa* 17.2: 105-34.

Nisbet, R.G.M. 1961 *Cicero In Pisonem*. Oxford: Oxford University Press.

Ogilvie, R.M. 1965 *A Commentary on Livy Books 1-5*. Oxford: Clarendon.

Opie, I. & P. Opie 1969 *Children's Games in Street and Playground*. Oxford: Clarendon.

Ortner, S.B. 1974 'Is female to male as nature is to culture?' in M.Z. Rosaldo & L. Lamphere eds *Woman, Culture and Society*. Stanford: Stanford University Press: 67-87.

Pagnotta, M. 1978-9 'Il culto di Fortuna Virile e Venere Verticordia nei riti delle calende di aprile a Roma', *Studi Classici, Annali della Facoltà di Lettere e Filosofia*, Università di Perugia: 145-56.

Palmer, A. 2000 'A peep at erotic Pompeii', *Sydney Morning Herald* 4 April 2000 (reprinted from the London *Telegraph*).

Parker, H. 1992a 'Love's body anatomized: the ancient erotic handbooks and the rhetoric of sexuality' in Richlin: 190-207.

Bibliography

—— 1992b 'Other remarks on the other Sulpicia', 1992a *Classical World* 86.2: 89-95.

—— 1997 'Women doctors in Greece, Rome and the Byzantine empire', in L. Furst ed. *Women Healers and Physicians: Climbing a Long Hill*. Kentucky: University of Kentucky Press: 131-50.

Parkin, T.W. 1992 *Demography and Roman Society*. Baltimore: Johns Hopkins University Press.

Passman, T. 1993 'Out of the closet and into the field: matriculture, the Lesbian perspective and feminist classics' in Rabinowitz & Richlin 1993: 181-208.

Paterson, J. 1982 ' "Salvation from the sea": amphorae and trade in the Roman west', *JRS* 72: 146-63.

Peacock, D.P.S. 1982 *Pottery in the Roman World: An Ethnoarchaeological Approach*. London, New York: Longman.

Peppe, L. 1984 *Posizione giuridica e Ruolo sociale della Donna romana in età repubblicana*. Milano: Giuffrè.

Peradotto, J. & J.P. Sullivan eds 1984 *Women and the Ancient World: The Arethusa Papers*. Albany: SUNY Press.

Petrikovits, H. von 1981 'Die specialisierung des römischen Handwerks', pp. 63-131, Teil I, H. Jankuhn, W. Janssen, R. Schmidt-Wiegand & H. Tiefenbach eds *Das Handwerk in vor-/frugeschichtlicher Zeit*. Göttingen.

Philippides, S.N. 1983 'Narrative strategies and ideology in Livy's "Rape of Lucretia" ', *Helios* 10.2: 113-19.

Plassard, J. 1921 *Le Concubinat romain sous le haut Empire*. Paris: Tenin.

Pleck, E.H. 1976 'Two worlds in one: work and the family', *Journal of Social History* 10.2: 178-95.

Pleket, H.W. 1984 'Urban élites and the economy in the Greek cities of the Roman empire', *Münstersche Beiträge z. antiken Handelsgeschichte* III.1: 3-36.

Pomeroy, S.B. 1975 *Goddesses, Whores, Wives and Slaves: Women in Classical Antiquity*. New York: Schocken.

—— 1976 'The relationship of the married woman to her blood relatives in Rome', *Ancient Society* (Louvain) 7: 215-27.

—— 1983 'Infanticide in Hellenistic Greece' in Cameron & Kuhrt 1983: 207-22.

—— 1984a *Women in Hellenistic Egypt from Alexander to Cleopatra*. New York: Schocken.

—— 1984b 'Selected bibliography on women in antiquity' in Peradotto & Sullivan: 315-72 (reprinted and updated from *Arethusa* 6, 1973).

—— 1991a ed. *Women's History and Ancient History*. Chapel Hill & London: University of North Carolina Press.

—— 1991b Preface to 1991a: xi-xvi.

Potter, T.W. 1987 *Roman Italy*. London: Guild.

Pugliese Carratelli, G. 1948 'Tabulae Ceratae Herculanensis II, Tavolette xiii-xxx', *Parola del passato* 3: 165-84.

Purcell, N. 1986 'Livia and the womanhood of Rome', *Proceedings of the Cambridge Philological Society* 212 (n.s. 32): 78-105.

Quinn, K. 1970 *Catullus. The Poems*. London: Macmillan.

—— 1973 'Trends in Catullan criticism', *ANRW* 1.3: 369-89.

Rabinowitz, N.S. 1993 Introduction to Rabinowitz & Richlin 1993: 1-20.

Rabinowitz, N.S. & A. Richlin 1993 *Feminist Theory and the Classics*. London, New York: Routledge.

Rawson, B. 1966 'Family life among the lower classes at Rome in the first two centuries of the Empire', *Classical Philology* 61: 71-83.

────── 1974 'Roman concubinage and other *de facto* marriages', *TAPA* 104: 279-305.

────── 1978 *The Politics of Friendship: Pompey and Cicero.* Sydney: Sydney University Press.

────── 1986a ed. *The Family in Ancient Rome: New Perspectives.* London: Croom Helm.

────── 1986b 'The Roman family' in 1986a: 1-57.

────── forthcoming: 'Children as cultural symbols: imperial ideology in the second century' in S. Dixon ed. *Childhood, Class and Kin in the Roman World.* London: Routledge.

────── ed. 1991 *Marriage, Divorce and Children in Ancient Rome.* Oxford: Clarendon; Canberra: Humanities Research Centre.

Rawson, B. & P.R.C. Weaver eds 1997 *The Roman Family: Status, Sentiment, Space.* Oxford: Oxford University Press.

Rawson, E. 1976 'The Ciceronian Aristocracy and its Properties' in Finley 1976: 85-102.

Richlin, A. 1981 'Approaches to the sources on adultery at Rome', *Women's Studies* 8: 225-50 (reprinted Foley 1981: 379-404 and, in condensed form, as an appendix to Richlin 1983).

────── 1983 *The Garden of Priapus: Sexuality and Aggression in Roman Humor.* Princeton: Princeton University Press (reprinted 1992, with a new introduction xiii-xxxiii).

────── 1984 'Invective against women in Roman satire', *Arethusa* 17.1: 67-80.

────── 1990 'Hijacking the Palladion', *Helios* 17: 175-85.

────── 1991 'Zeus and Metis: Foucault, feminism, classics', *Helios* 18.2: 1-21.

────── ed. 1992a *Pornography and Representation in Greece and Rome.* New York: Oxford University Press.

────── 1992b Introduction to 1992a: xi-xxiii.

────── 1992c 'Julia's jokes, Galla Placidia and the Roman use of women as political icons' in Garlick, Dixon & Allen 1992: 65-91.

────── 1992d 'Reading Ovid's rapes' in Richlin 1992a: 158-79.

────── 1997 'Pliny's brassiere' in Hallett & Skinner 1997: 197-220.

Riddle, J.M. 1992 *Contraception and Abortion from the Ancient World to the Renaissance.* Cambridge, Massachusetts: Harvard University Press.

Roberts, H.S. see Salskov Roberts

Rogers, B. 1980 *The Domestication of Women.* London: Tavistock.

Rose, C.B. 1997 *Dynastic Commemoration and Imperial Portraiture in the Julio-Claudian Period.* Cambridge & New York: Cambridge University Press.

Rostovtzeff, M. 1926 *Social and Economic History of the Roman Empire* (2nd ed. rev. P.M. Frazer, 1957). Oxford: Oxford University Press.

Rotondi, G. 1922 *Leges Publicae Populi Romani.* Hildesheim: Olms (Reprinted 1966).

Rouselle, A. 1988 *Porneia: On Desire and the Body in Antiquity.* Oxford: Blackwell (reprinted from French original 1983, Paris: Presses universitaires).

Rose, C.B. 1997 *Dynastic Commemoration and Imperial Portraiture in the Julio-Claudian Period.* Cambridge & New York: Cambridge University Press.

Rundell, 1979 'Cicero and Clodius: the question of credibility', *Historia* 28.3: 301-28.

Sahlins, M.D. 1966 'Poor man, rich man, big-man, chief: political types in Melanesia and Polynesia', in I. Hogbin & L.R. Hiatt eds, Readings in Australian and

Bibliography

Pacific Anthropology. Melbourne: Melbourne University Press: 159-79. (Reprinted from *Comparative Studies in Society and History* 5, 1963: 285-300.)

Saller, R. 1982 *Personal Patronage in the Roman Empire*. Cambridge: Cambridge University Press.

—— 1994 *Patriarchy, Property and Death in the Roman Family*. Cambridge: Cambridge University Press.

Salskov Roberts, H. 1977 'En piges chancer i oldtiden' in Salskov Roberts ed. *En Kvindes Chancer i Oldtiden*. Copenhagen: Museum Tusculanum: 9-47.

Salzman, M.R. 1982 'Cicero, the *Megalenses* and the defence of Caelius', *AJP* 103: 299-304.

Sasson, J. 1992 *Princess*. London: Doubleday.

Saylor, S. 1992 *The Venus Throw*. New York: St Martin's Press.

—— 1996 *A Murder on the Appian Way*. New York: St Martin's Press.

Schaps, D.M. 1979 *Economic Rights of Women in Ancient Greece*. Edinburgh: University Press.

Scheer, T. 2000 'Forschungen über die Frau in der Antike. Zele, Methoden, Perspektiven', *Gymnasium* 107.2: 143-72.

Scheid, J. 1992 'Myth, cult and reality in Ovid's *Fasti*', *Proceedings of the Cambridge Philological Society* 38: 113-31.

Scheidel, W. 1995 & 1996 'The most silent women of Greece and Rome: rural labour and women's life in the ancient world', Part I, *Greece & Rome* 42.2: 202-17; Part II, *Greece & Rome* 43.1: 1-10.

Schmitt Pantel, P. ed. 1990 *Storia delle donne I. L'Antichità*. Rome, Bari: Laterza.

Schuller, W. 1987 *Frauen in der römischen Geschichte*. Konstanz: Universitätsverlag.

Schultz, F. 1951 *Classical Roman Law*. Oxford: Clarendon.

Scott, J.W. & L. Tilly 1975 'Women's work and the family in nineteenth century Europe', *Comparative Studies in Society and History*: 36-64.

Scutt, J. 1976 'Reforming the law of rape: the Michigan example', *Australian Law Journal* 50: 615-24.

—— 1979 'The economics of sex: women in service', *Australian Quarterly* 51: 32-46.

Seager, R.J. 1996 'Clodia', article in *OCD*: 350.

Sebesta, J. & L. Bonfante eds 1994 *The World of Roman Costume*. Madison: University of Wisconsin Press.

Seltman, C. 1956 *Women in Antiquity*. London: Pan.

Setälä, P. 1977 *Private Domini in Roman Brick Stamps of the Empire: A Historical and Prosopographical Study of Landowners in the District of Rome*. Helsinki: Annales Academiae Scientiarum Fennicae (Diss. Hum. Litt. 5).

—— 1994 *Antikens Kvinnor* (Swedish translation of a Finnish original). Helsinki: Tidens Forlag.

—— 1998 'Female property and power in imperial Rome' in Larsson Lovén & Strömberg 1998: 96-110.

Setälä, P. & L. Savunen eds 1999 *Female Networks and the Public Sphere in Roman Society*. Rome: Finnish Institute in Rome (Acta Instituti Romani Finlandiae vol. xxii).

Shackleton Bailey, D.R. 1966 *Cicero's Letters to Atticus*, vol. 5. Cambridge: Cambridge University Press.

Sharrock, A. 1997 'Re(ge)ndering gender(ed) studies', *Gender and History* 9.3: 603-14.

Bibliography

Shatzman, I. 1975 *Senatorial Wealth and Roman Politics*. Brussels: Latomus (vol. 142).

Shaw, B.D. 1987 'The age of Roman girls at marriage: some reconsiderations', *Journal of Roman Studies* 77: 30-46.

—— 1991 'The cultural meaning of death: age and gender in the Roman family' in D.I. Kertzer & R.P. Saller eds *The Family in Italy: From Antiquity to the Present*. New Haven, London: Yale University Press.

Sherwin-White, A.N. 1966 *The Letters of Pliny: A Historical and Social Commentary*. Oxford: Clarendon.

Sienkewicz, H. 1895 *Quo Vadis?* reprinted 1973, Warsaw: Panstwowy Instytut. (and MGM film, 1951 directed by M. leRoy).

Sijpesteijn, P.J. 1965 'Die *chôris kyriou chrêmatizousai dikaiô teknôn* in den Papyri', *Aegyptus* 45: 171-89.

Singleton, D. 1972 'Juvenal VI.1-20, and some ancient attitudes to the Golden Age', *Greece and Rome* 19: 151-65.

Sirks, A.J.B. 1980 'A favour to rich freed women (*libertinae*) in 51 A.D. On Suet. *Cl.* 19 and the *Lex Papia*', *RIDA* 27 (ser. 3): 283-93.

Skinner, M.B. 1982 'Pretty Lesbius', *TAPA* 112: 197-208.

—— 1983 'Clodia Metelli', *TAPA* 113: 273-87.

—— 1986 'Classical studies vs. women's studies: *duo moi ta Noemmata*', *Helios* 12.2: 3-16.

—— 1987a 'Classical studies, patriarchy and feminism: the view from 1986', *Women's Studies International Forum* 10.2: 181-6.

—— 1987b 'Des bonnes dames et méchantes', *Classical Journal* 83: 69-74.

—— ed. 1987c *Rescuing Creusa: New Methodological Approaches to Women in Antiquity*. Special issue of *Helios* n.s. 13.2. Lubbock: Texas Tech.

—— 1987d 'Introduction' to Skinner 1987c: 1-8.

—— 1996 'Zeus and Leda: the sexuality wars in contemporary classical scholarship', *Thamyris* 3.1:103-23.

—— 1997 '*Quod multo fit aliter in Graecia ...*' in Hallett & Skinner 1997: 3-25.

Skoie, M. 1998 'Sublime poetry or feminine fiddling: gender and reception: Sulpicia through the eyes of two 19th century scholars' in Larsson Lovén & Strömberg 1998: 169-82.

Skydsgaard, J.-E. 1976 'The disintegration of the Roman labour market and the *clientela* theory', *Studia Romana in Honorem Petri Krarup Septuagenarii*. Odense: University Press: 44-8.

Solazzi, S. 1928-9 *Istituti tutelari*. Naples: Jovene.

Solazzi, S. 1973 '*Tutela e curatela*', entry in *Novissimo digesto italiano*, eds A. Azara & E. Eula, Turin.

Stehle, E. 1989 'Venus, Cybele and the Sabine women: the Roman construction of female sexuality', *Helios* 16.2: 143-64.

Sullivan, J.P. 1984 'The roots of anti-feminism in Greece and Rome', *Helix* 19/20: 71-84.

—— 1991 *Martial, the Unexpected Classic: A Literary and Historical Study*. Cambridge: Cambridge University Press.

Sullivan, J.P. & J. Peradotto eds 1984 *Women in the Ancient World: The Arethusa Papers*. Albany, New York.

Syme, R. 1939 *The Roman Revolution*. Oxford: Oxford University Press.

—— 1958 *Tacitus*. Oxford: Oxford University Press.

—— 1964 *Sallust*. Berkeley: University of California Press.

—— 1981 'Princesses and others in Tacitus', *Greece & Rome* 28: 40-52.

—— 1986 *The Augustan Aristocracy*. Oxford: Clarendon.

Bibliography

Syndikus, H.P. 1996 'Catullus', article in *OCD*: 303-4.

—— 1984-1990 *Catull. Eine Interpretation*. ed. with commentary on Catullus (3 vols). Darmstadt: Wissenschaftliche Buchgesellschaft.

Taylor, L.R. 1949 *Party Politics in the Age of Caesar*. Berkeley: University of California Press.

Thayer, J. 1929 *Lex Aquilia (Dig. IX.2); On Gifts between Husband and Wife (Dig. xxiv.1)*. Cambridge, Massachusetts: Harvard University Press.

Thomas, J.A.C. 1975 *The Institutes of Justinian*. Amsterdam, Oxford: North-Holland Publishing Company.

—— 1976 *Textbook of Roman Law*. Amsterdam, New York, Oxford: North-Holland Publishing Company.

Treggiari, S. 1969 *Roman Freedmen during the Late Republic*. Oxford: Clarendon.

—— 1976 'Jobs for women', *American Journal of Ancient History* 1: 76-104.

—— 1979 'Lower-class women in the Roman economy', *Florilegium* 1: 65-86.

—— 1981 'Concubinae', *Proceedings of the British School at Rome* 49: 59-81.

—— 1991 *Roman Marriage. Iusti Coniuges from the Time of Cicero to the Time of Ulpian*. Oxford: Clarendon.

Verdière, R. 1977 'À verser au dossier de la *Quadrantaria*', *Mélanges offerts à Leopold Sedar Senghor. Langues littérature histoire anciennes*. Dakar: Nouvelles éditions africaines: 479-94.

Versnel, H.S. 1987 'Wife and helpmate: women in ancient Athens in anthropological perspective' in Blok & Mason 1987: 59-86.

Veyne, P. 1957 'La table des Ligures Baebiani et L'institution alimentaire de Trajan', *Mémoires de L'Ecole française à Rome (MEFRA)* 69: 81-135.

—— 1958 'La table des Ligures Baebiani et L'institution alimentaire de Trajan II', *Mémoires de L'Ecole française à Rome (MEFRA)* 70: 177-241.

—— 1961 'Vie de Trimalchion,' *Annales* 16: 213-47.

—— 1979 'Mythe et réalité de l'autarcie à Rome', *Revue des études anciennes (REA)* 81: 261-81.

—— 1990 (orig. French 1976) *Bread and Circuses: Historical Sociology and Political Pluralism*. Harmondsworth: Penguin abridged edition from orig. French edition *Pain et cirques* Paris: Éditions du Seuil.

Villers, R. 1959 'Le statut de la Femme à Rome jusqu'à la fin de la République', *Receuils de la Société Jean Bodin XI, La Femme*: 177-90. Brussels: Éditions de la Librairie encyclopédique.

Virlouvet, C. 1994 'Fulvia, la passionaria' in Fraschetti 1994: 71-94.

de Visscher, F. 1963 *Le Droit des tombeaux romains*. Milan: Giuffrè.

Vogt, H. 1952 *Studien zum Senatusconsultum velleianum*. Bonn: Röhrscheid.

Walbank, F.W. 1979 *A Historical Commentary on Polybius*, vol. III. Oxford: Clarendon.

Walcot, P. & I. McAuslan eds 1995 *Women in Antiquity*. Oxford: Clarendon.

Waldstein, W. 1972 'Zum Fall der dos Licinniae', *Index III, Quaderni camerti di studi romanistici – Ommagio à Max Kaser*: 343-61.

Wallace-Hadrill, A. ed. 1990 *Patronage in Ancient Society*. London, New York: Routledge.

Walters, J. 1997 'Invading the Roman body: manliness and impenetrability in Roman thought' in Hallett & Skinner 1997: 29-43.

Waltzing, J.-P. 1895-1900 *Étude historique sur les corporations professionnelles chez les Romains depuis les origines jusqu'à la chute de l'Empire d'Occident*, 4 vols. Louvain, Charles Peeters.

Watson, A. 1967 *The Law of Persons in the Later Roman Republic*. Oxford: Clarendon.

Bibliography

———— 1971 *Roman Private Law Around 200 BCE*. Edinburgh: Edinburgh University Press.

———— 1975 *Rome of the Twelve Tables*. Princeton: Princeton University Press.

Westrup, C.W. 1943 *Recherches sur les formes antiques de mariage dans l'ancien droit romain*. Copenhagen: Munksgaard.

Wieacker, F. 1960 *Textstufen Klassischer Juristen*. Göttingen.

Wiedemann, T. 1987 *Adults and Children in the Roman Empire*. London: Routledge.

Wheeler, A.L. 1934 *Catullus and the Traditions of Ancient Poetry*. Berkeley: University of California Press.

Will, E.L. 1979 'Women in Pompeii', *Archaeology* 32: 34-43.

Williams, C. 1999 *Roman Homosexuality: Ideologies of Masculinity in Classical Antiquity*. Oxford: Oxford University Press.

Williams, G. 1958 'Some aspects of Roman marriage ceremonies and ideals', *JRS* 48: 16-29.

———— 1968 *Tradition and Originality in Roman Poetry*. Oxford: Clarendon.

Wiseman, T.P. 1969 *Catullan Questions*. Leicester: Leicester University Press.

———— 1970 'Pulcher Claudius', *Harvard Studies in Classical Philology* 74: 207-21.

———— 1971 *New Men in the Roman Senate 139 B.C. – A.D. 14*. Oxford: Oxford University Press.

———— 1974 *Cinna the Poet and other Roman Essays*. Leicester: Leicester University Press.

———— 1975 'Some imaginary lives', *Arion* n.s. 2: 96-115.

———— 1985 *Catullus and his World: A Re-appraisal*. Cambridge: Cambridge University Press.

Wissowa, G. 1912/1971 *Religion und Kultus der Romer.* Munich: Beck.

Wood, S. 1999 *Imperial Women: A Study in Public Images, 40 B.C. – A.D. 68*. Leiden/Boston/Cologne: Brill. (Mnemosyne Supp. 194.)

Woodcock, I. 1999 *Inventing the 'First Lady' Role: The Empress Livia and the Public Sphere*. Ph.D. thesis, University of Queensland.

Woodman, A.J. 1988 *Rhetoric in Classical Historiography. Four Studies*. London-Sydney: Croom Helm.

Wyke, M. 1987a 'Written women: Propertius' *Scripta Puella*', *Journal of Roman Studies* 77: 47-61.

———— 1987b 'The elegiac woman at Rome', *Proceedings of the Cambridge Philological Society* 213 (n.s. 33): 153-78.

———— 1989 'Mistress and metaphor in Augustan elegy', *Helios* 16: 25-47.

———— 1997 *Projecting the Past: Ancient Rome, Cinema and History*.

Yalman, N. 1963 'On the purity of women in the castes of Ceylon and Malabar', *Journal of the Royal Anthropological Institute of Great Britain and Ireland* 93: 25-58.

Zanker, P. 1988 *The Power of Images in the Age of Augustus*. Ann Arbor: Michigan University Press.

Zannini, P. 1976 *Studi sulla tutela mulierum*. Università di Torino, Memorie dell'istituto giuridico ser. II, memoria clix. Turin: Giappichelli.

Zetzel, J.E.G. 1980 'Horace's Liber Sermonum: the structure of ambiguity', *Arethusa* 13: 59-77.

Zimmer, G. 1983 'Römischer Handwerker', *ANRW* II, 12.3: 205-28.

de Zulueta, F. 1946-1953 *The Institutes of Gaius* (2 vols). Oxford: Oxford University Press.

Indexes

Index of ancient sources

This index includes authors and non-literary sources, arranged alphabetically. So for inscriptions, look under *AE* (*l'Année épigraphique*), *CIL* (*Corpus Inscriptionum Latinarum*) etc. References to the *Digest* (*Dig.*) and *Codex Iustinianus* (*CJ*) are under J for Justinian. Works known only by a collective title (*Anthologia Palatina*) rather than by author are filed under that title. Bold numbers refer to the pages and notes of this book.

AE (*l'Année épigraphique*): 1917-1918, 52, **186n.62**; 1940, 94, **187n.76**; 1946, 174, **188n.109**; 1964, 106, **188n.106**
Anthologia Palatina (*AP*): 5.46 & 101, **200n.68**
Appendix Vergiliana (*App. Vergil.*): 83, **172n.33**
APPIAN, Appianos, 2nd c. CE, from Alexandria (Egypt)
  Bella civilia (*BC, Civil war*), 1.1.7, **182n.8**; 1.20, **200n.71**; 4.32-4, **183n.19**; 4.37, **189n.123**
APULEIUS, b. *c.* 124 CE, Madaura, N. Africa
  Apologia (*Apol.*) 10, **196n.14**
  Metamorphoses (*Met.*) 2.9, **173n. 5**; 2.9-10, **41**; 2.9 & 16, **173n.45**; 2.16-17, **41**; 2.17, **xiv, 40, 41**; 17, **173n.43**; 87, **187n.85**
ARISTOTLE, 384-322 BCE, Chalcidice, N. Greece
  De generatione animalium (*On the generation of animals*) 7650, **172n.25**
  Politica (*Pol., Politics*) 1256-1328, **190n.2**; 1259b32, **172n.25**; 1260a14, **172n.25; 181n.16**
ASCONIUS, 3-88 CE, Quintus Asconius Pedianus, author of commentaries on Cicero's speeches
  Pro Milone (*On behalf of Milo*) 43C, **190n.15**
  In Pisonem (*Against Piso*) 10, **20, 199n.58**
AUGUSTUS, 63 BCE – 14 CE, b. Gaius Octavius, known as Octavianus (Octavian) after adoption by his

great-uncle Julius Caesar 45 CE; took the title 'Augustus' 27 January BCE
Res Gestae Divi Augusti (*RG, Achievements of the Divine Augustus*) 6, 8.5, **176n.3**
AULUS GELLIUS (Aul. Gell.) see GELLIUS
CALLIMACHUS, 3rd c. BCE, poet and scholar at the Ptolemaic court of Alexandria, b. Cyrene

  Epigrammata 25, **198n.36**
CASSIUS DIO see DIO
CATO the Elder (*maior*), Marcus Porcius Cato, 238-149 BCE, b. Tusculum, Central Italy
  De agricultura (*On agriculture*) pref. i-ii, **182n.4**
CATULLUS, Gaius Valerius Catullus, 84-54 BCE (but see ch.9), b. Verona, N.Italy: 2, **138, 197nn.21,22,25**; 2.1, **197n.26**; 3, **197nn.21,22**; 5, **140, 197nn.21,22,24,25,28**; 7, **140, 197nn.21,22,24,25,28**; 8, **138, 197nn.22,25,27**; **198n.36**; 10, **198n.37**; 10.9-13, **186n.63**; 11, **138, 140, 197nn.21,22,25,27**; 11.15, **197n.26**; 11.17-20, **37, 39**; 11.21-4, **198n.35**; 11.165-72, **42**;13, **197n.25**; 13.11, **197n.26**; 23, **173n.54**; 24, **197n.29**; 29, **198n.37, 200n.63**; 36, **138, 197nn.25,27**; 36.2, **197n.26**; 37, **197n.25**; 38, **197n.22**; 39, **173n.54**; 43, **197nn.24,25, 200n.70**; 48, **140, 197nn.28,29**; 51, **197nn.22,24,25, 198n.36**; 54, **198n.37**; 55, **140,**

General index

For definitions of legal terms (e.g. *patria potestas*), see Appendix 3. This index includes a selection of proper names, chiefly women's names. The names of imperial family members and well-known historical figures are under the most common initial or form, e.g. the empress Livia Augusta is under 'L', Caesar under 'C', but for most names rendered in English with 'J' (Julia, Junia, Julius etc.), see under 'I'.

235

241

Verginia xiv, 10, 46-7, 152
Verginius, father of Verginia 47, 48
Vestal priestess (= Vestal Virgin) 75, 102,
    104, 150, 180n.4, 202nn.93,94
vestiarii 124
Vettii, House of 125, 193n.57
Veturia Fedra 193n.52
Veturia Tryphera, freed slave of Decimus
    Veturius 124, 193n.50
Vibia Calybene, madam (*lena*) 116
Vibia Chresta, freed slave 116
victims: women as 10, 152; of sexual
    assault ch.4 *passim* esp. 50-1; poet as
    romantic victim 137, 139, 140
vilification 22, 137, 146-7, 152, 197-8n.32
violence 50, 54, 144; political 118
virginity 47-8, 52, 53, and ch.4 *passim*,
    174n.6
virtue, feminine 19, 33, 46, 52, and ch.4
    passim, 70, 89, 105, 117, 131 171n.3,
    182n.2, plate 8; asexual 40; the
    compliant or 'agreeable' wife 33;
    generalised depictions in iconography
    129; see also 'stereotype(s)'
Vitalis, Pompeian spinster 122
Voconian Law (*Lex Voconia*) of 169 BCE 84,
    94, 181n.40
Volumnia 186n.58, 189n.123
Volusii, monument of 187n.82
wall paintings 125, 131-2
ward (*pupilla* f., *pupillus* m.) 77; see also
    'children', '*tutela*'
wealth 89, 96, 118, 127
weavers xv, 116, 126, 127-8; in Roman Italy
    120; in Roman Egypt 192n.33; status
    70, 120; on the *monumentum
    Statiliorum* 192n.37; in Pompeii 122-3
wetnurses, wetnursing 61, 115, 129, 190n.8
widowers 107, 115
widows 52, 75, 79, 85, 95, 99, 135, 140,

141, 145, 147, 154, 155, 185n.45,
    202n.86
will (*testamentum*) 70, 72, 78, 79, 81, 95,
    106, 108, 109, 184n.21, 187n.75,
    188n.109; women's 76, 77, 79
wine: export 97, 98, 184n.33, 185n.40;
    production (by women) 97, 184 nn.33-4
wives 16, 117, 132; see also 'marriage',
    'married women'
womanly weakness 73-4, 81-4, 87-8 and
    ch.6 *passim*
women's health 63, 64, 179nn.39,43
wool-working (*lanificium*) 19, 56, 125
work, 19, 56, 69, 70, 72, plates 3, 7, 8, 9,
    10, 11, 15, 16; allocations 56, 116; as a
    bond 126; commemorations based on
    123-4, 131; culturally valued 132; and
    identity 130-2; modern vs ancient
    notions of 113, 130; paid 113, 116, 125;
    'real' 130; representations, iconographic
    130, ch.8 *passim*; representations,
    moral and social 114, 115
work, women's 19, 56, 69, 72, 114-15, ch.8
    passim; cloth production 70, 117-25;
    domestic 117, 132; élite 125, 193n.55;
    associated with virtue 117, 132; and
    Roman economy 120-2; idealisation of
    125; invisibility/low visibility of 116,
    125; multi-skilled 131; specialist 130;
    see also ch.8 *passim*
workers 105, 116, ch.8 *passim*; free 92;
    iconographic representations 125-9;
    rural 131, 195n.76
workplace 124, 128, 194nn.63-4; not
    separated from the home 130
workshops 132, 151; artisans' 120; in
    residential settings 122, 192n.41;
    weaving (*textrinae*) 116, 122-3, 128,
    194nn.63-4